The Mexican Reform, 1855-1876:
A Study in Liberal Nation-Building

Latin American Monographs, No. 49
Institute of Latin American Studies
The University of Texas at Austin

The Mexican Reform, 1855–1876

A Study in Liberal Nation–Building

by Richard N. Sinkin

Institute of Latin American Studies
The University of Texas at Austin

International Standard Book Number 0-292-75045-7 (paper)
0-292-75044-7 (cloth)
Library of Congress Catalog Card Number 78-620053

The Latin American Monographs Series
is distributed for the Institute of
Latin American Studies by:
University of Texas Press
P. O. Box 7819
Austin, Texas 78712

Contents

Tables

Acknowledgements

The writing of this book has been a personal odyssey. The journey brought me into contact with a number of individuals who have in some way influenced the outcome of this book. Above all, Charles Gibson first directed me toward the subject and encouraged me in my moments of deepest despair. Charles Hale read two incarnations of the manuscript and his suggestions and ideas permeate the entire book. Others who listened and suggested when I needed an audience and advice include Jan Bazant, Nettie Lee Benson, Romeo Flores Caballero, Gloria Grajales Ramos, Moisés González Navarro, Thomas F. McGann, Laurens Perry, Peter H. Smith, Ernesto de la Torre Villar, Paul Vanderwood, Josefina Vázquez, and John Womack, Jr. Under no circumstances are they responsible for what is wrong or inelegant in the following pages.

The book is based principally on archival material found in the following institutions: in Mexico the Biblioteca Nacional, the Hemeroteca Nacional, the Archivo General de la Nación, the Biblioteca de la Secretaría de Hacienda, the Museo Nacional de Antropología e Historia, the Colegio de México, the Centro de Estudios de Historia Mexicana at Condumex, S.A., and in the United States the library of the University of Michigan and the Nettie Lee Benson Latin American Collection at The University of Texas. To the directors and staffs of these libraries I extend my sincere thanks. To the Secretaría de Patrimonio Nacional of the federal government in Mexico I offer my gratitude for its generosity in giving me the volumes of Benito Juárez's correspondence edited by Jorge L. Tamayo.

The Foreign Area Fellowship Program funded the initial research and writing of this book. The Institute of Latin American Studies of The University of Texas at Austin provided funds for subsequent research trips to Mexico. The University Research Institute of The University of Texas supported computer programming and research assistants. I owe much to the special talents of Steven Neuse, Lucia Uhl, Michelle Holland, and Suzy Morrison. Virginia

Schneider expertly and cheerfully typed the manuscript.

Sue Sinkin and my daughters Patricia and Katherine lived with this project far too long; I only hope they think it worth the effort.

The Mexican Reform, 1855-1876:
A Study in Liberal Nation-Building

1. Nation-Building:
The Analytical Framework

In 1855 Mexico plunged into its most profound crisis of the nineteenth century. For more than two decades the crisis continued, and, when it was over, the survivors had to pick up the pieces of a country that had witnessed rebellions, civil wars, foreign intervention, a new constitution, a government in exile, a Hapsburg emperor, and human suffering on a scale unequaled since the ravages of disease had decimated the Indian population in the sixteenth century. This period—generally called the Reform—began in 1854 with the Revolution of Ayutla. The Ayutla movement was a coalition of local political chiefs who wanted to remove from office the current dictator, Antonio López de Santa Anna, and return to a loose confederation of states in which they were free to rule unfettered by national policy. And because Santa Anna had become more of a dandy than an effective politician, the local chiefs were successful. In their wake they carried to Mexico City a substantial number of liberal politicians who wanted to do more than just remove Santa Anna: they wanted to institute profound changes in the political structure of Mexico. Like engineers building a dam, they wanted to halt the flood of rebellions, new constitutions, counter-rebellions, and government by edict—all of which had characterized Mexico since its independence from Spain in 1821. And so they attacked the bastions of traditionalism: the military, the Catholic Church, the powerful economic guilds, the Indian communities. Their reforms were written into a new constitution in 1857.

Conservative opposition to the reforms produced a tidal wave of civil war. For three years, from January of 1858 until January of 1861, Mexicans killed each other with a ferocity unseen since the days of the conquest; the violence reached all sections of the republic and washed over all classes of society. Although the defeat of the conservatives in January 1861 temporarily ended the Reform War (or the Three Years War, as it is sometimes called), it did not resolve the political or ideological crisis. On the contrary, it forced the conservatives to seek other ways to destroy the liberal reforms. Casting their vision back to the "golden age" of Mexico's colonial past, the conservatives sought to reestablish the stability of monarchical rule. In this they were partially successful: they created a monarchy, but it produced more instability and more civil war.

The creation of the monarchy was as much the result of small personality quirks of the principal actors as it was the consequence of largely impersonal historical forces. Napoleon III, the emperor of France, wanted a Latin empire. His wife entertained intimately some exiled Mexican monarchists. For all of them the idea of establishing a throne in Mexico had tremendous appeal. And Maximilian, an Austrian prince, was available and gullible. In this way, the civil war in Mexico became an international conflict. By late 1861, foreign troops had landed in Veracruz and were beginning to advance inland. On the fifth of May, 1862, the Mexicans defeated the French army in Puebla, an event that astounded all concerned. But the French regrouped, and by the summer of 1863 they had driven the liberal government from Mexico City and into the northern desert.

As Mexicans had known for decades, setting up a government was one thing; making people obey it was something else. Maximilian had little more success than had dozens of caudillos before him. Even his own supporters turned on him when he, like the liberals, tried to maintain secular control in the face of ecclesiastical pressures. And though the Hapsburg court in Mexico City attempted to recreate the pomp and circumstance of majesty, the realities of wholesale civil disobedience always lurked in the background. When Napoleon, faced with his own threat in the form of an armed and dangerous Prussia, decided to withdraw his military support of Maximilian and his wife Carlotta, the phantom empire collapsed.

From the edges of the republic came the liberal armies, headed by a stolid Indian from Oaxaca, Benito Juárez. Since January, 1858, he had been the standard-bearer of the liberal cause; he had kept the movement together in the northern desert; and he had directed the six years of protracted guerrilla warfare until June 19, 1867, when Mexican soldiers executed Maximilian and his two closest advisers. The ritual killings were to cleanse Mexico of the torment of ideological warfare, anarchy, and, in Juárez's term, "nationcide." The killings were to symbolize the end of killing and the beginning of a period of independence and consolidation.

For a decade after the fall of the French empire, Mexico experienced an unusual situation: the government began to govern, and reforms actually reformed. The liberal victory had been total, and, though there was still violence in the countryside and even disagreement within the liberal camp, the Reform became a reality. Laws that had been issued during the Reform War—

like the nationalization of church property, separation of church and state, secularization of society, the forced sale of corporate property—were now backed by a legitimate government acting in the name of the Constitution of 1857. A new political elite had emerged and consolidated itself in power. The Catholic Church saw its power and property severely reduced. Local political bosses—the very ones who had inadvertently begun the Reform—lost absolute control over their independent territories. The striking mixture of personalism and constitutional legality that characterizes contemporary Mexican politics took on new forms. And Mexico reoriented its relationships with the rest of the western world.

When Porfirio Díaz launched the last successful coup of the nineteenth century at Tuxtepec in 1876, it was as if the parenthetical expression begun by the Ayutla movement had finally been closed. Coup d'etat began the Reform, coup d'etat ended it. But its achievements were lasting and profound. Painted with a broad brush, the comparisons between pre-Ayutla and post-Tuxtepec Mexico are remarkable. Before the Reform there had been forty-five governments in thirty-four years; in the thirty-five years after Tuxtepec there were only two governments. In contrast to the five constitutions and countless reform acts prior to the Reform, the Constitution of 1857 lasted until the revolutionary Constitution of 1917. From economic anarchy Mexico began the process of economic development. In short, no matter which variable is selected, the results are striking.

Everyone who has commented on the rapid and violent changes that took place in Mexico in the middle of the nineteenth century agrees that the transformations were profound and that they altered the course of Mexican history. The observers have not agreed, however, on how to interpret either the changes themselves or their consequences. Walter V. Scholes has offered the most cogent thesis in explanation of the Reform in Mexico.[1] He argued that the "really dynamic aspect of the period" was the "attempt to introduce democratic capitalism" into a backward Mexico. And he concluded that the leaders of the Reform "were successful in introducing certain aspects of democratic capitalism."[2] Yet Scholes never defined "democratic capitalism"; instead, democratic capitalism is introduced at the beginning and recapitulated at the end but plays no analytical role in between. The other major studies of the Reform make no attempt to offer an analysis of the period. The works of Justo Sierra concentrated on the role of the mestizo in the Reform movement.[3] Ralph Roeder provided a brilliant narrative, full of color and insight, that captures the spirit of the age but does not explain it.[4] Francisco Bulnes approached the Reform out of a desire to demote, if not destroy altogether, the almost mythical stature of Benito Juárez.[5] And though the works of Callcott were pioneering in their day, they provide little in the way of explanation.[6] Thus the Reform has had much attention but almost no analysis. It remains a subject of myth and imagery.

Yet throughout all these works runs a central implication: that somehow Mexico emerged from its crisis more of a modern nation-state than it had been before the Reform. The hypothesis is fundamental, but it remains untested and unanalyzed. This is particularly noticeable because in the last two decades North American social scientists have elaborated a complex set of assumptions about national development under the general heading of political "modernization" or "nation-building." Much energy and ingenuity have been devoted to developing theories that explain the emergence of the modern nation-state, but remarkably few actual situations have been analyzed carefully. The intensity of violence that accompanied the Mexican Reform, the striking number of changes that occurred, the emergence of new political forms and institutions— all indicate that the Mexican Reform experience provides an appropriate case study for the testing of the nation-building theories. At the same time, a detailed study of the degree to which the Mexican Reform fits the models may also help to answer some crucial questions: Why did the Reform begin when it did? Where did the leadership come from? What were the central issues of the Reform? What was the relationship between Reform politics and such other elements of modernization as economic development and education? And, finally, in what ways was Mexico a modern nation-state by the time Porfirio Díaz took power in 1876?

This final question of nation-building is the central concern of this book; all the others relate to it in one way or another. But, as with all such terms, "nation" and "nation-building" require precise definition before they can serve as analytical tools. Perhaps the clearest definition of "nation" comes from an essay by Carl J. Friedrich in which he defines a nation as "any cohesive group possessing 'independence' within the confines of the international order . . . which provides a constituency for a government effectively ruling such a group and receiving from that group the acclamation which legitimizes the government as part of the world order."[7] Karl Deutsch adds some specific qualities that all nations share. Among them are (1) independence from outside rule, (2) general social cohesion, (3) effective political rule, (4) political autonomy of the government through popular consent, and (5) internal legitimacy.[8] "Nation-building" refers to the processes by which certain groups in society act to attain political autonomy for their society. Nation-building should be viewed as only one aspect of the larger process of modernization, which can be generally defined as the expanding control over the environment through closer interaction among men.[9] Modernization thus implies a whole range of changes, including social mobilization, psychological transformation, and economic development. In the Mexican case, the broad social and economic changes did not occur until after the beginning of the political transformation, and for that reason this book will concentrate primarily on the political aspects of modernization—what is here called nation-building.

"Nation-building" is a term that describes the transition of a political structure from a traditional pattern to one that is more modern. This process has been the subject of an enormous amount of analysis and debate. Observers of the nation-building process have drawn on the analyses of sociologists such as Sir Henry Maine, Ferdinand Tönnies, Emile Durkheim, Max Weber, and Talcott Parsons and have applied them to the dynamics of political change.[10] They have identified three basic, interrelated characteristics of political modernization. The first of these is the creation of a strong central government.[11] Nation-building is most clearly related to the consolidation of policy-making that accompanied the technological revolution of the nineteenth and twentieth centuries. The consolidation process was the result of a basic desire on the part of political elites to rationalize and mobilize the total resources of society. Its ultimate goal was the achievement of greater control over the society, thus making politics more efficient and productive. In the public sector, the rationalization of authority takes the form of concentrating power within the structure of the nation-state. The centralization of authority contrasts sharply with traditional power structures in which the authority of the nation-state rarely reached the lower levels of society. Power in a traditional society was usually shared by several institutions, of which the state was only one.[12]

In Mexico prior to the Reform, intermediary institutions included the Catholic Church, the army, the private militias of the landed gentry, the guilds and commercial corporations, and even the Indian villages. These organizations existed in a privileged world, exempt from the authority of the state and subject to no control other than their own strength or weakness. Within the social context, these institutions performed numerous services for the people: the church educated those who were allowed into the schools; private armies supplied police protection in rural Mexico; Indian villages maintained a separate existence in almost all aspects of political and social life and provided maintenance for their members; the regular army maintained its own courts and way of life, thereby excluding its members and their families from civilian responsibilities; and the guilds and economic corporations carved out special niches for their members by maintaining their special privileges and exemptions. Thus intermediary agencies outside the control of the nation-state provided much of the education, transportation, communications, and social security in Mexico prior to the Reform. Nation-building suggests that the state reduced both the scope and the power of these organizations. And, as part of this process, the nation-state forced a transfer of the ultimate loyalty and commitment of large segments of society from primordial groups to the larger national political system. It is true that contemporary Mexico, like other modern political systems, is a fusion of centralism and corporatism. But nation-building indicates that the fusion took place only after the supremacy and dominance of the state had been firmly established.

With power localized in a traditional system, decisions tended to be arbitrary and personalistic. Political modernization thus involved a breakdown of arbitrary rule and its replacement by the rule of law. In fact, the central ethos of the liberal state-building model is juridical equality. Moreover, the centralization and rationalization of authority would not be possible without the establishment of rule by law maintained by a highly organized bureaucracy, principally because these processes involve the breakdown of intermediary institutions and the subsequent close rapport between the state and every member of society. As Cyril Black puts it: "Indeed, the replacement of the arbitrary administration of individuals by a legal system is the hallmark of modernization in the political realm."[13] Of course, arbitrary decisions continue to be made at all levels of the bureaucratic structure, but the range of these decisions becomes more restricted as the system is modernized. During the Reform in Mexico, as we shall see, the establishment of rule by law involved the writing of one of Mexico's most important constitutions.

Both the concentration of power and the establishment of rule by law seek to transform not only the way men are governed but also the way they perceive their relationship with the state. Basically the modern nation-state is, in the words of Reinhard Bendix, "the orderly exercise of nation-wide, public authority."[14] To accomplish this goal requires a fundamental transition on the part of individuals from subject to citizen, from passive acceptance of life-chances to active participation in shaping those chances. The orderly exercise of authority on a nation-wide basis thus dictates that individuals understand and accept their new roles and that, in some way, they register their comprehension and acceptance through elections or plebiscites. At the same time, the state stimulates these new feelings through the development of patriotism and nationalism. As Black observed, nationalism "has proved to be the most effective means of consolidating loyalties that would otherwise be divided by attachments to many other associations."[15] Nationalism thus provides the basis for what S. N. Eisenstadt calls a principal characteristic of modernizing societies: consensual mass tendencies.[16] The growth of consensus makes the role of ideology paramount in modernizing societies; the ideology serves to bind individuals to the state, thereby making the nation-state the ultimate arbiter of human affairs.[17] Nationalism, like the concentration of power and the establishment of rule by law, is a fundamental aspect of the nation-building process. In Mexico in the middle of the nineteenth century, nationalism was the ideology of both the conservatives and the

liberals. Both sought to preserve the nation, and both ultimately desired a
strong nation-state. The conflict between them centered not on whether
Mexico needed change—this they agreed on—but rather on what kind of change.
The liberals won the struggle, but not without intense conflict involving all
parts of Mexico and all classes of Mexicans.

Political nation-building is thus a process of transition from a more traditional to a less traditional political system. It involves three principal elements:
(1) the rationalization and legitimization of authority, (2) the establishment
of juridical equality and rule by law, and (3) the development of a unifying
ideology and national identity. These general hypotheses have been pulled
together by the Committee on Comparative Politics of the Social Science
Research Council. The committee has conceived of the "development
syndrome" as a "continuous interaction among the processes of structural
differentiation, the imperatives of *equality,* and the integrative, responsive,
and adaptive *capacity* of a political system."[18] The syndrome contains some
obvious contradictions that are inherent in any political transformation. The
committee argues that the working-out of the contradictions produces a
series of crises that it has labeled identity, legitimacy, participation, penetration, and distribution.

The identity crisis marks the point at which the people of a state come to
see themselves as parts of a single political community and also begin to sense
that their personal identities are in some measure defined by their adherence
to that community. The nation-building process involves the creation of a
new political community that brings the nation and the state into alignment.

The legitimacy crisis involves establishing an agreement about the exercise
of authority and the proper role of government; the participation crisis occurs
when new actors make demands on the limited resources of the political structure.

The penetration crisis occurs when the rulers attempt to create formal
political structures to implement and secure compliance with government
policies. Usually, penetration is marked by the growth of a centralized
bureaucracy with an increased capacity for regulation and taxation.

Finally, the distribution crisis has to do with the ability of the system to
respond to a situation of rising demands. Basically, it involves answering the
timeless political question, Who gets what, when, and for what purpose?

The particular pattern of political development in any society, according
to this set of hypotheses, will depend largely on the sequence in which these
crises arise and, of course, on the ways in which they are resolved. In Mexico
in the middle of the nineteenth century, not all of the crises arose at once.
Instead, the crises of the Reform seem to center on the questions of legitimacy,
identity, and penetration, and these will be the central points of focus in this

book. It should be obvious that these elements constitute only the primary stages of the total nation-building process. First of all, when the process is in its infancy the new organizations created or the old ones transformed have relatively limited scope. They touch primarily the upper and middle groups of society, which are predominant in the nation-building process. Only gradually will the process reach down into other levels of society. This first stage of political modernization also involves the secularization of society as part of the general pattern of the rationalization of authority.[19] And, finally, the most salient characteristic of the first stage of nation-building is the concentration of power.[20]

This study focuses primarily on the beginnings of *political* modernization in Mexico in the nineteenth century. Other kinds of modernizing processes— intellectual, social, economic, and psychological—are slighted in the interest of political analysis. Obviously all are interconnected, and any such separation does damage to the totality of the process. Yet the issues that matter during the Reform are so thoroughly political that the division seems not only justified but necessary. Thus when the concept of nation-building is used in the following analysis, it refers to the early stages of the process and implies a political emphasis.[21]

A second caveat is that, as a process, modernization requires the destruction of parts of the old system in order that the new may be created, and as such it can produce much human suffering. Conflict is a built-in ingredient of the nation-building process; the defenders of the old system will seek to thwart the purposes of the modernizers even to the extent of destroying them. At the same time, nation-building brings on a struggle over values and over claims to scarce status, power, and resources. Once the political issues become embodied in these terms, the conflicts that accompany political change reach a level of intensity never felt in the traditional society. Clearly, state-building is a mixed blessing at best. It is destructive, it creates chaos and disorder, it often causes great human suffering, and the end result may not be any "better" for the individual than the traditional system that the new politics displaced.[22]

A third restriction on the use of the concept of nation-building requires some explanation. When it first became popular as an analytical tool for the study of social change, its users conceived of two utopian or ideal models: tradition and modernity. The two were seen as mutually exclusive, which led observers to fall into the logical trap of identifying either the old tradition or the coming modern utopia as a "golden age." For some, modernity was seen as an unmitigated evil, bent on destroying what was good and simple and quietly elegant in traditional tribal structures. For others, tradition meant oppression, whereas modernity carried the implications of liberation, freedom, democracy, and "goodness."[23] Both of these positions make the mistake of

conceiving of modernity as something it can never be, a society totally without
a past. Such a concept is an abstraction without meaning. The problem has
arisen because analysts have not made the proper distinction between *tradition*
and *traditionalism.* Tradition refers to the beliefs and practices handed down
from the past; as history is rewritten, so too is tradition. Traditionalism, on
the other hand, is ideological and hence immutable. Traditionalists see the
world in static terms and look to the past for revealed knowledge. They see
innovation and change as threatening the order and stability of society. Traditionalism constitutes a major barrier to nation-building; tradition, on the
other hand, because of its flexibility in the light of history, poses no threat to
the modern nation-state.[24]

To relate this more specifically to Mexico in the nineteenth century, it is
obvious that Mexico was not a traditional society in 1855 if by traditional one
means "colonial." Independence had destroyed the upper levels of the political
structure, and power now resided with the local political bosses. On the other
hand, Mexico still retained many elements of her colonial heritage. Her
economy was essentially dependent on foreign markets, her social structure
was defined along racial lines, and colonial institutions such as the Catholic
Church and the hacienda continued to function in traditional ways. Nor
would most observers declare Mexico modern in 1876. The powerful colonial
institution of the hacienda persisted and even strengthened its position;
Mexico remained economically dependent within the world capitalist market;
and, though the social structure experienced some transformation, it nevertheless maintained many traditional patterns of relationship. Nation-building
involved destruction of *some* of the past. At the same time, much of Mexico's
tradition remained, perhaps to be transformed later, perhaps to persist within
the "modern" context of today.[25]

This study does not suggest that the period between 1855 and 1876 was
the only era of nation-building in Mexico. Indeed, political reform in Mexico
is a process that began with the eighteenth-century reforms of the Bourbon
monarchs and continues today. Rather, these years seem to mark the turning-
point in nineteenth-century Mexican history. All of the disparate themes, processes, and intellectual currents that surfaced during the Reform years had
been present and potent since the time of Mexican independence in the 1820s.
But in the 1855-1876 decades, the contradictory forces came to a violent confrontation in a struggle that allowed no quarter. Positions became polarized,
resolution by negotiation became impossible, and civil war became inevitable.
Why it happened at this particular moment in Mexican history will be the
subject of analysis in the third chapter. The point here is that the Reform
years should not be seen as containing something entirely new or unique.
They are best viewed as the culmination of a long historical process.

A final comment derives from these observations. The forces of nation-building cover an infinite range of possibilities. They touch almost every aspect of human life, from the structure of government to education to family organization. Because their effects are so broad, they are unevenly experienced; profound changes in one area do not automatically bring commensurate changes in another, and some groups are more immediately affected than others. This study will focus on the upper levels of government at both the national and the state level. It will not, except in passing, analyze the local manifestations of the early stages of nation-building.

2. Society and Politics: Roots of Reform

The Mexican Reform movement arose from three interrelated sources. The first of these was the collapse of the Mexican economy in the immediate post-colonial era. The second was the failure of the social structure to adapt to the critical changes that took place after independence. And the final source can be located in the failure of the post-independence political structure to provide regular and ample opportunities for advancement to those ambitious individuals who had little or no opportunity for success in the economic realm. Had any one of the root systems worked well and consistently, it seems likely that the Mexican Reform would have been substantially different, if it had taken place at all.

Although the Reform was a political process, it had its roots in the collapse of the economy after the decade of independence wars from 1810 to 1821. In the years immediately after independence, Mexico had nothing resembling a national economic system.[1] Because the rivers in Mexico tumble off high plateaus, few are navigable. There were even fewer railroad lines, and most commerce went by muleback. Even under the best of conditions, highway travel in early nineteenth-century Mexico was risky business. A merchant sending his goods by coach could count on at least two unwelcome experiences: constant breakdown of the stagecoach because of the disrepair of the roads, and highway robbery. Should a lucky merchant survive these plagues, he was still subject to the *alcabala,* a tax levied by each state on merchandise passing across its border. These taxes ranged from 3 to 12 percent of the value of the merchandise. In addition, the merchant could be taxed as he moved his wares through the various districts within a single state. And once he reached his destination, he could expect the municipalities to attempt to tax the sale of his goods at around 5 percent of the sale price. Because they constituted almost the sole source of state revenues, these taxes would prove extremely difficult to abolish in later years.[2]

After independence the principal economic activity in the country was agriculture, and of all the crops grown maize was by far the most important. Not only did it dominate in terms of the size of the crop but also in its value. Yet most of the maize grown in Mexico after independence was for home consumption. The same was true of other agricultural products such as wheat, beans, onions, fruits, and peppers. Because there is so little good land in a country dominated geographically by mountains, deserts, and jungles, Mexico produced little for export. Those crops that were grown for commercial agriculture—such as cotton, sugar cane, henequen fiber, and tobacco—were usually sold in the local markets. There the supply and demand market structure worked constantly against the farmer. A good crop inevitably meant low prices; a bad crop resulted in high prices, scarcity, and often severe hunger. The central problem was a lack of market outlets for the goods produced, not a lack of goods. Moreover, the agricultural techniques used on the haciendas, smaller private farms, and ejido lands were primitive, and productivity was extremely low.[3]

Mexico had not always had an economy dominated by agriculture. During the three hundred years of Spanish colonial rule, the principal economic force had been the mining of precious metals. The mercantile system devised by the Spaniards created a central mining core surrounded by an agricultural structure designed to supply the mining centers. In addition, an elaborate commercial system transported bullion from the New World to the metropolis and brought luxury goods from the metropolis to the colonial markets. At the heart of this complex system were the great mining centers of the Bajío, San Luis Potosí, Zacatecas, and Durango, whose mines appeared to be inexhaustible.[4]

But independence destroyed the mercantile system, not only because Spanish domination was removed, but because much of the fighting occurred in precisely those areas that had been tied to the mining economy. As workers left the mines to take up arms for the royalists or the insurgents, mines filled with water, timber rotted, shafts collapsed, machinery rusted, trained mining engineers were killed or migrated to safer locales, and some mining communities simply disappeared.[5] The heart of the colonial economy stopped beating, and there was nothing to take its place.

After independence, revitalization of the mines was impossible for several reasons. The first was the marked lack of capital in Mexico after independence. Even before the independence wars began, wealthy Spanish capitalists were leaving the country and taking their capital with them. They were reacting to the establishment of "free trade" by the Bourbon kings of Spain, a move that threatened their monopoly of the commerce of New Spain. In addition, the Spanish were horrified by the execution of the Consolidation Law of 1804, which ordered the seizure and sale of the assets of the Tribunal of Chaplaincies,

Testaments, and Pious Works of the Catholic Church. In effect, this law dismantled the single wealthiest organization in New Spain and the most important banking institution in the New World. The rationale for the law centered on Spain's need for funds to service its debt and fund its war with England. But the consequences for New Spain were disastrous. Not only did it raise questions about the utility of continuing the colonial relationship, it also shattered a thriving economy. Many of those in debt to the Tribunal left their lands; the value of real estate fell by one-half; the economic and political stability of the state wavered; and, with a war on in Europe, trade fell to a dangerously low level. To many Spaniards, especially those with money, New Spain lost much of its attractiveness as an investment opportunity.[6]

As soon as the anti-colonial independence wars were over, the victorious insurgents expelled the remaining Spaniards. In a series of laws enacted in 1827 and 1829, Mexico sent its Spanish population packing. Although many of the most wealthy continued some of their economic activities in Mexico through agents, the task was difficult and risky. During this time, no new Spanish capital flowed into Mexico. The result was that the mining industry had insufficient resources to stimulate its revitalization.[7]

In the climate of instability that characterized Mexico after independence, few investors were willing to take the enormous risks necessary to reopen Mexican mines. Mining entrepreneurs were faced with staggering production costs, exorbitant taxes, and high export tariffs. A few British companies, stimulated by the translation of the panegyrical works of Humboldt, took advantage of the relaxation of laws prohibiting foreign investments in mines and sunk capital in several revitalization schemes. Rarely did the investments pay off, and by the 1850s the Mexican mining industry had reached its nadir.[8] The principal economic activity of the colonial era no longer functioned to supply jobs, stimulate linking economic activity, or replenish Mexico's depleted capital.

Nor did other industrial enterprises move in to take up the slack. Only the textile industry, a legacy from the colonial period, made any advances during these difficult years. And they were paltry in light of Mexico's desperate straits. At the end of the colonial period the textile industry had employed around 60,000 workers. The independence struggles ruined the textile industry almost as thoroughly as they had mining. In an effort to increase the manufacture of cloth, the new governments raised tariff barriers against the importation of foreign textiles, lifted restrictions on the importation of machinery, and established the Banco de Avío in 1830 to stimulate investment in the necessary equipment. None of these measures produced the desired effects; by the early 1840s, only about half of Mexico's 5,832 looms were in operation, employing only around 9,000 workers. Most of the laborers were women and children who worked twelve to sixteen hours for less than half a peso a day. Mexican cloth continued to cost more than most could afford, and frequently textile mills went bankrupt for lack of cotton to spin and weave. Without sufficient power to drive the machines, lacking transportation for marketing the cloth, and plagued by high costs, the Mexican textile indus-try did little to stimulate economic development.[9]

World market conditions might have proved favorable for the Mexican economy if the country had had the resources to capitalize on the increase in demand for many of its products. But poor roads, lack of railroads, power shortages, primitive agricultural and industrial technology, restrictive taxation, regional isolation, and low literacy rates (5 to 10 percent) all worked to limit Mexico's potential in the world market. The trading that did take place con-sisted mainly of exporting gold and silver, which accounted for about 90 percent of all exports, and receiving in exchange manufactured clothing. Great Britain dominated the Mexican commercial houses, using her substantial mer-chant marine to undercut other European powers. Only the United States offered serious competition, but its efforts were weakened by the disastrous diplomacy of Joel Poinsett and Anthony Butler and the even more calamitous invasion of 1846-1848.[10]

The little capital available in Mexico in the middle nineteenth century went into the purchase of land. Traditionally, land ownership conveyed status, prestige, and, above all, political power. And in such a precarious economy, only land offered permanent security. Economically productive land was (and still is) scarce in Mexico. Only one-third of all the land is level enough to grow crops, and most of it is situated in the arid north and the waterless Yuca-tán peninsula. Barely 7 percent of Mexico receives enough rainfall to permit cultivation without irrigation, and another 10½ percent can be cultivated with partial irrigation.

Unfortunately, the actual configuration of land distribution in the middle nineteenth century is impossible to determine with the data now available. From the various travel accounts and contemporary comments, it seems clear that the hacienda dominated rural Mexico. It also appears that the haciendas frequently changed hands. Clearly the economic crisis following the indepen-dence wars had a serious effect. Land values, already depressed after the 1804 Consolidation Law, continued to decline, with the result that the burden of mortgages often became too great to sustain. In many cases, the debt-ridden haciendas were sold intact, but in some areas, particularly the Bajío and sur-rounding territory, there was a marked trend toward subdivision.[11] Even so, the common man rarely had access to them. Instead, families that had made their fortunes in mining or commerce sought large estates to confirm their social arrival; hence the proverb, "From grower to miner, a great fool; from miner to landowner, a noble gentleman."[12]

Contrary to much of the comment of the period, the Catholic Church possessed very little rural property, although those estates that it did own were generally prosperous and important. Church holdings were principally in the cities, towns, and villages; in fact, recent studies indicate that ecclesiastical corporations owned half the houses in Mexico City.[13]

The rural hacendado worked to make his hacienda as large as possible, and some haciendas covered more than fifty square miles. Frequently the hacendado would rent out portions of the hacienda to sharecroppers, who paid their rent in the form of produce. In the north of Mexico, the haciendas specialized in cattle ranching, although sheep raising also played an important economic role, particularly for tallow and meat.

The domination of the hacienda varied from region to region. In those areas that had been sparsely settled during the colonial period—particularly the north and Yucatán—the growth of the large estate had been rapid and thorough. In contrast, in regions where the Indian villages and small farms or ranchos had traditionally dominated, the growth of the hacienda was much slower and its influence far less pervasive. Indeed, in the middle of the nineteenth century most of central, south central, and north central Mexico exhibited landholding patterns that mixed hacienda, rancho (small farm), and village ejido or community property. Conflict between the owners of the various types of landholdings was a recurrent theme of the period. As the hacendados sought more land, they attacked Indian ejidos whose land titles were often lost or, if available, vague about the boundaries of the property. These villages of central Mexico had existed long before the hacienda began to threaten their existence, and they fought tenaciously to maintain themselves. During the colonial period, as the Spaniards sought to control and absorb the Indian villages, the villagers had reacted by closing themselves off from the outside world, forming semi-autonomous closed corporations. Poverty became a constant in village life, and deviance from the established norms of behavior was carefully excised. An individual windfall usually meant a village religious festival paid for with the sudden fortune. The result was a certain village egalitarianism of poverty. There was no incentive to achieve, self-promotion was deemed disruptive, and life revolved around the cycle of the harvest.[14]

The significance of these landowning patterns is that there was much competition over an extremely scarce resource; clearly, to become a landowner in mid-nineteenth-century Mexico was an extraordinarily difficult task. With opportunities in mining equally limited, with commerce at a standstill, with internal trade hampered by obstacles of gigantic proportions, few Mexicans possessed the resources, the entrepreneurial ability, or the incentives to seek advancement in the economic world. Those who wanted to get ahead sought other avenues.

Although the causal connections cannot be clearly drawn, certainly one aspect of the stagnant economic situation was the low rate of population growth. Almost everyone who has written on the subject of Mexican population in the middle of the nineteenth century agrees that approximately eight million persons inhabited the country.[15] Several important qualifications must be added to this observation. In the first place, the earliest official census was in 1895; prior to that time, all population figures are mere approximations. Second, if the eight million figure is correct, Mexico had experienced extremely slow population growth (around one-half of one percent per year) since the turn of the century, when Alexander von Humboldt estimated a total population of just under six million.[16] And this slow rate continued throughout the Reform period; by 1876 the population had risen to approximately nine-and-a-half million persons.[17] A third consideration is that the population was not evenly dispersed throughout the country. Indeed, the north, which represented almost half the land space, accounted for only one-eighth of the inhabitants. In contrast, the center of the country was densely populated; more people lived in the state of Mexico (before 1869 comprising what are now the states of Mexico, Hidalgo, and Morelos) than lived in the entire north.[18] Thus politics in the nineteenth century meant a struggle to control the fertile and populous core of the country.

Even though there is general agreement about the size of the population, almost no one is sure exactly how that population was divided. One reason for the wide variety of opinions is that Mexican society was in a state of transition from social differentiation based on ethnic or cultural criteria to one based on economic determinants. Colonial Mexico was, in the words of David Brading, a society of orders and estates, in which the privileges, functions, and comparative esteem of the various estates determined stratification and status. In New Spain the central criteria for status determination had been the five ethnic categories of Spaniards, mestizos, mulattoes, Indians, and blacks. But these increasingly came to be regarded more as cultural than racial categories, and movement between and among the estates was possible to a limited degree.[19]

By the middle of the nineteenth century, the top of the colonial social structure had been cut off. The Spaniards had been expelled from the country, leaving the high offices to those whites born in the New World, the creoles, who represented less than one-quarter of the population. It had been creoles who had led Mexico from Spanish domination during the wars of independence. Although their reasons for taking such a drastic step varied as widely as their economic interests, the one common ground was a hope for opportunities to reach the highest levels of economic and political life, which had been the increasingly exclusive preserve of the peninsular Spaniards. And once Mexico became an independent state, these creoles began the process of establishing themselves as the mighty of the land, or, in their words, the *gente decente.* They expelled the Spaniards and then took over the upper levels of the governmental bureaucracy; they became the highest clerics; they created both official and personal armies, which they commanded; and they solidified their positions as hacendados, rich businessmen, professionals, leading merchants, industrialists, and mine owners. In effect, they monopolized scarce resources, limited access to power and prestige, and attempted to re-create or maintain colonial structures and patterns. As one anonymous observer put it in 1850, "Once the creoles saw the lucrative top positions open, they took every place that the hated *gachupines* had possessed . . . and immediately became the new aristocrats."[20]

Because resources and mobility were so limited in these immediate post-independence decades, not all creoles were able to advance and prosper. Indeed, many, if not most, were faced with the prospects of living on the margins of power, seeking lower-level bureaucratic posts; begging a clerical chaplaincy; often sharecropping or eking out a minimal existence as an artisan.[21] In the fledgling society that emerged from the crisis of the independence wars, white skin was no guarantee of security; but without it, advancement to the top was nearly impossible.

The marginal whites clamoring at the doors of power were joined by a growing group of upwardly mobile mestizos. The mestizos were Mexico's largest ethnic group by the middle of the nineteenth century. At the end of the colonial period the mestizos had accounted for approximately 30 percent of the total population; by 1855 they made up almost 50 percent. In the colonial period these *castas,* part Indian, part white, had been accepted by neither Indian nor white society. For centuries they had existed on the margins of both worlds, seeking fortunes in the illicit dealings of the colonial underworld, serving their patrons on the haciendas, mastering the intricacies of survival in a world that did not recognize their existence. It was the mestizo who provided the contact between creole and Indian; it was the mestizo who carried Indian goods to market; and it was the mestizo who migrated to the city to seek his opportunity. By the middle of the nineteenth century, a few, perhaps 5 or 6 percent of the total population, had become a transitional group. Members of this group were socially ambitious, had received an education, and could be found in lower-level bureaucratic posts, working as merchants, lawyers, or journalists. A few sought military careers, and even fewer became landowners. Almost all participated in the fluid political life of post-independence Mexico. It was from this transitional mestizo group that the leadership of the Reform would eventually coalesce.[22]

The rest of the mestizos—some 45 percent of the total population—occupied an intermediate position in society. Approximately one-third of this group had some possibility for social mobility; they were the smaller farmers and shopkeepers, artisans, lower clergy, school teachers, overseers on the haciendas, mule-train drivers *(arrieros)*, notaries, scribes, and secretaries. But the vast majority of mestizos—peones, domestic servants, traveling vendors, urban proletariat, rank and file soldiers, and day workers—had no social cohesion and little hope for raising their low social standing. The possibilities for education simply did not exist; little land was available; economic stagnation meant few jobs and much unemployment. One estimate suggested that one-eighth of all creoles were out of work, and another indicated that almost one million men were unemployed in 1848.[23] Indeed, unemployment was so high among the lower-level mestizos that many of them hired out as soldiers of fortune to the highest bidder. As a result, there was a constant supply of soldiers for the guerrilla armies of the early nineteenth century.

The high incidence of social banditry is one of the clearest indicators of both the economic crisis of the middle nineteenth century and the large-scale social dislocation this crisis caused. Drawing on the large number of unemployed mestizos (and sometimes Indians who had left their villages), gangs of armed bandits terrorized villages, sacked haciendas, robbed stage coaches, and plundered the Mexican countryside. As Eric Hobsbawm has written, "Social banditry is universally found, wherever societies are based on agriculture . . . and consists largely of peasants and landless labourers ruled, oppressed and exploited by someone else—lords, towns, governments, lawyers, or even banks."[24] Social banditry was thus a form of rebellion within a pre-industrial society, and campesinos often looked on the bandits as heroes, defenders of village rights, and champions of justice. But for those in power, whether liberal or conservative, the social bandits were common criminals who threatened peace, order, and stability. It is not surprising that one of the central themes of the Mexican Reform was the establishment of law and order in the countryside.[25]

The Indians are the group most difficult to define. One problem is exactly what was meant by the term "Indian." For example, the estimates of the numbers of Indians in Mexico in the middle nineteenth century range from just over two million to over five million. Rarely are the criteria for adopting one figure over another explained, but usually nineteenth-century writers referred to Indians as those who did not speak Spanish, did not wear pants or shoes, lived in villages with communal property and traditional values, and, perhaps most important of all, considered themselves to be Indians.[26] But others have pointed out that it was not necessary to speak a native tongue or to be a descendant of Indians to be classified as an Indian.[27] Perhaps the best estimate of the total number of Indians in mid-nineteenth-century Mexico is the 3.8 million figure calculated by the Mexican sociologist Germán Parra.[28]

Whatever the actual number, the Indians constituted a large and abysmally poor segment of the Mexican population. Throughout the three-hundred-year Spanish domination, the Indians had been treated as a conquered people. They were forced to pay tribute to the Spanish crown; by law they were considered wards of the king; and, first through encomienda and then under repartimiento, they were forced to work for the state, or the church, or private individuals, with little or no compensation and frequently with great risk to their own health and family well-being. In addition, the Indians were subjected to restrictions on the types of clothes they could wear, jobs they could hold, money they could borrow, horses they could ride, and even meat they could buy. To protect themselves from white and mestizo exploitation, the Indians had retreated into their closed, corporate, communal villages, but even these bastions of defense were giving way in the late colonial period to the expanding haciendas and the lure of wage labor in the mining communities.[29]

Every now and then the Indians revolted against these oppressive conditions. But the uprisings were sporadic, localized, and easily suppressed by the Spaniards. There never was a concerted, organized, and widespread Indian threat to Spanish rule. The only notable exception to this was the series of Indian revolts that occurred in the mining region north of Mexico City called the Bajío. Here there was a fusion of all types of economic activity: mining, ranching, commercial agriculture, and commerce. Unlike the rest of Mexico, the Bajío represented a nascent free-market complex within the Spanish colonial mercantile system. Here the Indians sold their labor on the open market, and here the Bourbon reforms, which were designed to strengthen the mercantile system, created the most opposition. In 1767, the Indians rebelled against the expulsion of the Jesuits and against other measures such as the reimposition of dress codes and consumption restrictions. Although few Spaniards were injured in the revolt, the Spanish administration crushed it with great severity: public whippings and executions, stiff taxation, and strict limitations on Indian travel.[30]

The bitter legacy left by the 1767 revolt played into the hands of the local creoles who hoped for independence from Spanish rule. Their opportunity to arouse the Indian masses in revolt came during the constitutional crisis of 1808-1810. When Napoleon invaded the Iberian peninsula the Spanish crown disappeared, Spain collapsed into civil war, and some Mexicans, particularly in the capitalist Bajío, began to consider independence as a desirable alternative to colonial rule. Led by Father Miguel Hidalgo, a creole priest of the parish of Dolores, Guanajuato, hundreds of Indians and mestizos and a handful of creole leaders issued the Grito de Dolores on the evening of September 15, 1810, and began a concerted drive to rid Mexico of Spanish domination. The revolt spread rapidly throughout the Bajío region, culminating in an attack on the granary *(rlhóndiga)* in Guanajuato, in which hundreds of peninsulars and even a few creoles were massacred. With an army numbering almost seventy thousand, Hidalgo then marched toward Mexico City, where a ferocious but indecisive battle scattered the armed hoard from the north. In 1811, Hidalgo and his chiefs were captured, tried, excommunicated, and shot, but local guerrilla movements by survivors such as José María Morelos, a mestizo priest, kept the independence movement alive until 1821, when key creoles became convinced that it was in their best interest to sever the colonial ties.[31]

The vast and violent Indian uprising in 1810 left many scars and recurrent fears among the new ruling elite after independence had been achieved. Above all, it left a gnawing terror of "caste war," and prejudice against the "dangerous classes," particularly the Indians. And these fears received their worst confirmation in the 1840s, when once again large numbers of Indians took up arms against the white man. This time the revolt occurred in the southern Yucatán peninsula, where the Maya Indians rebelled against the voracious land-grabbing of the sisal haciendas. After much pillage, murder, rape, and attacks and counter-attacks, the Maya were driven deep into the jungles of Yucatán, where they listened to speaking crosses and plotted revenge on the ladino.[32] But throughout Mexico, the fear of caste war hovered in the Mexican consciousness and would play a key role in the Reform of the 1850s and 1860s.

Although the post-independence governments abolished most of the colonial legislation that discriminated against the Indians and other ethnic groups, legal equality brought few actual benefits to the Indians of Mexico. In fact, the Indians may have been worse off after independence than before; at least during the colonial period they had received some protection from the royal administration. Once independence removed that royal protection, the Indians were completely vulnerable to exploitation by both whites and mestizos. Throughout Mexico in the early nineteenth century, Indians were forced to join the army, were comandeered into work gangs, and were thrown off their lands. They rarely received justice in the courts and, because of centuries of Spanish tutelage, had neither the ability nor the inclination to enter into the political arena to defend their interests. Instead, the Indians retreated into their villages, rejecting the alien and brutal culture of the "Mexicans" and trying to the best of their ability to cut themselves off from the outside world. Francisco Pimentel, writing in 1864, described the basic nature of this conflict. He noted that the Indian cared nothing for white society and had no desire to become a part of it. For this reason Indians refused to learn Spanish, practice

Catholicism, learn useful skills, or leave their village. "For the Indian," in Pimentel's words, "there is no country, no government, no institutions; he sees everything with indifference."[33]

The wide diversity of ethnic groups and economic interests clearly presented an obstacle to national unity and nation-building in the eyes of Miguel Lerdo de Tejada, one of the leading liberal politicians. "This diversity of races," he wrote, "has been and continues to be a major obstacle to prosperity and development; because society is divided into different factions by birth, by education, by custom, and even by language, each part has divergent tendencies that prevent working in unison toward a common end."[34] And the staggering economic problems of post-independence sharpened and exacerbated the ethnic and racial conflicts. Given the bankrupt conditions of many haciendas, it is hardly surprising that the landowners failed to form a unified elite acting in concert for their best interests. Indeed, at all levels of society, class interests gave way to localism, petty struggles, and a distinct lack of national sentiment. Even the most effective conservative leaders—Anastasio Bustamante and Lucas Alamán—were unable to organize the great landowners into a viable political coalition. Certainly the diversity and competitiveness of the lower-level creoles and transitional mestizos prevented the formation of effective collective action. There were few explicit organized interest groups or voluntary associations such as trade or labor unions, agrarian leagues, or even political parties. And with the vast majority of Mexicans either peasants, or peones on the haciendas, or urban proletariat (often called *léperos*), barely surviving on wages of less than a peso a day, lower-class political activity was minimal.[35]

Nevertheless, all the social forces for political action were present by mid-century; what was needed to mobilize them was some precipitating event or series of events. The Mexican-American War of 1846-1848 was such a crisis; it brought the tensions, strains, and conflicts within Mexican society to the breaking point. And as with all such cataclysmic occurrences, it set in motion a chain of events that altered the course of history. In this case, it produced a political crisis that ended only after twenty years of turbulence, civil war, and foreign intervention—that monumental upheaval known in Mexican history as the Reform.

In the spring of 1846, following a border skirmish along the Rio Grande, the United States went to war with Mexico. Zachary Taylor, the U.S. commander in the north, marched inexorably southward, overwhelming Monterrey and Saltillo and beating Santa Anna. From the east came Winfield Scott, who led his army from Veracruz over the same path of conquest the Spaniard, Cortés, had traversed more than three centuries earlier. Although there was scattered Mexican resistance, the vast majority of Mexicans simply did not take up arms against the invading armies, and by the summer of 1847 Mexico City was in foreign hands. Six months later, in February 1848, Mexico signed a humiliating peace treaty in which the United States acquired half of the territory Mexico claimed to possess.[36]

Stunned by the rapid defeat, humbled by the Treaty of Guadalupe Hidalgo, and fearful of the future, educated Mexicans began to wonder out loud about Mexico's continued existence. Obviously the United States could have absorbed all of Mexico had it so desired; clearly, too, there would have been little Mexican resistance to national disintegration. As one pamphleteer put it, "Wherever we cast our view, we see that everything is decaying, everything is degenerating."[37] And Mariano Otero, one of the leading opponents of signing the peace treaty, summarized a general feeling: "In Mexico there is not, nor has there ever been able to be, anything called national spirit because there is no nation."[38]

Such feelings produced a rash of publications concentrating on self-criticism and the problem of national existence. Perhaps nowhere was this tendency more clearly illuminated than in the number and kinds of newspapers founded in Mexico City during these years of crisis. After the war, at least four major daily newspapers carried on an extensive and often acrimonious debate over great national issues. On the left was the liberal *El Monitor Republicano;* on the right were the staunchly conservative *El Universal* and *El Tiempo;* in the middle, although generally somewhat liberal, was *El Siglo XIX.* In their pages, articulate Mexicans waged an ideological battle over why Mexico had failed and what measures, if any, could secure her continued existence. In addition to the newspapers, many pamphlets, broadsides, speeches, and books flowed from the pens of such thinkers as Lucas Alamán, the major architect of the conservative movement, and liberals like Mariano Otero and Francisco Zarco. And as the decade of the 1840s terminated, the debate became more intense, positions became hardened, and political ideologies—which had hardly existed prior to the war—became polarized into irreconcilable visions of the solutions to Mexico's problems.[39]

The liberal analysis of the situation took a complex form. At its heart was a view of Mexican history that disparaged the independence movement. For the liberals, the independence movement had failed to rid Mexico of the vestiges of colonial mentality. The Indian past was a history of barbarity, and the centuries of Spanish rule had done little, from the liberal point of view, to change things. Instead, the Spaniards had instituted absolute monarchy, religious intolerance, ecclesiastical education, and social rigidity. Mexican liberals recapitulated the traditional Protestant Black Legend of Spanish despotism and fanaticism. The failure of Hidalgo was that he operated without a clear notion of the evils of the Spanish system, and so, for liberals like

José María Luis Mora, Hidalgo's movement was simply "pernicious and destructive."[40]

No colonial legacy received more attention than the social structure. In a remarkable essay published in 1847, Mariano Otero attempted to account for Mexico's defeat at the hands of the North Americans. What concerned him most was the question of why Mexicans did not rise up in defense of their homeland as the Spaniards had done in response to the Napoleonic invasion of 1808. The difference, Otero argued, could be found in the social problems of Mexico. Whereas in Spain there was a sense of common national spirit and harmony, in Mexico there was only hopeless internal division. Otero divided Mexican society into three classes: the "people in general," or Indians; the "productive classes," or those engaged in commerce and agriculture; and the "unproductive classes," or privileged groups. None of these had a stake in a Mexican victory. Clearly the Indian had no interest in defending his exploiters against foreign invasion. Nor did the shopkeepers and farmers have strong desires to defend a system that only burdened them with high taxes, corrupt government officials, and onerous tariffs. And as for the unproductive— principally the clergy and military—in Otero's view they were so degenerate and corrupt that they were incapable of defending Mexico against the invasion. In fact, when the Catholic Church was faced with the responsibility of financing the national defense effort, it supported a military revolt against the government. Thus, given the social and economic crisis of post-independence Mexico, there was no one to defend the *patria*.[41]

The liberal vision of the future encompassed a federal democratic republic, governed by representative institutions (although "representative" had an extremely restrictive meaning for nineteenth-century liberals) and based socially on a mixture of small proprietors, yeoman farmers, and master craftsmen. Their ideal was the Jeffersonian agrarian democracy in which individual interest prevailed over restrictive legislation and such artificial privileges as the *fuero* (a set of exemptions from legal sanctions and taxation granted to a corporation). Borrowing freely from European liberals, Mexican liberal thinkers assumed the correctness of Adam Smith's invisible hand and were confirmed individualists. In their view, the good of the individual harmonized with the good of society. Any institution—including the state—that interfered with the free play of individual interest was to be excised from society. Thus the liberal program, as it developed from the 1830s and became solidified after the Mexican-American War, sought to remove all vestiges of colonial forms.[42] In the liberal view, the reason Mexico had failed to respond to the challenge of national defense was that the independence movements had failed to alter the basic colonial structures, attitudes, and values.

No institution more represented the failed colonial heritage than the

Catholic Church. Unarguably the most powerful institution in post-independence Mexico, the church exercised what seemed to the liberals an unwarranted and downright dangerous political and economic power. It had been the church that had financed and promoted the military Polkos revolt during the American attack on Mexico City; it had been the church that seemed to monopolize most of the productive land; it was the church that received more income than the national government; and it was the church that existed as a separate entity within the state with its own courts and privileges. Indeed, for Mexican liberals the church embodied all the worst elements of the colonial heritage, and for them the only hope for national survival lay in a severe reduction of the power of the Catholic Church. Although, as we shall see, the liberals were often in disagreement about the timing and severity of the measures to be adopted, all agreed that something had to be done to subordinate the eccesiastical corporation to the will of the nation-state.[43]

If in the minds of the liberals the church represented the chief obstacle to the formation of the Jeffersonian utopia, the Indian communal property system (the ejido) was a close second. Like the church, the ejido had become an encysted institution outside the control of the nation-state. And, like the church, it had removed large numbers of individuals from direct contact with the state, thereby making them more loyal to their local communities than to the nation. In addition, the ejido acted as a brake on agricultural development, the very heart of the liberal program for national salvation. It was, in the liberal view, an institution designed to curb individual initiative and prevent the free circulation of private property, both essential to the establishment of an agrarian democracy.[44]

Although the liberal reforms envisioned a society in which private property would be the foundation, liberals were careful to limit the scope and power of the state. In fact, this was the basic liberal dilemma: how to carry out the comprehensive reforms that were necessary to rid Mexico of its colonial heritage while at the same time restricting the authority of the national government. The liberals saw clearly that the large hacienda, another principal colonial legacy, inhibited the creation of a nation of small landowners; yet the liberals also feared the authoritarian heritage of the Hapsburg and Bourbon monarchs. Monarchy was for them an anachronism, a vestige of the dark ages, and, above all, an intolerable interference in the free play of individual interest. Powerful presidents were seen as being little better than masked dictators. And yet, to accomplish the needed reforms, a strong central authority became a dire necessity. The tensions within a philosophical system that held out the ideal of the small proprietor while simultaneously denying the means to achieve this goal would provide the dynamic for Mexican liberalism in the age of reform.

Mexican conservatives were not faced with these dilemmas. For them, the answer to the puzzle of national survival was a return to the colonial traditions. While liberals saw the solution in a thorough abolition of the past, conservatives offered a program that envisioned the restoration of Bourbon rule in Mexico. Indeed, to conservatives the reason Mexico had failed to defend itself was that too much of the colonial tradition had been lost in a disastrous experiment with alien, republican forms of government. The result had been internal anarchy, excessive regionalism, and a collapse of those common bonds that hold nations together.[45]

The conservative position found its spokesman in Lucas Alamán, creole son of a wealthy Guanajuato mining family and member of the Third Order of the Franciscans.[46] Like the liberals, Alamán turned his attention to interpreting Mexico's history; but unlike his liberal counterparts, Alamán gloried in Mexico's colonial heritage, disparaged Hidalgo's revolution, and openly praised the 1821 creole effort, led by Agustín Iturbide, to establish an independent, monarchical Mexico. In two huge and magisterial works, the *Disertaciones* and the *Historia de Méjico* (the Iberian spelling of Mexico emphasized its peninsular roots), Alamán carefully built his case for the desirability of restoring colonial values, institutions, and behavior.[47] The purpose of the *Disertaciones* was to prove the significance of Cortés and the conquest in the establishment of orderly society in the New World; the function of the *Historia* was to demonstrate the folly of Hidalgo's "rising of the proletarian class against property and civilization."[48] The hero of independence for Alamán was Iturbide and his Plan of Iguala, which had promised unity, Catholicism, and independence.

If the root of the problem of Mexico's continued existence was the failure to maintain Iturbide's vision of an independent Mexico, the solution was clearly simple: restore the old order, return to those twin bastions of stability, the Catholic Church and the monarchy. For Alamán and fellow conservatives such as José María Gutiérrez de Estrada and Luis Cuevas, the bulwark of Mexican society prior to independence had been the church. In Alamán's words, the Catholic Church was "the only common bond that unites all Mexicans when all other ties have been broken and the only one capable of sustaining the Spanish American race and protecting it from the great dangers to which it is exposed."[49] Indeed, the church had come through the independence movement relatively unscathed and still maintained much of its political, economic, and social power. For Alamán, the church was the essence of order and stability. As he wrote toward the end of his life, "In the midst of an upheaval in all sections of society, the Church is the only element which has remained unchanged."[50] And because it occupied such a vital position, it had to be protected from all assaults on its privileges, property, and prerogatives.

While Alamán was composing his defense of the old order, others, such as Gutiérrez de Estrada, another creole aristocrat, were actively working to make it a reality. As early as 1840, Gutiérrez had been openly advocating the establishment of a constitutional monarchy in Mexico.[51] With the Mexican defeat and the horrors of the 1848 revolutions (particularly the overthrow of the July Monarchy in France) fresh in his mind, Gutiérrez began a diligent campaign to locate a member of a European royal house whom he could persuade to come to Mexico, a campaign that would eventually be successful in the early 1860s.[52] Meanwhile, conservative newspapers harped on the difference between the peace of the colonial golden age of monarchy and the apparent chaos of republican Mexico.[53]

If the liberal dilemma was how to resolve the paradox of an ideology that advocated both reform and weak government, the conservatives had a similar, and in the end fatal, dilemma. Alamán and the conservatives envisioned a society dominated by the "clase propietaria," the "gente decente" of large landowners, high clergymen, and the military elite. And yet the landowners had never mobilized into a unified collective group and certainly had no stake in a conservative victory. In the first place, many were liberals hoping for a thorough destruction of the Indian ejido so that more land would be available. Obviously, liberalism posed no threat to their property. In addition, many feared the kind of authoritarian system that conservatives promised to restore. After all, a powerful national government would eventually begin asserting authority over the local dominance wielded by the hacendados. Why should they support a system that might mean the end of their power? Thus, the ultimate weakness of nineteenth-century Mexican conservatism was not so much in its ideas as in its lack of a social base. As we shall see, liberalism had a strong social base in poor creoles, transitional mestizos, liberal hacendados, and a few emancipated Indians.

In the late 1840s and early 1850s, these problems were not at all clear to either liberals or conservatives. And the immediate post-war years saw the intellectual lines hardening as Mexico experienced a period of relative political calm. Constitutional president José Joaquín de Herrera defeated the incessant rebel, Mariano Paredes y Arrillaga, and was able to step out of office without a coup. His constitutional successor, Mariano Arista, ruled a peaceful land until conservatives, led by Lucas Alamán and Antonio Haro y Tamariz, began plotting to begin the process of establishing monarchy in Mexico. When their efforts to persuade a European prince to occupy the Mexican throne met with no favorable response, they turned to the last of Mexico's great caudillos, Antonio López de Santa Anna. Their hope was that the national reputation of Santa Anna would be sufficient to begin the process of forming a monarchy.

He was to be the temporary agent while the search for a dynasty went on. So it was that in September, 1852, a local revolt against a progressive governor in the state of Jalisco became a national rebellion. Rushing to Guadalajara, the capital of Jalisco, the conservative leaders suborned the military officers, enlisted the aid of the archbishop, and began a military push to oust Arista. By the beginning of 1853, Arista was in deep political trouble as a result of the revolt. He had requested from a liberal-dominated Congress special authority to carry out a military campaign against the rebels in the north. Congress refused, and, after much wheeling and dealing, Arista was impeached. On March 17, Santa Anna was declared president-elect; on April 20, he took office. Alamán headed the conservative cabinet and proposed a general program for the new regime. It was to have five main points: (1) absolute religious intolerance, (2) strong government, (3) abolition of federal systems and popular voting, (4) reorganization of the army, and (5) no congresses. In Alamán's words: "Santa Anna well-counseled—that will be the whole Constitution." And to top it off, Santa Anna gave himself the title of "His Most Serene Highness."[54]

The conservative program finally had a political reality, and the attempt to reincarnate Iturbide's Plan of Iguala appeared to be successful. Yet, unobtrusively, the new monarchy was playing an unexpected role: it was molding the leadership of the liberal Reform effort. And it is to how the liberals united that we now turn.

3. The Reform Leadership

By the spring of 1855, "His Most Serene Highness" was hardly serene. Accusing "His Highness" of every type of malfeasance in office, plan after plan had demanded the end of the perpetual dictatorship of Antonio López de Santa Anna. On March 1, 1854, in the village of Ayutla in the southern state of Guerrero, General Juan Alvarez, Colonel Florencio Villarreal, and Colonel Ignacio Comonfort withdrew recognition of the Santa Anna regime and called for a constitutional congress. In Jalisco, Santos Degollado formed guerrilla armies to fight the dictator, while other powerful caudillos—those local chieftains who ruled their territories like absolute monarchs—such as Santiago Vidaurri in Nuevo León and Manuel Doblado in Guanajuato, issued plans of their own, expelled Santa Anna's deputies, raised armies, and joined the Ayutla movement. Even Antonio de Haro y Tamariz, one of the architects of the Santa Anna dictatorship, issued a plan in San Luis Potosí calling for the destruction of his own creation. When Haro turned against him, Santa Anna began planning his retreat. Eventually someone in almost every section of the country revolted, and, though few major battles were fought, the rebels won repeated victories. When the port city of Veracruz lent its support to the Ayutla movement on August 9, 1855, Santa Anna decided that his time had come. He sneaked from the capital that day, issued his abdication statement three days later, and boarded a steamer, once again bound for exile. The Ayutla movement had triumphed over the tawdry dictatorship that was the last of Santa Anna's eleven presidencies. In October, 1855, the old cacique from Guerrero, Juan Alvarez, became president of Mexico.[1]

Two years earlier, things had looked much rosier for Santa Anna and the conservative solution to the crisis of national survival. In January, 1853, Mariano Arista, the only president since independence in 1821 to achieve office through natural and legal succession, had been overthrown by the combined forces of upper clergy, powerful landowners, and military officers.

Under the tutelage of the creole conservatives Lucas Alamán and Haro y Tamariz, the perennial caudillo again returned to office, this time with unlimited powers for life. Once in office, Santa Anna set about pacifying those who were responsible for bringing him back from Turbaco, Colombia, where he had been living in exile since his last dictatorship during the American invasion. For the conservatives there was a centralized administration to replace federalism and a state council of "notables" to fill the legislative void created by the abolition of congress. For the militarists there was an army expanded beyond their wildest dreams, and though the number of troops did not reach the projected 96,000, it did soar from approximately 10,000 to over 46,000—many more than the dictatorship could afford. For the upper clergy there were special honors: the presidency of the council of state went to the bishop of Michoacán; in the newly revived Order of Guadalupe, high-ranking prelates held three of the seven Grand Crosses, half of the commanderships, and fifteen of the ninety-four commisions as knights. For landowners there were tariff restrictions, reduced taxes, new import privileges, prohibitions against the incorporation of peones into villages, and even control over some of the customs revenues. With a sense for the dramatic, Santa Anna gave symbolic expression to his complete authority with the grandiose title of "His Most Serene Highness." To all appearances, liberalism was crushed and the conservative, creole domination of Mexico was as complete and thorough as it had ever been since the days of Iturbide.[2]

But the very success of the centralized dictatorship carried with it the seed of its own destruction. With his large-army policy, Santa Anna based his regime on the military. The expenditures necessary to maintain 46,000 men under arms were more than the treasury could bear, and when funds ran out, so did the support of the army and of all those who had depended on Santa Anna's strong military posture. Nor were the merchants happy over the financial straits of the dictatorship. The business community found itself taxed more heavily with excessively high tariff barriers, and public administration was more corrupt than ever. Santa Anna's obsequious behavior toward the church infuriated some conservatives, not to mention moderate and radical anti-clericals, while at the same time his efforts to reform the clergy won him the enmity of some high-ranking clerics. Above all, the attempt to rule without legal or moral restrictions alienated those who had been working for personal advancement within the political system. Liberals such as Benito Juárez, Melchor Ocampo, and José María Mata found themselves in exile abroad because they had opposed Santa Anna's arbitrary rule. All segments of Mexican society—conservatives, clerics, generals, merchants, and liberal politicians—found their position weakened by the strength of the dictatorship. Later these groups would unite briefly in common cause against Santa Anna.[3]

In no area was the process more marked than in the centralization of public administration. Usurpation of the powers of the states began immediately after Santa Anna assumed office. All state legislatures were closed, and each governor became responsible solely to the dictator. The central government took over the operation of all major highways, and, ultimately, all state revenues were allocated to the national coffers. To insure complete central authority, the local ayuntamientos, or village councils, were disbanded and the governors were granted full administrative authority, including the right to appoint all officials within the state. As Lucas Alamán, the intellectual leader of the conservatives, phrased it: "Let us leave the states their sovereignties and their farces, and let us take the money from them."[4]

Such stringent centralization eventually undermined the dictatorship because it threatened too many vested interests. With the first movement toward independence from Spain and the accompanying breakdown of political authority throughout New Spain, a power vacuum had been created on the national level. As insurgent army followed insurgent army, royal authority could no longer dominate local areas, particularly in remote, hard-to-reach regions. One result had been the rise of local caciques who proceeded to rule their territories like autonomous lords. They were the power brokers in the post-independence political structure, and the president was often little more than a cacique who had the support of the majority of the other caciques. The rapid turnover of presidents from 1824 to 1853—there were forty-six changes of government in those thirty years—can be explained in part by the unwillingness of the caciques to support another of their group for very long. Mexican political life, at least up to the Mexican-American War, was thus non-ideological. Caudillos tended to be federalists to preserve their local autonomy, but they were willing to support anyone, including avowed centralists, who promised to leave them alone. The Santa Anna centralization threatened to end the caudillo system by making all local officials dependent on one dominant, permanent chief.

One region in Mexico that Santa Anna could not control was the province where the revolt broke out, Guerrero. It had been ruled by Juan Alvarez in a semi-feudal, semi-patriarchal manner since the days of Vicente Guerrero. Alvarez, protected from outside interference by high mountains, impenetrable jungles, and fiercely loyal subjects, clearly recognized the danger that Santa Anna's centralization posed for his rule, and he gathered support for a revolt. Such support was not hard to find, for Santa Anna had angered a number of southern politicians. Fearful of the use to which potential rebels might put the port of Acapulco, Santa Anna had removed its administrator, Colonel Ignacio Comonfort, and tried to substitute one of his supporters.[5] Other actions by the dictator, such as granting mining concessions without consulting Alvarez, infuriated the southerners and raised them to a fighting pitch.

Thus the growing threat to local autonomy and the weakening support for the dictatorship combined to produce the Revolution of Ayutla.

The revolt that began in Ayutla has commonly been treated as more than just another of the barracks revolts, or cuartelazos, of cacique against cacique that had plagued Mexico since independence. And yet there is little in either the Plan of Ayutla or the reformation of that plan in Acapulco to suggest that social concerns played a role in the movement against the dictatorship. The Plan of Ayutla called for the end of the Santa Anna regime because "it had trampled those individual guarantees that even the least civilized countries respect." The plan itself was remarkably federalistic, requiring each state to draw up its own code of laws, and asserting only that "the nation is and will be one, indivisible and independent." Once established, the new government was to convoke a constitutional congress "to turn the Nation into a popular, representative Republic." The Acapulco reformation toned down the excessive federalism of the Plan of Ayutla and strengthened the executive by giving him supreme powers "with no other restrictions than that he should inviolably respect individual guarantees."[6]   In neither plan was there any expression of concern for the social ills of nineteenth-century Mexico; there was no mention of the church and its wealth or of the Indian and his poverty. Both plans were aimed exclusively at Santa Anna and his unlimited, centralized dictatorship.[7]

Most of the historical literature views the Plan of Ayutla as, in the words of one official historian, "an expression of authentic social and political revolution" and "the first banner of the revolution that gave Mexico its definitive character and structure."[8]   This view is exaggerated and incorrect. The Ayutla movement was not a revolution. But it was more than just another in Mexico's seemingly interminable cuartelazos, since it served as the catalyst for a ten-year holocaust that involved both a civil war and a foreign intervention. These consequences would suggest that much more was at stake in the Ayutla movement than a mere transfer of power from one caudillo to another. What began as a traditional barracks revolt ended up as a full-scale conflict between disparate political ideologies. The last Santa Anna regime was more than traditional caudillismo desperately trying to hang on to the reigns of government for a few months; instead, it was the first attempt since the days of Iturbide to reestablish Bourbon rule in Mexico. It represented the conservative vision of Mexico's solution to the problem of national survival. As such, it was opposed to the extension of liberalism, the continuation of federal republicanism, and the secularization of society. At its inception, the Ayutla movement was concerned only with the problem of centralization of power, and Juan Alvarez would have accepted any government that promised him local autonomy. But the movement had others in its ranks who had a much broader conception of the struggle. For these liberals—Benito Juárez, Melchor Ocampo, Ponciano

Arriaga, Ignacio Ramírez, the brothers Lerdo de Tejada, to name a few—the overthrow of Santa Anna was the renewal of the liberal struggle to complete the work of independence by removing the last vestiges of Mexico's colonial heritage.

In October, 1855, Juan Alvarez led his army of *pintos* (so-called because of their dark skin) into an exhausted Mexico City and assumed the presidency. In his wake he brought with him a group of liberals who assumed high positions in the new government and who began using those positions to make dramatic changes in government policy. The liberal leadership obviously chose to follow the risky course of reform for complex reasons. And yet this important problem has never been systematically analyzed in the voluminous literature on the Reform movement. In order to suggest some of the motivations behind the liberal program and to explain why the program took the particular form that it did, I have selected thirty-six liberal leaders—see Appendix A—to study in some detail.[9] The criteria used for the selection were two: (1) the individuals had to have been among the original supporters of the Ayutla program, and (2) they had to remain loyal to the liberal cause during the Three Years War (or War of the Reform) and the French intervention (if they lived that long). The first criterion seemed appropriate because the focus of the analysis here is on the origins of the movement. But the second was necessary for several reasons. Most important of all, many supported the Ayutla movement at its inception solely because of opposition to certain programs of the Santa Anna regime (like Bishop Munguía), or in the hopes of destroying what was considered a false monarchy in favor of a true European royal monarch (like Antonio Haro y Tamariz), or simply because the rebellion provided an opportunity for a power move on the local level (like Santiago Vidaurri in Nuevo León and Coahuila). Those who joined for these reasons did not remain with the liberals when the Reform program produced civil war and foreign intervention. In fact, a number of participants in the Ayutla movement were instrumental in fomenting both the Reform War and the French empire. Thus the second criterion served as a screen to filter through those who were committed to the liberal vision of Mexico's future.

The question still remains, Who were the men who came to power with the Ayutla movement? The remainder of this chapter will explore the social bases of the liberal leadership. Seven areas of inquiry will be considered: age, regional origins, education, social status, religious experiences, occupation, and political career.[10] The data for this analysis are discouragingly scarce and do not lead to decisive conclusions; instead, all that can be offered here are some suggestive patterns and, it is hoped, fruitful speculation.

Age

When the literature on the Reform does speculate about the leadership and the social base of the movement, almost invariably it mentions that the Reform movement was a generational conflict.[11] And yet that explanation does not account for either the form that the liberal program took or the intensity of the conflict that it produced. Nevertheless, like many such considerations, the generational question does play an important role in the analysis of the motivation for the Reform. The data on the thirty-six leaders indicate clearly that they were a new generation in Mexican politics. As table 1 demonstrates, only three were born before 1810 and none were born in the eighteenth century. Over half (53%) were born after 1820 and almost one-fifth after 1830. The largest single category is made up of those born during the tumultuous years of the independence movements between 1810 and 1821.

TABLE 1
AGE DISTRIBUTION OF LIBERAL LEADERSHIP

Decade Born		Number	Percentage
1800–1809		3	8
1810–1819		14	39
1820–1829		12	34
1830–		7	19
	Totals	36	100

Several suggestive conclusions can be drawn from these data. One of the most important is that the Reform liberals were the first generation to mature after independence. Indeed, in contrast to the men who made up Santa Anna's last cabinet, there was clearly a generational conflict in the Reform movement. Santa Anna's ministers were, with two exceptions, born before 1811. The backbone of the Santa Anna cabinet, Lucas Alamán, was born in 1792, and another key minister, José Alcorta, was born in 1787. Not one of Santa Anna's ministers was born after 1815. Many of the cabinet members had even been active in the Trigarante army of Iturbide's empire in the early 1820s, at a time when half of the Reform leadership had not yet been born.

A second conclusion that can be drawn from these data is that because the liberal elite was born primarily during or after independence, they were products of the chaotic conditions of their age. In fact, chaos seems to be a constant in their lives: born in times of rebellion, growing up in times of great instability, and reaching political adolescence at precisely the moment Mexico suffered its most severe political crisis, the Mexican-American War. It is not surprising that one of the central themes of the Reform movement, as we will see, was the almost desperate search for law and order, a search that would ultimately lead to authoritarian rule.

Nor is it surprising that the Reform program took the form of a thorough rejection of colonial traditions. After all, the leaders of the Reform had been born during the collapse of the colonial structure. They had no roots in or emotional ties to colonial institutions, values, or political patterns. Their experience had been republican, federal, and democratic, not monarchical, centralized, and authoritarian. As teenagers they had observed the aborted liberal reforms of Gómez Farías and Mora; as young adults they had watched the United States humiliate the Mexican republic; and in the 1850s, as maturing political participants, they would try to redress these wrongs.

Regional Origins

The Reform was more than just a movement of young against old; it was also an attack by the periphery on the center. An analysis of the birth places of the Reform leadership indicates that the principal liberals came from what could be called the "liberal circle," a vast arc of territory that slices from Veracruz up through San Luis Potosí, Zacatecas, Guanajuato, Jalisco, then back down through Michoacán, and ends in Guerrero and Oaxaca.[12] With the notable exceptions of the Riva Palacios, Leandro Valle, Guillermo Prieto, and Manuel Payno, the leading liberals overwhelmingly came from the periphery of the old colonial empire. Veracruz produced the brothers Lerdo de Tejada: Miguel, who authored the Ley Lerdo disamortizing corporate property, and Sebastián, who became Juárez's successor as president. Also from Veracruz came the merchant Manuel Gutiérrez Zamora, the physician José María Mata, and the general Ignacio de la Llave. San Luis Potosí produced one of the leading intellectuals of the Reform, Ponciano Arriaga, and neighboring Guanajuato contributed three of the Reform's most distinguished leaders, Santos Degollado, Manuel Doblado, and Ignacio Ramírez. From the far northern states of Nuevo León, Coahuila, Durango, and Zacatecas came such liberals as Mariano Escobedo, Francisco Zarco, Juan Antonio de la Fuente, and Jesús González Ortega. Even Texas made a contribution in the person of the hero of the Fifth of May, Ignacio Zaragoza. But perhaps the most distinguished group came from the state of Jalisco with its sophisticated capital, Guadalajara. Frequently in opposition to the dominance of Mexico City, Guadalajara was a natural site for the development of provincial liberals. And from Jalisco came the general Pedro Ogazón, the lawyer Ignacio Vallarta, and the journalist-lawyers Juan José Baz and José María Vigil.

But the question still remains: What was it about this fertile circle that produced the leadership of the Reform? The lack of data prevents a clear-cut set of answers. If anything comes out clearly from the evidence at hand, it is that a wide variety of local conditions produced the liberal leadership. As has already been mentioned, one element in the complex situation was the tradition of provincial opposition to the dominance of the core and particularly Mexico City. Although Guadalajara stands out as the prototype of the anti-Mexico City sentiments, it was by no means alone. Veracruz, too, had a long tradition of distrust of the exploitative nature of the port's relationship with the metropolis. And the Bajío, with its unique capitalist development during the eighteenth century, had been the starting point for Hidalgo's rebellion against the colonial system.

The importance of Veracruz as a participant in the Reform cannot be emphasized enough. Five of the thirty-six Reform leaders came from the Veracruz area, and it was to Veracruz that Juárez fled when the conservatives launched a concerted effort to remove the Ayutla government. Indeed, Veracruz was consistent throughout the Reform and the French intervention in its support for the liberal reform movement. Clearly the Veracruz merchants had much to gain from a liberal victory: a laissez-faire economic structure, reduced tariffs, increased trade, and local autonomy. Whereas conservatism allied itself with Mexico City, industrialism, and monarchy, liberalism promised anti-clericalism, republicanism, and an economy based on trade and commerce. For these reasons Veracruz had been for some time a bastion of anti-clerical sentiments. As José María Mata put it to the 1856 Constitutional Congress: "In 1848, just as the press and private circles began to discuss the question of religious liberty, *only one town in the Republic,* Veracruz, the capital of my state, actually presented to Congress demands that it declare religious toleration."[13]

Jalisco, too, was a logical source of liberal support. Isolated from the center of Mexico by the Sierra Madre Occidental mountains, traditionally independent of Mexico City, and economically self-sufficient, Jalisco became one of the centers of liberal support for the Reform movement. The University of Guadalajara, located in the capital of Jalisco, had produced some of Mexico's leading early liberal writers: Mariano Otero, Carlos María Bustamante, and Ramos Arizpe. Since the 1830s Jalisco had experienced a constant struggle between the secular state government and the powerful ecclesiastical hierarchy. It was from the quills of Guadalajara prelates that hundreds of anti-liberal clerical pronouncements flowed. Much of the strong anti-clerical sentiment of the Jalisco reformers can be traced directly to the long tradition of church-state conflicts.[14]

The liberal circle supplied the leadership for the Reform movement for another, and more complex, reason. In marked contrast to the conservative core area of Mexico City, Puebla, Querétaro, Toluca, and Pachuca, the liberal circle showed a highly varied social and economic system. The core area had been the heart of the colonial empire. Here the sharp dichotomy between hacendado and peon, between landed rich and debt-bonded poor, left little room for middle groups composed of small proprietors and tenant farmers. The periphery, on the other hand, seems to have evolved a remarkably complex agricultural and social structure. Although there is no systematic study of the entire area, scattered recent studies of haciendas, mining communities, and agricultural production in such areas as San Luis Potosí, the Bajío, and Los Altos of Jalisco and Michoacán suggest substantial variety in class structure and methods of production.[15]

The most striking economic difference between the core and the periphery was the large number of independently owned small farms or ranchos in the periphery. The ranchos were prosperous, although frequently they were so clustered together as to form minifundia. Interspersed among the ranchos were the larger haciendas. But many, if not most, had been forced to rent a large proportion of their land to sharecroppers and tenant farmers. Peonage was thus a relatively insignificant labor form in the periphery. More usual was the hiring of day laborers—jornaleros—to plant and harvest the crops. In addition, the lower classes of the periphery were made up of yearly tenants, sharecroppers, and sometimes simply squatters who worked the land left vacant by unprofitable haciendas. Thus, while the core of central Mexico was a generally closed society in the middle of the nineteenth century, the near north, the ports, and the near south were more capitalistic and socially more fluid.

Social Status

The social fluidity of the periphery was the result of a long heritage of race mixture. Since the days of the Aztecs, the periphery (with the obvious exception of Veracruz) had been outside the imperial domain. During the three hundred years of colonial rule, the periphery had been settled sparsely, and even then only around the great mining centers. It was in this area that the mestizo found opportunities for advancement. In fact, the large number of mestizos that played a prominent role in the Reform has led many observers to comment that the Reform was, for all intents and purposes, a mestizo movement against white, or creole, rule. Andrés Molina Enríquez was one of the first to observe that the group was primarily mestizo. As he forcefully expressed it:

Since the mestizos were united with the Indian race by blood, since they
carried with them a great store of energy, since they did not have monarchical traditions, since they did not have religious traditions, since they
did not have aristocratic traditions, and since upon taking over the country
they have bettered [its] condition, it can be said with justice that they were
the true patriots, the true founders of our nationality . . . . Now it is understood why the national instinct gave to the Revolution of Ayutla the proportions of a social revolution.[16]

Molina Enríquez overstated the case. As far as can be determined only two-
thirds of the Reform leadership were mestizos. Most of the rest were creoles
from poor families who did not benefit from the distribution of power within
their caste. Creoles such as Matías Romero, Manuel Doblado, Ezequiel Montes,
Ignacio Comonfort, José María Lafragua, and the Lerdo brothers did not come
from aristocratic families but rather from those on the bottom rung of the
creole ladder. Doblado and Lafragua came from abject poverty; the Lerdo
brothers benefitted little from their father's merchant enterprises. Only
Comonfort came from a wealthy creole family, but he had supported liberal
causes and presumably was not considered a member of the conservative creole
elite. Some creoles, like Mariano Riva Palacio, took mestiza wives. Riva
Palacio's wife was the daughter of the mestizo independence caudillo, Vicente
Guerrero, and his son, Vicente, was therefore a mestizo. Although the Ayutla
group included creoles, they were not of the landed, creole ruling elite.

Also in the group were two Indians, Benito Juárez and Ignacio Altamirano,
and properly speaking neither should be considered racially mestizo. Yet
they did not consider themselves part of traditional Indian society. Juárez
left his village behind and submerged himself in the half-caste world of Oaxaca
City. To solidify his place in mestizo culture the Oaxacan Indian took a wife
of Italian origin, Margarita de la Maza, and bred mestizo children. It is a striking
fact that in all the correspondence of the Juárez Archive in Mexico City there
is practically no mention of Indians. For Juárez, the Indian past was dead; the
mestizo present was his reality.

Similarly, Altamirano fled from his Indian village in Guerrero, sought education in Toluca, and entered the world of those between hacienda and Indian
village. His experiences in that world led him to sympathize with the plight
of the mestizo, and he offered this acute analysis of the situation: "The mestizo," he asserted in a patriotic speech glorifying Hidalgo,

. . . could not feel a part of the European blood he had in his veins. Social
considerations forced him to deny the Indian blood that mixed with [the
European]. He was forbidden to study the sciences and thus was unable to

become more than an obscure worker. In the high speculation of commerce he could become no more than a peddler in the market or a mule driver. In the military hierarchy he could become little more than a common soldier.[17]

Manuel Payno made the same evaluation of the condition of the mestizos and made their cause his as well. As a poor creole he had been excluded from the higher ranks of power and felt the sting of social discrimination. Payno wondered, as the conservatives were waging desperate war against the liberal program in the three years from 1858 to 1860,

... why, after years and years and after a new family, a third race, has flowered and grown that can and ought to live free, earning their own incomes, cultivating their fields, living under their own laws, there is an oppressive and terrible force that sends soldiers, cannons, and weapons of death to stop them?[18]

Francisco Zarco, a mestizo and spokesman for the Reform goals through his newspaper *El Siglo XIX,* echoed the same theme of social discrimination. In a series of editorials entitled "The Third Estate" he explored the nature of the new elite and its members' common bonds. Zarco described the group as "the strongest part of the nation, the hardest working, the most industrious, and doubtless the most politically enlightened, since it includes lawyers, doctors, industrialists, and merchants." Although these were the elements of a strong and stable society, Zarco noted that in Mexico they had no place in the two-caste structure. "Intolerance," he argued, "was carried to the extreme of not admitting to the clergy, courts of justice, and high military those individuals who did not belong to the titular nobility . . . closing the door to ability and merit with monopolies while at the same time obstructing the formation and development of the middle class."[19]

This sense of uniqueness as a group and hatred for discrimination produced in the liberal elite a positive attitude toward their condition in life. They developed a new self-awareness that did not deprecate their condition but instead glorified it. The mestizo often was given attributes that combined the best of both his heritages. Ignacio Ramírez, in a patriotic speech, asked the overriding questions in the minds of the new group: "Where did we come from? Where are we going?" His answer was that they were neither Aztec nor Spanish but something unique and new. "We are," he said, "descendants of the people . . . born struggling . . . for all the symbols of emancipation."[20] Eventually the glorification of the mestizo became so intense that all historical reality was lost. One deputy in the congress, carried away by his enthusiasm, claimed that all Mexico's heroes were mestizos. He correctly stated that "we are descendants of two races" and just as incorrectly argued that "from this mixture came such men as Hidalgo and Iturbide, Morelos and Bravo, Matamoros and Guerrero, Zaragoza, Juárez, and many others." He pointed out that even the name "Mexico" was a mixture of two languages, Náhuatl and Spanish, and that it was therefore the appropriate name of the nation.[21] Melchor Ocampo described the mestizo liberals as "noted for their energy of character, the simpleness of their habits, the independence of their social ties and means of subsistence." He concluded with an awareness of the rootless position of the members of the liberal elite when he wrote: "We are not well classified in Mexico."[22] The Reform group began to see itself in a positive light, as a unique and new body of men destined for power. An anonymous author summarized all these feelings: "We are another class of men, new men, enlightened and unfanatical, children of reason."[23]

The deep sense of self-awareness on the part of the provincial liberals inspired an equally profound hatred for what they termed the conservative aristocracy. Guillermo Prieto, in a circular from the Minister of Hacienda to the governors of the states, blamed Mexico's problems on "all the frauds of privilege, all the foul cunning of the *fuero*, all the corruption of the aristocracy."[24] José María Lafragua accused the conservative aristocracy of encouraging political chaos and civil war in order to maintain its control. As he viewed the aristocrats' strategy: "They want disorder . . . because this incessant anarchy adds to their fortunes . . . forcing the people to succumb to the oligarchy, exchanging liberty for peace and their rights for tranquility."[25]

Throughout the liberal leadership ran the feeling that the aristocracy was only interested in its own well-being and was willing to sacrifice national interests for its own. Francisco Zarco, in an editorial entitled "The Reaction," branded the conservative elite "criminals" and accused them of "separating their cause from that of the people." "Privilege, *fuero*, and caste interest are . . . their traditions."[26] Similarly, the governor of the northern state of Tamaulipas exhorted his citizens to resist the aristocracy because "we know the privileged classes want to dominate and make sure that private interests prevail over the great majority of the nation."[27]

A general feeling existed among the liberals that the creole elite was an anachronism, belonging to another age that had long passed. The liberal newspaper *El Republicano* best expressed this view in an editorial justifying attempts to disamortize church property. The paper argued that history had taught that in times of ignorance and anarchy a privileged class made up of nobility and clergy was necessary to provide stability. "The clergy cultivated the sciences and the arts while the nobility was strong, intrepid, valorous, heroic, rich, and generous, and defended the national independence, but . . . Oh, how much, how far have the nobility degenerated!" Thus the utility of the traditional social structure was called into question. For the new liberals the conservative elite had monopolized all power and status in the state and yet served no social function. It had maintained all the privileges, as had the French aristocracy before the French Revolution, but had abdicated all its responsibilities. The good parts of the colonial system had disappeared and only the onerous remained. *El Republicano* vehemently denounced the creole elite and called for its destruction. "The aristocracy and clergy, unable to defend the kings, cannot and will not defend the people."[28]

What emerges from these comments by the liberal leaders is a strong sense of rootlessness, a feeling of resentment against the established order that has attempted to exclude them from the opportunities of office, wealth, and prestige. Certainly the number of mestizos in the leadership group would suggest a social dimension to the Reform movement. But it would be a mistake to push the racial component of the Reform movement too far, because there were other and, in many ways, more important social and cultural variables that made the Reform take the form and content that it did. One such element was the educational background of the liberal leadership.

Education

The social tensions that permeated Mexican society had been thrust upon the liberals at the time they entered school, and their educational experiences continued to color their later political views. The most famous case of social strain in education was that of Benito Juárez in the Royal Academy of Oaxaca. Unable to speak Spanish, the young shepherd knew that the only way to learn was to take up domestic service in Oaxaca City. Once in the city he enrolled in the Royal Academy. There he was placed in a separate class made up of poor students while the "decent ones" [*gente decente*] had a special class. When he was asked to do a difficult lesson, he could not do it and was severely punished. The event left its mark on the young Indian. Years later he bitterly remembered his experience:

This injustice offended me profoundly, and so did the inequality with which instruction was dispensed in that institution . . . for while the master taught a certain number of so-called respectable pupils correctly in a separate room, I and the other poor boys like myself were relegated to another room, under the direction of a man who called himself the Assistant, and who was as little qualified to teach, and of a character as harsh, as the master himself. I was disgusted with this wretched method of teaching.[29]

If he learned anything at the school it was class consciousness, a hatred for the *gente decente* who had punished and segregated him. But because the church controlled almost all education, Juárez was forced to continue in such schools, eventually choosing a career in the clergy. The social tensions and the boredom of ecclesiastical education later caused him to drop Moral Theology, and when a secular school, the Institute of Sciences and Arts, was established in 1827, Juárez enrolled. With that move the clergy lost its weakening hold on the young man; his future allegiance was cast to the secular state.

The Oaxacan institute produced not only Juárez but also Porfirio Díaz, José María Mata, Ignacio Mariscal, and Manuel Ruiz. The liberal, secular attitudes of the professors at the institute created a generation of young men eager to put those values into practice. At the same time the Oaxacan upper classes condemned the institute as "a house of prostitution" and the students and faculty as "heretics" and "libertines." There were good reasons for the epithets. The faculty was teaching that ecclesiastical control over civil authority, family, and all secular society was dangerous and had to be destroyed. So vehement was the ecclesiastical attack on the school that good families refused to send their children and, as Juárez put it, the students who did attend were "excommunicated by the immense majority of that ignorant, fanatic, and unfortunate society."[30] Thus the school became a training camp for those on the margins of Mexican society, for those who had no family reputations to ruin and no deep social roots to destroy. The rootless, the orphans, the poor, the mestizos, the socially "excommunicated"—these were the new wards of secular education and future agents of liberal, secular reform.

Half of the liberal leadership were educated by the new secular institutes, principally in the area of jurisprudence. The lawyers found themselves studying other legal systems in addition to the traditional canon law. Natural, civil, and constitutional law were taught in comparative law courses, undermining the tradition of dogmatic authority. In practically every state the institutes were taking in the young and ambitious who found no home in Catholic education. This new generation of students with a legal and secular point of view provided the leadership for secular nation-building in Mexico.[31]

For those who did not study law there was always a military education, and here, too, secular instruction molded men with viewpoints and values that differed sharply from those taught in traditional church-oriented schools. Leandro Valle, for example, began his studies in the Colegio Militar at the age of eleven years. His experience with secular education led him to question the value of ecclesiastical control over secular affairs as well as the alliance between the military and the church, an alliance that had resulted in the formation of a conservative party whose goals were to protect the special privileges and prerogatives of the two corporations.[32]

Religious Conflict

Another common and recurring pattern in the development of the Reform leadership was the seemingly inevitable conflict with the Catholic Church. As generally rootless and secularly educated, liberals had felt the pressures of social discrimination and had been taught to question the accepted values that produced that discrimination. Because they had no roots in the established social structure they could consider remolding society to include themselves. Such questioning of traditional customs and values led them into severe conflicts with the clergy, and these clashes were to color their attitudes toward the ecclesiastical establishment once they seized the reins of power. Juárez discovered in his law practice that the clergy and the civil authorities worked hand in glove to give the church "an almost omnipotent influence." As a lawyer he found that the ecclesiastical *fuero* prevented secular law from touching the clergy and led to "all kinds of excesses and all kinds of injustices." When Juárez attempted to defend the villagers of Loricha against the excessive demands of the local curate, he found the leading villagers jailed by the ecclesiastical judge. When he appealed the unjust incarceration he discovered that the clergy controlled the high court of Oaxaca, and "the doors of justice remained closed." One midnight Juárez was arrested on the order of a high church official for stirring up a riot in Loricha—a village he had never visited! It took nine days of appeal to obtain his release and he never forgot the experience. He described the event with great passion in his "Notes to My Children."

> Because I and others suffered these blows almost daily at the hands of the privileged classes in partnership with the civil authorities, I became strikingly aware that society would never be happy as long as they and their alliance existed, and I affirmed my goal of constantly working to destroy their evil power.[33]

Of such experiences reformers are made, and Juárez was no exception. What happened to him in the 1830s was to influence his attitude toward the ecclesiastic elite and the church when power was finally his.

Juárez was not alone in clashing with the ecclesiastical corporation. In 1851 Melchor Ocampo, shocked by the refusal of a priest to bury a dead man for lack of funds to pay for the service, launched a campaign to reform the practices of parochial fee collections for performance of the sacraments. According to legend, the priest involved, Augustín Dueñas of Maravatío, Michoacán, told the dead man's widow to eat the body rather than ask for alms. Ocampo was horrified, and a large-scale polemical battle ensued between

two individuals representing two opposing world views: the theocratic absolutism of the church and the secular liberalism of the new generation.[34] Two
years later, in 1853, Ocampo was arrested and sent into exile, and his property
was threatened with confiscation by the clerical-supported Santa Anna regime.
Such was the price of crossing the clergy.

Ignacio Vallarta learned the same lesson. He began his political career supporting the privileges and prerogatives of the church until the arch-conservative
Bishop of Guadalajara, Pedro Espinosa, bitterly attacked him for his liberal
views. The result of the attack was that Vallarta became a leading anti-cleric.[35]
In the life of almost every member of the Reform leadership a conflict with
the church figured prominently and provided a common bond among all the
new political elite of Mexico after Ayutla.

Occupation

Because the opportunities for employment were so limited during the nineteenth century, most Mexicans who were not farmers had multiple occupations.
Table 2 indicates the principal occupations of the thirty-six liberals.

TABLE 2
PRINCIPAL OCCUPATIONS OF LIBERAL LEADERSHIP

Principal Occupation	Number	Percentage	Cumulative Percentage
Lawyer	15	41.7	41.7
Military	8	22.2	63.9
Bureaucracy	5	13.9	77.8
Journalist	4	11.0	88.8
Education	1	2.8	91.6
Medicine	1	2.8	94.4
Landowner	1	2.8	97.2
Merchant	1	2.8	100.0
Totals	36	100.0	

Lawyers, soldiers, bureaucrats, and journalists dominated the liberal movement. Almost 89 percent came from just these four professions, and most of
those who were bureaucrats or journalists had studied law at some point in
their lives. Many young lawyers were unable to find enough work simply to

practice law and frequently sought other ways to supplement their income. In doing so, they invariably ran into conflicts with the conservative administration established by Santa Anna and Alamán in 1853. Manuel Doblado, for example, overcame a destitute childhood, obtained a law degree in Guanajuato, and taught law before finding it more lucrative to serve as a justice on Guanajuato's supreme court. Highly ambitious and with talent to match, Doblado then became governor of his state at the age of twenty-eight. He used that office to mold a power base and transform himself into a local cacique. He was later one of the caudillo leaders in the revolt against Santa Anna and a stalwart of the Reform movement undertaken by the Ayutla group.[36]

Many others of the liberal leadership followed the route from lawyer to politician. Benito Juárez, an Indian from the southern state of Oaxaca, was, as we have seen, orphaned at the age of three and lived with his Zapotec grandparents in the tiny village of Guelatao high in the mountains surrounding the valley of Oaxaca. Too ambitious to be contained in the closed community, Juárez left his home at the age of twelve and walked to the state capital in the valley below. There, under the guidance of Dr. Antonio Salanueva, a lay brother in the Third Order of Saint Francis, Juárez received his ecclesiastical education, preparing himself for a clerical career. When the ecclesiastical education in its turn proved too confining he switched to the newly established secular Institute of Sciences and Arts, which awarded him a law degree. He then began his political adventures. In 1831, at the age of twenty-five, he was elected to the city council, and two years later, during the liberal regime of Valentín Gómez Farías, to the national congress. Rapidly progressing up the political ladder, Juárez was named secretary general to the governor of the state of Oaxaca in 1844, grooming himself for the office of governor, which he won in 1847. From then on he built a reputation as a fair and honest—if unspectacular and conservative—administrator and as a shrewd politician. His only mistake was once to snub Santa Anna, and for this he was exiled from Mexico in 1853. That experience changed the latent liberal into the ardent reformer and made Juárez one of the leaders of the movement.[37]

Not all the lawyers came from the absolute poverty known by Juárez and Doblado. Some, like Melchor Ocampo, were at the other end of the economic spectrum. Unlike Doblado and Juárez, Ocampo was born into wealth and security, in the valley of Maravatío in Michoacán. Of unknown parents, he was raised by the creole owner of the increasingly impoverished hacienda of Pateo, Doña Francisca Xaviera Tapia, and it was from her that he inherited his land. Leaving Michoacán, Ocampo went to Mexico City, where he enrolled in the university and studied law. Later he served as a liberal senator from Michoacán and twice as governor of the state. He cultivated a keen interest in scientific experimentation and French philosophy, which led him to conduct sophisticated botanical studies and to read widely in the works of Voltaire, Diderot, Benjamin Constant, and Proudhon. When Santa Anna became dictator in 1853, he removed the increasingly liberal Ocampo from the governorship and exiled him from Mexico. Ocampo met Juárez for the first time in their New Orleans exile—an event ripe with future significance for the development of the Reform in Mexico.[38]

Most of the lawyer-politicians experienced neither the extreme poverty of Juárez and Doblado nor the downward mobility of Ocampo. They usually came from families with small incomes and large ambitions. Santos Degollado lived in Doblado's state of Guanajuato. His father's property had been confiscated during the Hidalgo revolt because the family supported the rebel priest. Young Degollado studied law, entered both politics and the military, and became a local political boss. Similarly, Juan Antonio de la Fuente, a poor, mestizo orphan, rose to the rank of lawyer and became a leading politician in the state of Coahuila. Others who followed this lawyer-politician route to power were poor creoles such as Ezequiel Montes in Querétaro and Matías Romero in Oaxaca, and mestizos such as Vicente Riva Palacio, son of the governor of the state of Mexico.[39]

Some members of the liberal leadership sought law degrees as means to careers in public service. José María Lafragua of Puebla was born in 1813 of creole parents and began his public career as soon as he received his law degree in 1835. By 1842 he was serving in the Constitutional Congress and in 1846 he became minister of foreign and internal affairs for President Salas. He made his mark as a liberal, and when Santa Anna seized power in 1853, Lafragua was ordered arrested. In this way another creole ousted from the ruling elite was to become an implacable foe of the conservative establishment. Ignacio Vallarta pursued a similar career, no sooner receiving his law degree from the University of Guadalajara in 1854 than Santos Degollado named him his private secretary. From there Vallarta took up the teaching of law and finally became a judge. By the end of his life Vallarta had served as a congressman (1856-1857), secretary of gobernación (1861-1863), governor of the state of Jalisco (1871-1875), secretary of foreign affairs (1876-1878), and justice of the Supreme Court (1878-1882).[40]

Ponciano Arriaga was a lawyer who never practiced law. Born in San Luis Potosí, he received his law degree before he was twenty years old, but he sought other means of livelihood, particularly politics. He served on the ayuntamiento of San Luis Potosí, then as a deputy in the state legislature, and finally as secretary general of the state government. When Santa Anna exiled Arriaga for his political liberalism, he joined Juárez and Ocampo in New Orleans to begin plotting for the expected seizure of power. Others who joined Arriaga in exile were Miguel María Arrioja and Jesús Terán, both of whom had served in diplomatic posts, and two bureaucrats, Manuel Ruiz and Ignacio Mariscal.[41]

Because few sources of power were available to members of the growing professional group, many of the lawyers found journalism a comfortable outlet for pent-up grievances against the political system. In print they could express ideas that they could not put into practice. Ignacio Ramírez and José María Vigil both studied law and then pursued careers in the world of newspapers and pamphlets. After graduating from law school, Ramírez, along with Guillermo Prieto, established the witty and sarcastic newspaper *Don Simplicio*. When Santa Anna suppressed it during the American invasion, Ramírez worked on another paper, *La Insurrección*. His first political venture was as deputy to the Constituent Congress in 1856-1857. Later he served Juárez as minister of justice, public instruction, and development. From 1868 to 1879 he was a justice on the Supreme Court. Similarly, Vigil had studied law but made his reputation writing for *El País* of Guadalajara and *El Monitor Republicano* in Mexico City. Eventually Vigil became the semi-official historian of the Reform movement when he wrote the fifth volume of Vicente Riva Palacio's monumental *México a través de los siglos*.[42]

José María Iglesias was another lawyer-journalist who incurred the wrath of Santa Anna. After studying in the Colegio de San Gregorio and the Academia Teoricopráctica de Jurisprudencia, Iglesias taught at the Colegio de San Ildefonso. In 1848 he was named editor-in-chief of the leading liberal newspaper in Mexico City, *El Siglo XIX*. With Guillermo Prieto and Manuel Payno, he wrote a history of the Mexican-American War that so outraged Santa Anna that when the dictator once again had power he fired Iglesias from his bureaucratic post. Later Iglesias served Prieto in the treasury and became minister of justice and ecclesiastical affairs under Comonfort.[43]

Francisco Zarco, like some others, went directly into journalism because an education was impossible to obtain. Zarco's father was a colonel in the military and a minor bureaucratic official in the distant province of Durango. The family was too poor to provide an education for their son, who was forced to quit school and seek work. As in the case of many young liberals, Zarco migrated to Mexico City and went to work where he could. Eventually he became the editor of *El Siglo XIX*, following the illustrious footsteps of Iglesias. His editorials attacking the military and the creole establishment prompted Santa Anna to send the fiery journalist into exile and close down *El Siglo*. The effect of this on Zarco was profound. He returned on the heels of the Ayutla movement determined to stamp out of Mexico forever the twin horrors of military dictatorship and press censorship.[44]

Unlike Zarco, Guillermo Prieto entered journalism indirectly. Born in Molino del Rey near Mexico City, he lived comfortably until his father suddenly died and his mother went mad. For all intents and purposes an orphan, Prieto had to work in a clothing store to keep up his education. Luckily, some of the poetry he wrote to express his sorrow came to the attention of Andrés Quintana Roo, then minister of justice, who was so moved by the poems that he agreed to support the rest of Prieto's education. Shortly thereafter President Anastasio Bustamante made Prieto editor of the *Diario Oficial* and brought him to live at the presidential palace in 1837—all this at the age of nineteen! In 1841, when Santa Anna overthrew Bustamante, Prieto left the *Diario* and went to work at the anti-Santa Anna paper *El Siglo*. Later he switched to another crusading newspaper in the capital, *El Monitor Republicano,* and edited, with Ignacio Ramírez, *Don Simplicio.* Under the pen name of "Fidel" he attacked the Santa Anna dictatorship, and for this he was arrested in 1853 and exiled to Cadereyta in the state of Querétaro, where he remained under house arrest for six months. The conservative military dictatorship had made another implacable enemy.[45]

The second-largest occupational category was the military. Many were mestizos who found the upper ranks closed to them but who did find a chance for some advancement through the lower ranks. Jesús González Ortega, for example, came from a poor mestizo family in the state of Zacatecas. Unable to receive an education, he enlisted in the military in the hopes of advancing through the ranks. Finding the upper echelons closed to mestizos, he became increasingly liberal, attracted to the emphasis on equality found in nineteenth-century liberalism. Santa Anna, desiring to sweep the army clean of liberal influences, was aware of González Ortega's views and offered a bounty for the person who successfully murdered the young military figure.[46]

Ignacio Zaragoza, on the other hand, came from a military family that knew the effects of discrimination. The life-long military career of Zaragoza's father had brought him only to the rank of captain. Born in Bahía de Espíritu Santo, Texas, young Zaragoza had hoped to avoid a military career and wanted to enter business, but, thwarted by Mexico's devastated economy, he followed his father's advice and entered the service. There he encountered the same problems of advancement his father and other mestizos were facing. The biographies of mestizos like Leandro Valle, Ignacio de la Llave, Mariano Escobedo, and Porfirio Díaz indicate that all experienced discrimination based on their race and humble origins.[47]

Ignacio Comonfort presents a striking contrast to the preceding figures. Unlike the young mestizos, Comonfort was the son of a rich creole who had sided with the Spaniards rather than with his own class during the independence struggles. Young Comonfort entered the military at the age of eleven and advanced rapidly, reaching the rank of colonel. In all probability and in spite of his moderate views he would not have been among the liberal group had not Santa Anna summarily removed him from his comfortable job as head of the Acapulco customs house. Thereafter he harbored a hatred for Santa Anna that was every bit as profound as the hatred of those who found themselves in exile. Respect for his honesty led many of the Reform leaders to support him for the presidency, which he achieved in 1855.[48]

Those creoles who did not come from families of the ruling elite, and who did not enter the military, chose careers in government bureaucracy. Manuel Payno worked in the tobacco administration before becoming a section chief in the ministry of war. A moderate liberal, he was exiled by Santa Anna, and he eventually made a name for himself in economics, in journalism, and as a novelist whose book *Los Bandidos de Río Frío* has become one of the best-known literary works of nineteenth-century Mexico. Miguel Lerdo de Tejada came from a merchant family in Veracruz and pursued business as a career until entering the government bureaucracy at a low level. His younger brother, Sebastián, entered the priesthood, a common practice among second-son creoles, who hoped to reach the upper levels of the clerical hierarchy, which were generally closed to mestizos and Indians. Sebastián, after taking minor orders, found the clergy too limited for his taste; he switched to secular education, becoming the rector of San Ildefonso in 1852—a position he held for eleven years.[49]

Although the predominant occupations were in the law, journalism, the bureaucracy, and the military, some other professions were scattered throughout the liberal group. José María Mata was a doctor in Jalapa, Veracruz. As an outspoken liberal he was exiled by Santa Anna. He ended up in New Orleans, joining Juárez, Ocampo, and Arriaga in the long wait for the fall of His Serene Highness. Manuel Gutiérrez Zamora, also of Veracruz, was a merchant with little education but with strong liberal views, which led Santa Anna to exile him; he went to Paris to wait. With the success of the Ayutla movement, Gutiérrez Zamora returned to become the mayor of Veracruz and then governor of the state. It was because of Gutiérrez Zamora's sympathy for the liberal cause and his identification with the Reform movement that the Juárez government sought refuge in Veracruz during the three-year War of the Reform.

The central pattern that emerges from the analysis of the occupational structure of the liberal leadership is one of young professionals who were moving rapidly and successfully up the political ladder until the establishment of the Santa Anna dictatorship. Then their world collapsed; the bright future dimmed immediately; most were exiled and the high hopes of continued advancement faded as rapidly as the Mexican shoreline they were forced to abandon. The Reform can be explained in large measure by the desire of the exiled professional class to regain its position in Mexican society and politics.

The Santa Anna dictatorship provided the precipitating ingredient for the Mexican Reform. With two exceptions, everyone in the group had held political office by 1853. Yet, at the end of that year not one was in office. Santa Anna, a representative of the reaction that looked with fear at the advancing liberals, wiped them out of office in one broad stroke. The more successful of them—somewhat more than a third—were exiled. At least half were imprisoned, ordered shot, subjected to property confiscation, or in other ways molested by the conservative regime. Those not directly attacked went into a "moral exile," withdrawing from public life for fear of being physically harmed by the vindictive emperor. But once again the very success of Santa Anna's policies—this time the silencing of his enemies—produced totally unexpected results.

One result of the exile experience was a unique opportunity for men of different views and backgrounds to meet and discover their common experiences. Social communication in Mexico was extremely difficult in the first decades of the nineteenth century, and the liberal group had been forming on the geographical edges of the nation. Hence, there had been little opportunity for them to meet, and indeed they might never have met had not misfortune lumped them in the infested climate of New Orleans. There a transformation took place. Juárez, for example, had been outstanding for his efficient and honest administration as governor of Oaxaca, but there was little in his past policies to indicate that he would become the leader of a reform movement. In Oaxaca he had generally cooperated with the church, extolled a philosophy of federalism that bordered on state sovereignty, and, by the time of his exile, established himself as a moderate and careful man. The influence on Juárez of Ocampo, who was a large step ahead of Juárez as a reformer, was to bring out the latent radical tendencies that had been sown in Oaxaca. Thus, once the group was established in New Orleans, its members formed a revolutionary government in exile that plotted to overthrow Santa Anna and bring themselves to power. Ocampo was the leader and Juárez second in command. They saw the Ayutla movement as the opportunity for their seizure of power and they cultivated their relationships with the southern rebels through their agent in Acapulco, Ignacio Comonfort. Knowing that individually they could do nothing, they stressed the group aspect of their job. Juárez and Mata summed up this emerging group attitude when they wrote: "Each one of us counts for little or nothing, but our united efforts will count on the scales that today weigh the destinies of our unfortunate Mexico."[50]

Once the group reached a certain level of self-awareness as a unit of collective behavior, the final element necessary for collective action was a generalized belief that served as a guiding principle. As the liberal professionals discovered their common cultural heritage, as they discovered that others too had been excluded from power and status, they began to project onto the society as a whole a common emotional force, the passion for liberal reform. From exile it was easy to see that what Mexico needed was an end to the weak and unstable caudillo system and the substitution of a strong, secular nation-state established by a republican constitution. In response to Santa Anna's authoritarianism, rule of law through the constitution was to become a major tenet of the new group's brand of nationalism. Such a system was essential, in Ocampo's view, "if Mexico is to continue being a nation."[51] Juárez expressed the same concern about rule of law when he wrote to Ocampo—who had gone to Brownsville, Texas, to set up a revolutionary junta— that though Santa Anna must fall "there is not sufficient learning and patrio- tism to establish liberty without committing excesses." Juárez feared that "ambitious persons" would control the movement and that personalism would continue.[52] Both Juárez and Ocampo desired an end to caudillo rule, an end to the system that had resulted in their performing menial tasks— Ocampo was a potter and Juárez a cigar maker—in exile in a foreign country. They and others like them joined the Ayutla movement in order to wage total war not so much against Santa Anna as against the historical logic that made *santanismo* possible.

Exile strengthened the reforming sentiments of the elite group and made them more aware of what it meant to be "Mexican." Melchor Ocampo wrote from New Orleans that now he better understood Mexico and the problems that beset it as a nation. He listed the major characteristics that prevented Mexico from becoming a modern nation-state: the boredom of most Mexicans with public affairs, the exploitation of public office, the toleration of vice, and the lack of public instruction. These had been supplemented with four other dangerous aspects of Mexican life: the unnatural control over property by the clergy, the inordinate wealth and laziness of the church, the lack of responsi- bility in public expenditures and tax collection, and "the prostitution of the so-called administration of justice." Ocampo wondered whether the Mexicans would ever be able to establish a true nation-state. "The Hispanic-Mexican race can never establish a free country because it does not have a deep feeling of rights and duties; all oppression is accepted if not applauded." Ocampo blamed this state of affairs on the clergy, "who have turned their back on the nation" and "who have no national loyalties."[53]

Juárez, too, analyzed the weaknesses of the Mexican political structure and came to some important conclusions for his later activities as president and leader of the Reform movement. He became convinced that rule by caudillos would only perpetuate the chaos that made Santa Anna possible. What was needed was a concerted effort by the liberal leadership to create a strong secular nation-state. And he was optimistic about their chances for success. As he put it from his run-down hotel room in New Orleans: "It seems to me that a unanimous effort by the few good men who are interested in the good of the nation will be enough to destroy the tyranny."[54]

Exile also made men deeply concerned with patriotism itself, not just with the weaknesses that made patriotism difficult. When the Santa Anna regime tried to stir up support by publishing reports that the exiled liberals were organizing a filibustering army in the United States to raid Mexico, the exiled group responded vigorously. In a public manifesto they posed the fundamental question: "What is the fatherland for us?" Their answer: "Everything!" They vehemently denied that they wanted to remain in the United States, as the *santanista* propaganda had claimed, "because here we would lose our nationality as Mexicans." Exile, they said, had made them better Mexicans because "there are in the hearts of good men innate sentiments that are inseparable from their honor. . . and these feelings are those of patriotism. Instead of dying in us they have become more and more alive, they have rooted more and more in our hearts in spite of the bitterness of our disgrace."[55]

The Santa Anna dictatorship was thus the precipitating event in the development of a liberal Reform movement in Mexico. The weakness of the political structure was made evident, the social tensions were heightened to the breaking point. In exile the disparate individuals discovered their common cultural heritage and their common ideology, liberalism. By glorifying the nation-state at the expense of the traditional corporate society that had excluded them, the exiles no longer felt the sense of isolation and rootlessness; all men of all classes were equal before the might of the nation. Liberals stressed the opening of the political structure to merit and talent, not birth and caste. In their desire to channel all individual loyalties to the secular state, they promised a vigorous attack on sources of intermediate loyalty such as the church the military *fuero* , the local cacique, and the semi-autonomous economies that prevented the creation of a national spirit. In this sense the Mexican liberals of the mid-nineteenth century represent classic examples of a nation-building elite. Their rootlessness, their historical experiences, their occupations, their personal crisis of participation and exile—all are compatible with the concepts of deliberate, reform-oriented kinds of change as suggested by the nation-building approach to political development.

4. The Constitution of 1857

After the triumph of the Ayutla rebellion, the first task of the new government was to write a constitution. Both the Plan of Ayutla and its reformation in Acapulco had made the drafting of a new constitution a high priority of the liberal movement. In contrast to the conservative abrogation of constitutionalism in favor of "Santa Anna well counseled," the Reform leadership wanted a formal, written constitution that made the new government legitimate. Ignacio Comonfort, who had taken over the presidency from Juan Alvarez in December 1855, wrote to state governors that "the nation will be able to rehabilitate itself and pursue a regular and progressive course in public political affairs only when those that lead and those that follow comply with their strict mutual obligations."[1] These obligations had to be codified and publicized for all Mexicans to know and obey. "Nothing," asserted Francisco Zarco, "is more important than the establishment of national unity; without it there is no hope for this nation."[2] For Zarco and the liberal leaders the path to unity was through a national constitution that reflected the new realities of political life. This constitution was to be an instrument through which the new elite would rule. It was to create a political structure that opened up a closed political system, allowed a circulation of elites through the channels of power without violence, and broke down the barriers that had prohibited the establishment of a meritocracy. Guillermo Prieto, giving the first public oration after the Ayutlan triumph, injected these social considerations into the political realm. He stressed that moral organization brings with it social reorganization and argued that the constitution would assure the "development of the life of our people, the affirmation of their rights." From these elements would come a good political constitution that would be neither American, nor English, nor Spanish but a "national constitution based on our necessities, on our racial differences."[3] Above all, the new constitution would provide the legitimacy that had disappeared with the Spanish crown in 1821.

Mingled with the need for legitimization was the growing sentiment of liberal nationalism. Nationalist agitation began immediately after the government took office, and its focus was principally on the writing of a viable national constitution. Noting that the Plans of Ayutla and Acapulco had called for a new national code, José María Lafragua, minister of gobernación, stated that the "first, most holy, indispensable duty of this government is to affirm the nationality of the nation." Lafragua argued that this could be achieved only when all men in the nation were "Mexicans above all else." The dictatorship of Santa Anna had submerged both the national and the public interest under the whims of personal power, and the results had been civil war, chaos, and misery. Not far from Lafragua's mind were the disastrous debacles of the Mexican War and the Gadsden Purchase, and he insisted that the best way to prevent further national disintegration was through a workable constitution. Meanwhile, Lafragua and the rest of the cabinet issued a position paper stating that the first goal of the new regime would be to frame a constitution that established "the rightful supreme authority of the nation."[4]

The new political elite conceived of the constitution as a means not only of legitimizing its rebellion but also of regenerating the nation. Throughout their speeches and writings the liberals insisted on the regenerative qualities of their movement, invariably linking regeneration with the constitutional convention scheduled to meet on the 16th of September, 1855, because, as Mariano Riva Palacio put it, they hoped for the "regeneration of the nation . . . on the anniversary of its independence."[5] Similarly, Benito Juárez, the new minister of justice and ecclesiastical affairs, described the Ayutla movement as a "regenerative and humanitarian revolution" that would "happily finish the difficult job of regenerating the nation."[6] Although both Riva Palacio and Juárez left the exact meaning of regeneration vague, they still managed to convey the impression that it referred to the growth of a modern political system, one free of the legacies of both colonial and conservative rule. This system would have at its base a constitution that synthesized the conflicting tendencies in Mexican political life and harmonized divergent interests into a national whole. Thus regeneration in this context actually meant liberal nation-building with its elements of legitimization and nationalism. For this reason Juárez referred to the entire process of regeneration through a new constitution as an "eminently nationalist goal."

The men of Ayutla placed great faith in the Constitutional Congress, and when it finally met in February 1856 they were well represented. Among the delegates who gathered in Mexico City were Ponciano Arriaga, Francisco Zarco, Juan Antonio de la Fuente, Ignacio Vallarta, Ignacio Ramírez, Melchor Ocampo, Guillermo Prieto, Valentín Gómez Farías, José María Mata, and many others.

Although the social composition of the Constitutional Congress has received much attention, little systematic research has been done on the exact structure of the Congress.[7] Instead, various authors have offered unsupported generalizations. One historian, Jesús Romero Flores, asserted that the members of the Mexico City Congress were "the most distinguished men of the epoch," with "the majority dedicated to diverse occupations: farmers, shopkeepers, journalists, and a few military officers."[8] Francisco Bulnes, on the other hand, argued that of the 154 delegates to the Congress, 108 were lawyers and the rest were soldiers and bureaucrats.[9] Similarly, Walter Scholes concluded that the delegates were lawyers, journalists, teachers, and government employees.[10] Table 3 summarizes the occupational structure of those delegates for whom information was available.[11]

TABLE 3
OCCUPATIONAL STRUCTURE OF THE CONSTITUTIONAL CONGRESS

Principal Occupation	Number	Percentage*
Law	35	45.5
Military	16	20.8
Journalism	9	11.7
Bureaucracy	7	9.1
Medical	4	5.2
Education	1	1.3
Other Professional	3	3.9
Other Non-Professional	2	2.6
Total	77	

*Cumulative percentage varies from 100 because of rounding.

Although reliable information could be found on only half the delegates (77 out of 154), the data do suggest that Romero Flores's description of the social composition of the convention is inaccurate. Among the 77 there were no farmers, few shopkeepers, and a large number of soldiers (in fact, the military were the second largest category). The estimates by Scholes and Bulnes seem to be much closer to the actual situation. And many of those who were journalists and bureaucrats had received a legal education but could not find enough clients to sustain a law practice. Thus, rather than being a popular convention representing all groups in society, the Constitutional

Congress that met in 1856 represented a professional class and, in a country where few could read and write, a social elite.

In addition, table 3 bears striking resemblance to the structure of the Reform leadership discussed in the preceding chapter. Over 80 percent of the sample were either lawyers, journalists, bureaucrats, or soldiers—the same categories that prevailed for the leadership of the liberal program. And like the liberal leadership, the delegates to the Constitutional Congress seem to have been young men who were making their way up the political ladder. The average age of the delegates was just under forty, and 60 percent of the delegates had entered politics within a decade prior to the opening of the Congress, that is, during the ten years following the American invasion of Mexico. And like the liberal elite, the delegates came primarily from the liberal circle. The states of Veracruz, San Luis Potosí, Zacatecas, Guanajuato, Jalisco, Michoacán, Guerrero, and Oaxaca supplied seventy constituents, or 45.2 percent of the total.[12] Even this figure does not tell the whole story of the periphery's influence on the Congress. Because the Congress allowed multiple representation, some delegates—like Ponciano Arriaga, Melchor Ocampo, Guillermo Prieto, and Ignacio Ramírez—represented more than one state. Arriaga, Ocampo, and Prieto not only represented their homes states but also the more conservative state of Mexico surrounding Mexico City. Both Ocampo and Arriaga also were part of the five-man Mexico City delegation. Obviously, conservatives were systematically excluded from the delegations.[13]

The liberal leadership dominated the Constitutional Congress; every important position was in their grasp. Ponciano Arriaga was elected president of the Congress and Francisco Zarco became secretary—both by acclamation. The key commission appointed by the president was the committee in charge of drafting the new constitution. Arriaga placed himself as well as Melchor Ocampo and José María Mata on the committee along with some moderate liberals. And that was not all; the liberal elite controlled every other important committee. Mariano Riva Palacio chaired the committee on internal affairs (gobernación); Zarco served on the foreign affairs committee (relaciones); Guillermo Prieto directed the finance committee (hacienda); Ponciano Arriaga and Vicente Riva Palacio were charged with the committee on the national guard (guardia nacional); and José María Romero Díaz chaired the all-important committee on ecclesiastical affairs (negocios eclesiásticos).[14] These were the committees before which the urgent issues of mid-nineteenth-century Mexico were to be resolved. The nature of power in the political system, the role of the church and military in political affairs, the crisis of public finance, and the position of Mexico before the world—these were the critical issues that the committee had to face in the struggle to modernize the political process.

Liberal political reform promised the spread of potential power to wider groups in society. And, in the eyes of the Reform leaders, the failure of creole politics after independence had been precisely the inability to expand and incorporate new groups into the political arena. Power in the old system had been monopolized by a few caudillos who passed office back and forth among themselves. The example most often used by the new elite was the frequency of Santa Anna in the presidential chair. Thus one of the first acts of the Constitutional Congress was to annul the official decrees of Santa Anna's last dictatorship. Santa Anna, himself a symbol of personalistic rule, became the object of vicious personal diatribes in which the deputies castigated him for everything from gross public display to treason. On March 28 Melchor Ocampo and José María Mata, both victims of Santa Anna's attempt to destroy liberalism, produced to a surprised Congress documents clearly proving that Santa Anna had conspired with North American adventurers to make Texas independent in 1836. Santa Anna was accused of "selling the nation for gold, establishing tyranny, and making and unmaking laws for money."[15] In session after session the liberals produced evidence of the dangers of personal politics and characterized the rule of the caudillos as the dark ages of barbarism when men ruled at will and laws ratified unjust acts. Perhaps Ponciano Arriaga best expressed the liberal longing for regular, established, constitutional government: "For years the Mexican people—suffering the dreary consequences of civil war, the extortions of despotism, the evils of anarchy, the disasters of personalism, and the bad faith of petty rulers—hoped that someday . . . a constitution would rule."[16] For the new reformers, constitutional government was the symbolic panacea for Mexico's problems: all other constitutions had failed because they had allowed the caudillos to perform. Now the need of Mexico demanded a political change that put laws over men. Government by law—this was the ideal of the liberal reformers.

But though the delegates to the Congress were of similar social and ideological backgrounds, they nevertheless wrangled bitterly over the key issues of the day: the role of the president, the position of the church, the composition of the legislative sector of government, the abolition of the death penalty, and many more. Those who have commented on the bickering have identified two major groups, or voting blocs: the moderates (called *moderados*) and the radicals (called *puros* or *jacobinos*).[17] In addition, much has been made of the church-state conflict during the Congress. Walter V. Scholes has argued that "in the minds of the leaders *the* question was the clerical one."[18] And Justo Sierra characterized the politics of the period as a "war between the lay and the ecclesiastical state."[19] These comments and others have established the conventional wisdom that the issue producing the most severe moderate-radical conflict at the Congress was the question of the church and its relation to the secular state. And yet, none of the authors who have commented on the issues and voting blocs has used the available roll-call voting to test these hypotheses. The official records of the Congress contain over 200 roll-calls taken during the year-long session.[20] Of these, 161 had statistical significance in terms of opposition voting (unanimous votes were considered separately). From the 161 votes, 70 were selected for quantitative analysis on the basis of a stratified random sampling technique: four votes were chosen for their importance in the literature (the vote to defeat an attempt to restore the Constitution of 1824, the vote to approve the Ley Juárez limiting *fueros* of the Catholic Church and the military, the vote to include in the constitution the Ley Lerdo prohibiting corporations from owning property, and the vote on religious toleration), and the rest were chosen with the aid of a table of random numbers.[21] (The votes, their substance, and Riker coefficient of significance are listed in Appendix B.)

Several mathematical techniques have been developed to utilize these votes to analyze and measure the degree of conflict and the principal issues. Experimentation with three such methods—Guttman scaling, cluster-bloc analysis, and factor analysis—revealed that factor analysis gave the clearest picture of the dimensions of conflict within the Constitutional Congress.[22] Factor analysis is a procedure that measures the underlying relationships among all variables and produces mathematical statements of the common relationships. It begins by measuring the degree of association (or correlation) between pairs of variables (in this case votes). The program then analyzes the degrees of association between sets of variables and discovers those sets that vary in similar ways in the body of data. The result in the case of roll-call votes is the identification of groups or clusters of votes that are closely related and are most meaningful in explaining variability in the voting patterns. These groups are called factors. Individual votes that account for most of the variance within each factor are said to have "high loadings" on that factor. The votes with high loadings ( ) ± 0.5) are used to identify the meaning of the factor. Table 4 summarizes the votes with high loadings on the five factors that emerged from the factor matrix of the roll-call votes in the 1856-1857 Constitutional Congress.[23] (The absolute mathematical loadings on the five factors are given in Appendix C.)

The factor analytic technique identifies common relationships among votes that have high loadings on a single factor but does not provide the interpretation of their common meaning. In light of the conventional wisdom about the principal issues at the Congress, it might be expected that the church-state question would dominate the first and most important factor. A careful analysis of the votes with high loadings on Factor I does reveal some important church-state votes. Most obvious are the defeat of religious toleration (article

TABLE 4
SUMMARY OF HIGH LOADINGS IN ROTATED FACTOR MATRIX

Roll Call		Factors				
		I	II	III	IV	V
4.	Executive Council (defeated)				x	
5.	Repeal executive budget (defeated)				x	
6.	Approval of Vidaurri (defeated)				−x	
9.	Congressional autonomy				−x	
13.	Mail seizure (defeated)					−x
17.	Freedom of religion (defeated)	−x				
18.	Freedom of education	−x				
21.	Trial by jury (defeated)	−x				
22.	Discuss abolition mutilation (defeated)	−x				
23.	Expulsion of ministers	x				
24.	Unicameral legislature	−x				
25.	Procedure: To debate death penalty abolition					−x
26.	Abolition of death penalty					−x
27.	Size of congressional district			x		
29.	Residency requirements for Congress		−x			
31.	Congress has authority to allow states to divide			x		
39.	Jury trial in federal cases	−x				
41.	Prohibit state alliances			−x		
46.	Limit tax powers of Congress (defeated)		−x			
47.	Trial of government officials (defeated)	−x				
50.	Prohibit shackles, chains, and irons (defeated)	−x				
56.	D.F. in Querétaro (defeated)			x		
57.	Cuautla and Cuernavaca to Guerrero (defeated)	−x				
58.	Maintain boundaries of state of Mexico	x				
62.	Licenses by Congress	x				
64.	Death penalty time limit (defeated)					x
67.	Remove all congressional residency requirements (defeated)		x			
69.	State support for clergy (defeated)		x			

15 of the proposed constitution) and the vote on freedom of education in the face of Catholic domination of the educational system. But the rest of the votes have little or nothing to do with the church; instead they are a defeat of trial by jury in criminal cases, a defeat of an attempt to bring onto the floor for debate a move to abolish mutilation as a punishment for crimes, a secret vote giving the Constituent Assembly the right to expel cabinet ministers from the hall when the Congress discussed their office, the establishment of trial by jury in federal cases, defeat of an article that would have abolished shackles, chains, and irons as legitimate punishments for crimes, defeat of an attempt to remove the cities of Cuernavaca and Cuautla from the state of Mexico and give them to Juan Alvarez's state of Guerrero, a vote to uphold the prevailing boundaries of the state of Mexico (including Cuernavaca and Cuautla), a vote giving Congress the authority to issue licenses to high government officials to leave the capital, and, finally, a vote creating a unicameral legislature.

Although it is clear that the church-state issue was not the dominant meaning of Factor I, the wide variety of votes does not readily yield a defining category. There seems to be a mixture of votes relating to religion, criminal punishments, congressional powers and structures, and local boundary disputes. But the striking number of votes pertaining to criminal justice provides a clue to the meaning of Factor I. They suggest that the principal dimension of conflict at the Constitutional Congress of 1856-1857 was the issue of law and order or a fear of anarchy.

The problem remains to reconcile the seemingly aberrant votes on church, boundary, and congressional issues with this common theme of law and order. To do that, a careful reading of the debates further clarified the significance of Factor I. The debate on article 15, which would have established religious toleration, indicates the law and order dimension. As one delegate, José María Castillo Velasco, put it: "The question before us is not a truly religious one but, rather, essentially social and political."[24] In this vein, the debate focused principally on the effects religious toleration would have in Mexico. Marcelino Castañeda predicted that toleration "will bring on rebellion," and he concluded gravely: "Ultimately, fellow delegates, the domestic home will disintegrate into chaos . . . because religious unity is the only possible social source of morality, order, and patriotism."[25] José María Lafragua, minister of gobernación and delegate to the Congress, articulated the central fear underlying the debate on article 15, arguing that religion per se was not at issue; instead, it was a question of law and order. Lafragua was convinced that admitting alien religions into Mexico would produce only national disintegration. He asked the delegates to the Congress to imagine what would happen if all religions were legal. He pictured the central plaza of Mexico City with the Cathedral, a synagogue, a Protestant church, and an

Aztec temple on each side, and in the middle a raging religious war. Playing on the fears of more caste wars, Lafragua concluded with a dire warning: "The Indians are agitated, and for this reason it is very dangerous to introduce a new element that will be exploited by the enemies of progress in order to immerse us in a truly frightening anarchy."[26]

The fear of anarchy pervaded the debates on the other votes with high loadings on Factor I. The apparent contradiction between defeating religious toleration and then establishing secular education can be explained within the framework of the law and order hypothesis. The Congress passed the freedom of education bill because an educated public would be less prone to civil disturbance. In the opinions of the delegates, the clergy had failed to instill the necessary patriotism through education. As Manuel Soto expressed it, "Civilization is impossible without the development of intelligence."[27]

Similarly, profound distrust of popular instincts produced the defeat of trial by jury. Ignacio Vallarta, in one of his few speeches before the Congress, argued that Mexico was still in an infancy "corrupted by an uninterrupted series of rebellions" and that to allow trial by jury would only perpetuate the anarchy.[28] The fear of popular rebellion also figured significantly in the debates on the removal of Cuautla and Cuernavaca from the state of Mexico and placing these important cities in the state of Guerrero. Obviously a move to reward Juan Alvarez for his leadership of the Ayutla movement, nevertheless the plan produced a bitter outcry from the residents of the two towns. Petitions flowed into the Congress demanding that the state boundaries be maintained in their present form. Many of the petitions threatened rebellion if the transfer went through. When the issue came up for debate, Prisciliano Díaz González warned the Congress that to change the boundaries would produce local rebellion, chaos, and anarchy. Troops would be required to put down the rebellion, and the net result would be a complete breakdown of law and order.[29] Thus the defeat of the attempt to alter the boundaries and the subsequent vote to uphold the traditional state lines was a vote for law and order.

The votes on the legislative questions that loaded highly on Factor I also had as a principal component of the debates surrounding them a pronounced fear of anarchy. In particular, the establishment of a unicameral legislative body was a direct reflection of the liberal fear of a continuing breakdown of law and order. The endless conflict between the Senate and the Chamber of Deputies promised to retard and perhaps even negate all efforts at reform. And when the drafting committee presented its proposed constitution to the delegates, it contained a single legislative body. Ponciano Arriaga, the chairman of the drafting committee, went to great lengths to explain the necessity of a unicameral legislature. He argued that while the Senate in the American system of government had been established to check the passions of the lower house, in the Mexican case the Senate had served only as the "blind and systematic opposition . . . to all progress and reform." Instead of giving equal representation to all states, the Mexican Senate had favored the more powerful; instead of being the voice of reason, it had become the source of conspiracies against the people; in place of providing a forum for reflection and debate, it had adopted the pretensions of an "exclusive superiority." Arriaga argued that a Senate could not exist in Mexico as long as the ambition, avarice, and vanity of a small number of powerful men took advantage of the ignorance and apathy of the masses. Echoing Arriaga's sentiments, Francisco Cendejas declared that the Senate "has never represented anything more than the interests of certain social classes allied to colonial government, and it cannot represent anything else since . . . it is always separated from democratic principles." And even those arguing for the Senate put the debate within the law and order context. Francisco Zarco expressed the fear that the single body would represent only the larger states, thereby impelling the small frontier states to use extra-legal means to achieve their goals.[30] Those on both sides of the argument agreed ultimately that the solution to the problem of law and order was a strong legislature, one that would check the president and his cabinet. Thus, the last two votes that had high loadings on Factor I were symbolic but emotional votes to control the physical movement of the president and to establish the right of the Congress to expel a cabinet minister from the chamber during debate on that ministry.

If legislative power was to be the solution to the problem of anarchy, then the composition of the unicameral Chamber of Deputies became a crucial issue. It is not surprising, therefore, that Factor II clearly concerns the composition and power of the Congress. Two of the five votes that loaded highly on Factor II deal directly with the residency requirements for election to the Chamber; another is a defeat of an attempt to limit the tax power of the legislative branch. A fourth vote concerned the attempt to transplant the Federal District from Mexico City to Querétaro. The move was defeated principally because most delegates felt that Mexico City had been too well entrenched in the popular mind as the center of government and feared that any move would seriously weaken the prestige and power of the legislature.[31] Thus the second principal dimension of conflict can be labeled "the power of Congress."

Factor III identifies a "centralist-federalist" split in the Constitutional Convention. Each of the three votes with high loadings on Factor III involves the relationships between the national power (Congress) and the state governments. And in every case the delegates decided that power would rest ultimately with the national government, thus calling into question the general

assumption that the Reform liberals were also federalists. Indeed, the struggle
in the Constitutional Congress was not one of national authority versus state
authority; rather, it was a question of where national authority would reside:
in the presidency or with Congress.

Factor IV indicates clearly the president-versus-Congress dimension of
conflict. The votes that loaded highly on this factor all concern conflict between
President Comonfort and the Congress. None of these four votes was a constitutional issue; rather, they were attempts to limit Comonfort's authority.
Since the Congress was sitting not only as a constitutional body but also as a
working legislature, many delegates argued that it was necessary to check
Comonfort's policy-making authority. Thus when Comonfort proposed the
formation of an executive council to help him rule, the delegates turned the
proposal down on the grounds that it violated the principle of legislative dominance. Similarly, the delegates voted down the proposed budget for the
president's office and staff because it was excessive. When Comonfort
requested formal congressional approval for his attempt to appease the
powerful northern caudillo, Santiago Vidaurri, by approving Vidaurri's illegal
unification of the states of Nuevo León and Coahuila, the Constitutional
Congress turned him down. And when Comonfort protested, the delegates
responded by declaring that the president had no authority to make objec-
tions or even observations about the decrees and resolutions of the sovereign
Congress.[32] Thus Factor IV can be labeled "Congress versus the president."

Taken together, Factors, II, III, and IV suggest a strong centralist tendency
in the Constitutional Congress. In reaction to the dictatorial power exercised
by Santa Anna, the liberals of the 1850s wanted power vested in a representative, unicameral, and sovereign legislature. Nor did the delegates want
independent local power to be the counter-balance to presidential absolutism.
In the face of the political crisis facing Mexico, they wanted, above all,
regularized, effective, and strong central government. Francisco Zarco
explained the new political structure. "Our Constitution," he wrote,
"establishes neither [the American nor the British] system. . . . It does not
make the chief of state inviolable, as in constitutional monarchies, nor does
it make him the sole authority, as in the United States. Instead, it establishes
a mixed system, a complex responsibility, extending to the president and the
ministers."[33] And León Guzmán, vice-president of the Constitutional Congress,
asserted that the constitution "proclaimed the dogma of the sovereignty of the
people . . . . All power derives from the people; people govern people; people
legislate."[34]

The factor analysis produced one final factor that had four variables with
high loadings. Three of the four votes concerned the abolition of the death
penalty. The fourth vote, a defeat of an article that would have permitted the

national government to seize personal mail "in times of grave crisis," seems to be an anomaly. Although mathematically independent of Factor I, Factor V bears a close relationship in meaning. The proposal to abolish the death penalty engendered the same kind of debate on law and order as did the votes that loaded highly on Factor I. Yet the factor analysis identified the death penalty issue as an independent dimension. Therefore, Factor V can be called "death penalty." After much debate and several votes, the Constitutional Convention wrote into the new constitution that the death penalty would be abolished on the completion of a national penitentiary system.[35]

The factor analysis of the roll-call voting at the 1856-1857 Congress identified five principal dimensions of conflict. Statistically the most important was the "law and order" dimension. The other four were "power of Congress," "centralism versus federalism," "Congress versus the president," and "death penalty." (See Table 5 for the distribution of variance in the rotated factor matrix.) What is striking about these factors is what they *do not* concern.

TABLE 5
DISTRIBUTION OF VARIANCE IN ROTATED FACTOR MATRIX*

Factor	% of Total Factor Variance	% of Total Variance
I. Law and order	35.8	14.9
II. Power of Congress	19.4	7.1
III. Centralism vs. federalism	15.2	5.2
IV. Congress vs. president	14.5	4.0
V. Death penalty	15.1	3.8
	100.0	35.0

*Rotating the factor matrix reduces the percent of variance explained by
 Factor I while increasing the percent of variance explained by the other
 factors.

Clearly the church-state issue did not generate significant conflict during the year-long session.[36] Although it is true that the Constitutional Congress met in the midst of a vicious church-state struggle, the statistical analysis suggests that it was not a major source of conflict within the Congress. In fact, the delegates were of a similar mind on the need to break the political and economic power of the Catholic Church, and the votes on these issues, such as the limitation of ecclesiastical privileges and the disamortization of church property, were nearly unanimous. Those votes on the church that did show up in the factor analysis indicate that the church-state issue can most profitably be considered as an integral part of the larger issue of ordering and stabilizing Mexican society and politics. The struggle to secularize society was thus a function of the attempt to build a liberal nation-state.

A second issue that did not appear in the factor analysis but one that has been the subject of much comment is the problem of equality before the law. In his massive study of early Mexican liberalism, Jesús Reyes Heroles argued that the principal issue before the Congress was equality before the law. Clearly there was unity among the delegates about what kind of equality should be established through the new constitution.[37] Early nineteenth-century liberalism had seen society as having a relatively static, machine-like quality. Adjust the gears and the machine would run.[38] But the new men of the 1850s had a much different vision. For them society was constantly in flux. Rather than being a machine, society was undergoing constant change, a world in motion with infinite fluctuations. This world view reflected the rootlessness and upward mobility of the group that dominated the Congress, and the liberals made sure that the constitution contained provisions creating official justice. As chairman of the committee in charge of drafting the constitution, Ponciano Arriaga expressed the views of the new political elite: the liberal political system was to be based on the equality of all men. "The great principle of equality," he emphasized to Congress, "is incontrovertible because divine right, privileged castes, classes born exclusively to direct and govern are discredited theories that civilization, after centuries of struggles, has declared absurd."[39] Thus the first section of the constitution was entitled "The Rights of Man" and included an impressive array of individual rights. Article 2 abolished slavery and declared that all men were born free. Article 4 provided that every individual had the right to choose whatever profession, industry, and labor he wanted to pursue without hindrance or limit. Although on the surface this right seems obvious and simple, it was in fact a revolutionary statement. Now the *gremios*, or guilds, which had exercised authority over many of the artisan professions, could no longer maintain their traditional monopoly. Equally revolutionary was article 5, which prohibited the entering into any contract that might sacrifice or destroy the liberty of the individual. Clearly aimed at religious vows that bound the clergy to the church, article 5 had a more widespread revolutionary potential. In a country where four-fifths of the population labored in debt peonage, such a provision struck at the heart of the prevailing labor system. Combined with article 17, which said that no one could be imprisoned for debt, article 5 destroyed the power of the employer to set working conditions and then enforce them. Under the new law employees could bargain over wages and quit their jobs if they did not like the terms. Had these provisions been strictly enforced, the large maguey and sugar plantations would have been severely damaged. In effect, articles 5 and 17 meant a complete and thorough restructuring of nineteenth-century Mexican society. To cap this radical restructuring, article 13 abolished the *fuero*, declaring that no individual could be judged by exclusive jurisdictions or special tribunals. Every man had to answer to the judicial system of the nation; no longer could the *fueros* of the military and the church protect a soldier or cleric from the judgment of the secular nation-state. Article 13 said: "In the Mexican Republic no one can be judged by private laws or special tribunals. No person or corporation can possess *fueros*." All men, no matter what their station in life, no matter what their occupation, or wealth, or race, were now citizens of the nation-state, members of a national community and equal before the law. As one broadside summarized the situation, Mexico had not experienced a social readjustment since 1810. But now the Ayutla movement had become a "social struggle between the masters and the dominated," in which the dominated were fighting for an open society "without monopoly, favoritism, or secret powers." Others saw the transformation as one in which "the social system of privilege, restrictions, and monopoly gave way to ideas of justice, complete and harmonious with the spirit of progress." No one doubted that these changes were the product of pressure for a restructuring of society by new political groups.[40] The liberalism of the mid-nineteenth century not only sought law and order but conceived of a political system that removed norms of government based on privilege.

The equalization program of the reformers did not limit itself to the correction of ancient abuses but also moved into the realm of establishing new civil rights for all men. Freedom of education, freedom of thought, freedom of expression, freedom of petition, freedom of association, freedom of travel without passports and safe conduct passes, protection from illegal search and seizure, elimination of torture, and strict limitations on the death penalty— these were the civil rights of all men in Mexico. Their goal was to make all men equal before the law; their consequence promised a revolution in the civil and political rights of Mexicans. León Guzmán, vice-president of the Congress and its spokesman on the day of promulgation, hailed the coming meritocracy: "Equality will now be the supreme law of the Republic; virtue will be the only merit."[41] And Ignacio Ramírez put the constitution into the social context: "For half a century the nation has studied and learned about itself; it has discovered in its veins Aztec, African, Asiatic, and European blood, and so as not to injure anyone, it has declared the equality of all men."[42]

A third major debate that did not show up in the factor analysis was the issue of property. By far the most radical provision of the new constitution was article 27. It upheld the concept of private property and prohibited the state from confiscating or otherwise expropriating private property without consent of the owner. Should the owner consent, the state was required to pay a fair price and even then the government could act only with the authorization of Congress. These aspects of article 27 referred specifically to individual private property; most corporate property, on the other hand, was declared illegal. No corporation of whatever character was allowed to own real estate except that land used directly in service of the corporation. Any property not directly used by the corporation had to be sold. This was not confiscation, however. Rather than deprive the corporations of their wealth, article 27 changed the form of the wealth from land to capital. Although the article was aimed directly at the church and its fabled (though vastly overestimated) landed wealth, it struck as well at the community property of the Indian ejidos and the holdings of such economic corporations as the conservative-dominated artisan guilds *(gremios)* and merchant organizations *(consulados)*. Its purpose was to liberate the land held by these corporations and make it available to the new power elite.

There were other proposals more radical in scope and content suggested to the Constitutional Convention, but all of these were rejected for being excessive and dangerous, as a threat to law and order. The most startling was Ponciano Arriaga's suggestion that all ecclesiastical property be immediately nationalized so that the income from the sale of church land would accrue to the state and not the church. He also proposed that the great haciendas be broken up, the land be redistributed, and the role of the rural proletariat in Mexico be recognized.[43] Had these programs been adopted in the middle of the nineteenth century, there probably would not have been a Mexican Revolution at the beginning of the twentieth. But this group of ambitious mestizos and upwardly mobile professionals who wanted access to land, prestige, and wealth was not about to tamper with what they conceived of as the very basis of the economic structure. What tampering did occur was to focus on corporate or collective property, not private holdings. The goal was to open the paths to power, not to destroy power itself. Thus it was inconceivable, given the assumptions and goals of nineteenth-century liberalism, that the reformers would invite anarchy by destroying private property.

A consideration of the issues that did not produce deep divisions in the roll-call voting indicates that the delegates were of like mind on several important questions. They agreed that the state should exercise effective control over the political activities of the Catholic Church. They wanted to preserve the absolute right of private property. And they established the protection of individual liberties and equality before the law as the cornerstone of the new liberal republic. The cleavage over the law and order issue suggests that although the delegates agreed on the need for basic human liberties and equality, they were divided on how far that process was to proceed. If the moderate-radical split existed at the Congress, it was over how far the liberal impulse was to go.

Factor analysis not only provides a means of identifying the underlying dimensions of conflict within the voting patterns of the Congress, it also supplies a technique for grouping delegates by how they vote on each factor. The method gives each delegate a "score" on the factor, and delegates with similar scores can be considered to form a voting bloc.

A constant theme running throughout the literature on the constitutional convention was a sharp and bitter split between those who wanted to move slowly in the area of reform and those who wanted to strike while the iron was very hot. Although no one provides a formal list of this moderate-radical division, invariably such men as Ponciano Arriaga, Francisco Zarco, Ignacio Ramírez, and José María Mata are linked with the radicals. Others—such as Marcelino Castañeda, Antonio Aguado, Juan Barragán, and Mariano Arizcorreta—are usually classified as moderates.[44] An analysis of the factor scores on the law and order factor of the seventy delegates who voted more than fifty times does not confirm such a split. Grouped together at the positive (or radical) end of the scale are Ignacio Ramírez (as expected) and Marcelino Castañeda (unexpectedly). Zarco and Mata fall at opposite ends of the scale, and Arriaga scores in the middle. The factor scores seem to indicate that at least on the most significant issue of law and order the moderate-radical split did not exist.

This judgment is confirmed by a scalogram of the factor scores.[45] It indicates the distribution of the factor scores. If clearly defined voting blocs existed, the graph would have clusters at either end of the scale and relatively low numbers in the middle. As it stands, however, the graph has the largest categories in the center of the factor score scale and very few scores at the extremes.

Nor does a factor analysis using the delegates instead of the votes as variables demonstrate a clearly defined moderate-radical split. In this Q-analysis each delegate was given a loading on the five factors.[46] Those with high positive loadings on Factor I were Santos Degollado, José María Mata, Ponciano Arriaga, and Gregorio Payró. Those with negative high loadings were Benito Quintana, José de la Luz Rosas, Rafael María Villagrán, and Francisco Guerrero. Table 6 compares the factor scores of each group. In both cases there is a general tendency, but the relationships are too slight to identify a defined cleavage within the Congress. What seems likely is that while there was indeed much cleavage within the Congress, the conflict was among constantly shifting coalitions.

SCALOGRAM OF THE DISTRIBUTION OF FACTOR SCORES ON FACTOR I

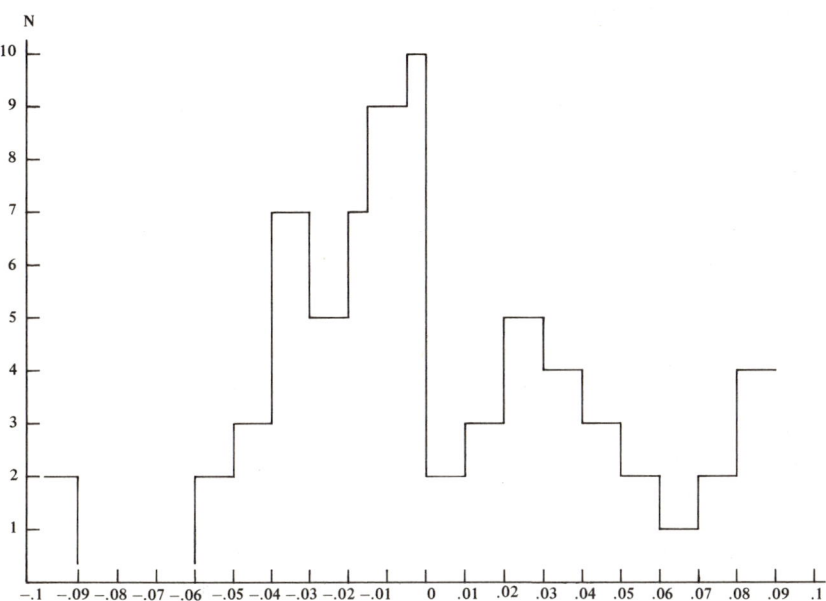

TABLE 6

COMPARISON OF Q-ANALYSIS AND FACTOR SCORES

+ High Loadings	Factor Score	−High Loadings	Factor Score
Arriaga	.0150	Guerrero	−.0132
S. Degollado	−.0306	Quintana	.1034
Mata	−.0076	Rosas	.0100
Payró	−.0391	Villagrán	.0017

The quantitative analysis of the social compositions and voting patterns in the Constitutional Congress yields a number of significant conclusions.

1. The delegates were young professionals. Most had studied law though they may have practiced another profession. In general, they seem to reflect the familial and social patterns of their leaders. Many had found the paths

of advancement closed to them during the Santa Anna years, and came to
the Congress determined to make the protection of individual liberties
the heart of the new government.

2. At the same time, the delegates did not agree on how much liberty to
allow in a society that had seen so many years of anarchy. They agreed
that powerful corporate interests had to be subordinated to the state, but
they disagreed sharply on how much individual liberty could be permitted.
The law and order dimension indicates a deep fear of anarchy and chaos
and an overwhelming concern for the establishment of stability.

3. The liberals of the mid-1850s were moving away from the basic federalism
of the earlier nineteenth-century liberals. Instead, as the high loadings on
Factors II, III, and IV indicate, one of the principal aims of the delegates
was the establishment of a centralized, rational, and regularized political
system in contrast to the previous system of alternating presidential
absolutism and anarchy. A powerful unicameral legislature, regularly
elected and supreme in authority, was seen as the optimum solution.

4. Although law and order proved to be the principal dimension of conflict
within the Congress, it did not produce the expected clear-cut moderate-
radical voting bloc split. Neither regional identification, nor occupation,
nor age, nor social status played a major role in determining voting positions. Instead, voting seems to have been issue-oriented, with constantly
shifting coalitions.

The constitution of 1857 was a flawed document. It represented the liberal
vision, not the realities of nineteenth-century Mexico. In a territory where
fully 90 percent of the inhabitants were illiterate a bill of rights would be
practically inoperable. Forcing the Catholic Church to sell its property still
left it with funds to defeat the Reform. Particularly important was the un-
resolvable dilemma of envisioning a nation of small landowners without providing a mechanism to implement these aims and to resist the reaction that the
reforms provoked. By protecting the concept of private property and denying
the executive the power to act, the liberals of the Constitutional Congress
created an ideological framework whose success would, as we shall see, entail
the destruction of liberalism itself.

Perhaps the most serious political failing of the new constitution was contained within the paradox of the law and order dimension. In a territory that
had written much law and established little order, the possibility of the unicameral revolutionary assembly bringing peace and tranquility was remote at
best. Just as the liberal vision failed to provide a mechanism for establishing a
Jeffersonian yeoman farmer class, so too did it fail to provide a workable solution to the crisis of anarchy in mid-century, particularly in a country where

respect for men outweighed respect for law.

But in the euphoria that accompanied the promulgation of the new constitution on February 5, 1857, few of the delegates were aware of the problems raised by their work. Instead, they saw the new constitution as the fulfillment of a dream. Guillermo Prieto foresaw an age "without fanaticism, inequality, hatreds, and poisonous miseries." This was to come about because "the Constitution symbolizes all our dreams of good, all our hopes for happiness."[47] Others predicted that the new political system would put an end to the "ruinous ambitions of some, the established power of others, and the disunity found among almost all the inhabitants of the Republic."[48]

So that all Mexicans would realize the importance of the new system, the constitution required everyone to swear "with great solemnity" an oath of loyalty. And in great solemnity it was done. Juárez, dressed as usual in his black suit, swore before the Oaxacan congress. Juan Alvarez, who always had a touch of the dramatic, lay prostrate before a church altar with one hand on the Bible and the other on the constitution. There he took the oath.[49] All across Mexico the people were required for the first time in the nation's history to declare their loyalty to the constitution and the national government. In this manner, the new political elite forced Mexicans to choose between traditional society and the modern, secular nation-state. The forcing of Mexicans to make such a choice was an important part of the Reform strategy, and this was the first time in Mexican history that men had to make choices between competing political cultures. The purpose was to make their fellow countrymen see the differences, and making Mexicans choose between them marked the beginning of the nation-building process.

All the evidence indicates that the choice was not an easy one. Letter after letter poured into the offices of state governors and high government officials from local office holders who refused to take the oath. Most acted out of fear of clerical reprisals, and many lost their jobs because of their refusal.[50] Despite vigorous ecclesiastical opposition, however, large numbers did take the oath, thus beginning the process of building a national consciousness. These individuals would eventually provide the support the liberal leadership needed when conservative opposition to the new politics finally resulted in civil war.

The concern for law and order, the emphasis on national power, the oath of loyalty—all indicate that the major crisis on the minds of the new liberal elite was the question of legitimacy, one of the dominant themes of nation-building. Clearly, since the fall of the imperial government in 1821 no constitution had been accepted as the legitimate instrument of government. Each coup prior to the Reform had been launched in an attempt not only to overthrow the existing government but also to write a new national constitution. The Ayutla movement was no different. Of course, writing a constitution and converting it into a symbol of legitimate national authority are two entirely separate processes. And the dilemma the liberals faced in February 1857 was how to accomplish what others had failed to do.

5. The Constitutional Dictatorship

To make the liberal nation-building program a reality, the liberals had to abandon some of their most fundamental beliefs. And in no area is the process of compromise and abandonment clearer than in the relationship between the new Constitution of 1857 and the structure of national power.

The authors of the Constitution of 1857 drew on a long and varied constitutional history. Prior to the Ayutla movement, Mexico had experienced seven constitutional congresses, one Constitutive Act, a Reform Act, and four constitutions—all in just over four decades, from 1814 to 1855. The constitutions had run from the most extreme localism, through national legislative dominance, to the most arbitrary dictatorships. The Constitution of Apatzingán and that of 1824 are representative of a trend towards legislative dominance. Power concentrated in the hands of a powerful executive marked the First Empire of Iturbide (1821-1823), the Organic Laws of 1843, and the last dictatorship of Santa Anna. The 1836 Constitution of Seven Laws was an interesting but unsuccessful attempt to synthesize these conflicting tendencies. By the time the liberals reached power the question of authority was unresolved.

Even the Plan of Ayutla failed to resolve the fundamental dilemma. With rare exceptions the Plan of Ayutla has been treated as an entity, a single call for action that rallied those opposed to the ways of Santa Anna. In fact, there were two plans written in those troubled days of 1854, and they differ as radically from one another as do the Constitution of Apatzingán and the *Bases Orgánicas.* In their differences the two plans represent the contradictions between legislative and executive dominance that had characterized pre-Ayutlan political life. The first of the two plans, the one that correctly deserves the name "Plan of Ayutla," was written in March 1854 by a group of dissident army officers gathered to declare war on Santa Anna. Fiercely loyal to their local chief, Juan Alvarez, these militarists wanted an end to federal intervention into local affairs. They wanted to keep Guerrero free of meddling by unsympathetic bureaucrats from Mexico City; they wanted to keep their army independent of the generals from Puebla and Jalisco and loyal to the caudillo of the south, Alvarez. In short, they wanted local autonomy. And so the Plan of Ayutla was proclaimed in the name of federalism, local autonomy, and a weak central government. A close scrutiny of the principal provisions of the plan illustrates this conclusion. Like all of Mexico's pronunciamentos, the Plan of Ayutla called for an end to the present government, cited the grievances on which the revolution was based, and required the quick convocation of a constitutional congress. The constitution was to create a federal republic with popular representation. In the meantime, the commander-in-chief of the armed forces was to rule the country.[1] There is little that is extraordinary in this plan; it is typical of almost every plan that accompanied cuartelazos in the first half of the nineteenth century.

If the Plan of Ayutla left some doubt as to the strength of the chief executive, Comonfort's Plan of Acapulco (March 11, 1854) cleared the picture. In it the executive ruled "without any restriction other than to respect inviolably individual rights." These rights remained ominously unspecific. At the same time the duty of the president was to maintain the security and independence of the nation, reform all areas of public administration, and do whatever was necessary for the prosperity, growth, and progress of Mexico.[2] Such a regime would mean an end to Ayutla's vision of a federal republic with local autonomy. In the Acapulco revision the only attribute of a monarch the president lacked was the title; otherwise, he was free to operate as he wished as long as unspecified individual rights were respected. The shift from Ayutla's traditional federalism to Acapulco's strong-man vision is best reflected in the language used in the two documents. In the Plan of Ayutla the states are referred to as "Estados"; in the Plan of Acapulco they are described as "Departamentos," the term used by the *Siete Leyes* of 1836 and Santa Anna's dictatorship. The choice of words seems to be a deliberate imitation of the 1836 code with its attempt to prevent tyranny from either a monarch or a divisive federalism, but it also echoes the aspirations of strong presidents. Thus from the outset the Ayutla movement was confined within a paradox: on the one hand, a revolt against a strong-man dictatorship in the name of local autonomy and legislative dominance; on the other, a revolt against dictatorship in the name of liberalism but subscribing to omnipotent executive power within the juridical structure of the nation. The failure of the Ayutlans to resolve immediately this internal contradiction within the movement was to be the source of titanic political struggles. These struggles lasted until the nation-building elite could work out a unique solution to the paradox; by

1876 the process was complete and Mexico had a constitution that stood as a national symbol while the president ruled unchecked.

The oath of loyalty was only the beginning of a long and violent saga out of which the constitution emerged as a potent political symbol. The process began immediately after its promulgation and was complete by the time Porfirio Díaz launched the 1876 Revolution of Tuxtepec. No sooner had the constitution been published and the oaths of loyalty taken than anti-constitutional plotting began. Such plotting and scheming was not confined to reactionary clerics and generals; liberals too began to suspect that the whole system was fatally flawed and should be junked. Manuel Payno, for one, met with conservative military leaders and discussed with them the best way to remove the constitution as the law of the land. Although Payno's motives must be suspect, one element was his concern that the system was unworkable, especially since the president had no real power.[3] Thus both the liberals and the conservatives, who had always supported the concept of the strong president, could agree on a coup d'etat against the constitutional Comonfort government. Even Comonfort, after much hesitation and soul-searching, joined the rebellion in January 1858. The rebels issued the Plan of Tacubaya, which focused directly on the Constitution of 1857. No longer were revolts to be against men; now they were focused on political symbols. Thus the Constitution of 1857 became the object of scorn for those who supported Tacubaya and the object of vigorous defense for those who opposed it.

Politics had become ideological. After the overthrow of the Comonfort government the conservatives immediately annulled the constitution and established military rule. The liberals, although routed and in complete disarray, proclaimed the legitimacy of their cause. Manuel Doblado feared that Mexico had returned to the "vicious circle of revolutions with no chance of ever recovering the thread of legitimacy." He blamed "the privileged classes" for the coup and predicted that "if the cause of legitimacy does not triumph, the result . . . will be schism, anarchy, and the loss of our nationality."[4] The Juárez government condemned the creole generals for creating anarchy and optimistically declared: "When we are victorious there will be a return to a reign of law, not [government] by the ridiculous aristocracy."[5]

Thus the War of the Reform was launched. Not since Hidalgo's revolt in the Bajío had social issues led Mexicans to war. For three years (1858-1860) the future of Mexico hung in the balance. On the one hand stood the anti-constitutional forces of tradition in Mexico City. Here Miguel Miramón and Félix Zuloaga struggled to maintain a traditional system dominated by the church, the military, and wealthy landowners. In Veracruz, where the constitutionalists were confined, the ideological nature of the struggle was becoming apparent. In January 1858, Melchor Ocampo issued a statement on behalf of the government asking each governor to choose between the regime of "*fueros* and privileges" and the regime of the constitution, "reform and progress."[6] In this way the liberals made the constitution a national symbol, and as the war dragged on the importance of the constitution increased. When the liberals finally achieved victory, the constitution was the banner of their cause. As such it received a veneration unknown in Mexican history. "From now on," declared Juan de Dios Arias, "the law and only the law will be the great principle supporting public liberty, independence, and the future destiny of the Mexican nation, which has conquered inch by inch the legality represented by its constitution."[7] And the constitution was indeed honored as no document had ever been. When the constitutional army entered Mexico City on January 1, 1861, the reception was triumphant. Every street was decorated with banners and streamers. Arches adorned the main street leading to the Plaza de la Constitución, the last topped by a figure on whose forehead shone a star and in whose hand was a copy of the Constitution of 1857.[8] León Guzmán, in a speech to the reestablished Congress in 1861, summarized the nationalist feeling about the constitution. From 1821 to 1855 Mexico had been ruled by the aristocracy, high clergy, and military. The many coups, revolts, and uprisings of those years were the result of these elites' trying to keep others out of power. But, Guzmán declared, "in 1855 things changed; the people decided to form a new constitution," a new political system. This constitution, he concluded, established a rule of law and not men, thus becoming the very heart of the liberal struggle to create a modern nation-state.[9] And Francisco Zarco, as minister of foreign relations and thus head of the cabinet, summed up the importance of the constitution in a circular to the governors announcing the return of the government to the capital.

> "Constitution and Reform" has been the slogan on the banners of the people in their heroic, magnanimous, and bloody struggle against their oppressors; "Constitution and Reform" has been the war cry that for three years has unceasingly resounded across the entire Republic; "Constitution and Reform" has been the aspiration of all thinking men and of the unfortunate classes that have the desire to better themselves; "Constitution and Reform" has been the hope of all the political prisoners and the redemption of all who have died on the gallows; "Constitution and Reform" is, ultimately, the hope the civilized world has for our existence and our nationality.[10]

The growth of the Constitution of 1857 as a national symbol did not stop with the end of the Reform War. Hardly had the constitutional government reestablished itself in the capital than another threat loomed ominously on the horizon. Rumblings about foreign intervention had been heard in Veracruz as early as 1859; by 1861 these rumblings had turned into a veritable tempest. From every European capital came word of planned intervention in Mexico; rumors of scheming by conservative agents in European courts received disturbing confirmation. And on October 30, 1861, England, France, and Spain signed a tripartite agreement to intervene in Mexico to collect outstanding debts. The Reform War had been over for less than one year, yet Mexicans of all political persuasions now realized that the last few months of peace had been only a hiatus. More war was to follow; civil war was to be transformed into international war. No longer was it just Mexicans against Mexicans, now it was Mexicans against foreigners aided by Mexican allies. And for five years (1862-1867) the struggle spread throughout Mexico, from the isolated regions of Oaxaca and Yucatán in the south to the northern desert states of Chihuahua, Sonora, Coahuila, Nuevo León, and Tamaulipas. On one side stood the French-backed empire of Maximilian and Carlotta with their court of conservative dandies, brilliant young military officers, aging hacendados, and shrewd prelates. On the periphery struggled the remnants of the Constitutional Army with Benito Juárez at its head surrounded by the "immaculates": Sebastián Lerdo de Tejada, José María Iglesias, Ignacio Mejía, and Blas Balcárcel. Their claim to power was the Constitution of 1857, and they fought against the French as they had fought against the Tacubaya movement: in the name of the constitution.

As the government was driven north by the French army in the summer of 1863, it struggled desperately to maintain the semblance of constitutional government. When, in June, Juárez and his cabinet reached San Luis Potosí, he ordered that the Supreme Court and Congress continue to meet as if in Mexico City. The purpose was to show to the world that the constitution still reigned, that Mexico's sovereignty had only been disrupted, not destroyed. As Zarco put it: "The meeting of Congress in this city, under these circumstances, and on the day designated by the Constitution, would be an important victory for the cause of Mexican independence because it would demonstrate that the presence of the enemy was no obstacle to the continuing rule of those institutions which the people are defending with as much fervor as our autonomy."[11]

Although a quorum never gathered and Congress never officially met, the banner of the constitution played an important role in the psychological warfare launched by the government. In his New Year's declaration in 1865, Juárez touched time and time again on the theme of law and justice as represented by the constitution. After three years of bloody and unequal battle, he wrote, the Republic still stands. "We have been unfortunate, that is true;

fate has been against us many times, but the cause of Mexico, the cause of law and justice, has not succumbed . . . because there are still dedicated Mexicans in whose hearts burns the fire of holy patriotism." Juárez then added: "The existence of arbitrary power is a permanent violation of law and justice . . . and must be destroyed for the honor of Mexico and all humanity."[12]

One significant indication of how important the constitution had become as a national symbol during the French intervention was the constitutional crisis in November 1865. According to the constitution, Juárez's presidential term was to end on the last day of November. If no elections had been held by then the office was to be occupied by the president of the Supreme Court, in those days General Jesús González Ortega, thoroughly infused with the feeling that no other person could save the Republic, and convinced that the omnipotent powers granted by Congress provided the legal basis for dramatic action, Juárez prolonged his term of office until the end of the war. At the same time he declared that González Ortega was, by virtue of his unauthorized absence in the United States, no longer president of the Supreme Court.[13] Reaction among some of Juárez's closest advisers was swift and vigorous. Manuel Ruiz, a fellow Oaxacan who had played an important role in the writing of the Reform Laws and who now served on the Supreme Court, renounced his position and retired to private life. He explained that he was taking such action because of the "violence and damage to the fundamental law" the prorogation had done.[14] González Ortega branded the move "immoral and unwise" and "illegal, arbitrary, and unjust." The extension of the term of office, said González Ortega, destroyed the republican principle and "the base of legal order which is the form of government established by the Constitution." He declared that the action was an "insult to the Mexican people" and all those fighting to defend the constitution against the foreign imperialists.[15] Guillermo Prieto, a member of the Constitutional Congress and close friend of Juárez, also announced his separation from the government.[16] One of the clearest statements of the strong constitutional feeling that permeated the liberal camp can be found in a letter from José María Patoni to Benito Juárez. For Patoni the great conquest achieved by the Ayutla movement was that the question of persons had been abolished forever and with the Constitution of 1857 the rule of law had supplanted the personalism of caudillo politics. The extension of office was a "usurpation . . . an inheritance from the days of Santa Anna" that "exposes the country to anarchy, weakening it, and highly damaging our name abroad." All of this at a time when Mexico was being invaded by the French with the justification that Mexicans did not know how to rule themselves. The constitution had given the liberal cause its legitimacy, and it was "that indispensable condition . . . for the salvation of our Independence." Patoni feared that without strict constitutionality the cause of Mexico would be lost.[17]

As the war against the foreigners turned in favor of the constitutionalist cause, Juárez increasingly used the Constitution of 1857 as the symbol of Mexican victory. In October 1866, fearful of Prussia and its rapid expansion, Napoleon III removed his troops from Mexico, thus leaving Maximilian totally dependent on a conscripted and disloyal army. The end was clearly in sight, and the liberals took the opportunity to stress the constitutionality and legality of their cause. They chose the form of an interview between Juárez and a reporter from the *New York Herald* that appeared on December 16, 1866. Juárez noted that Maximilian's army was deserting the empire and explained that this was happening because Mexicans were choosing the cause of legality and nationality over usurpation and foreign domination. "This," he declared, "is the result of our long revolution against the reactionary elements in our country." When Iturbide declared independence the country was left in the hands of only one class, a class that the Catholic Church and the military dominated. They preferred a foreign prince to Mexican leaders and wanted to maintain the vestiges of traditional colonial rule by preserving the privileges and wealth of these anti-national institutions. With the Congress of 1824 the battle began. A small number of reformers were determined to incorporate into the new constitution truly liberal principles, but they were only partially successful. "The church still governed with an iron hand; the military, under the control of the church, was the scourge of the country; and the extraordinary privileges of the clergy and military still crushed the liberties of the people." The situation changed in 1857, however. "The Constitution of 1857 initiated the liberation from all this misery, and the Reform Laws, issued in Veracruz, completed the job." The people, concluded Juárez, are beginning at last to understand these great principles and "we are now ready to initiate a new era." The new era was to have the constitution as its dominant symbol, a symbol of nation-building and reform.[18]

When Juárez finally entered Mexico City on July 15, 1867, after four years of exile in the north, he did so in the name of the Constitution of 1857. To the enormous crowd that met him in the Plaza de la Constitución he addressed these words: "Today, upon our return to the Capital, I have the pleasure to inform you that, in spite of having been terribly battered, neither the Constitution nor our independence has been damaged."[19] On the same day the government issued a proclamation to the Mexican people. In it the victors emphasized the legality of their cause and linked it to the future of the Mexican nation. "The Government left," read the declaration, "in order to defend the flag of the Patria as long as necessary to obtain the triumph of the holy cause of independence and the institutions of the Republic." The proclamation went on to affirm that the government had complied with its duties;

it had made no agreement that would hurt "the independence and sovereignty of the Republic, the integrity of its territory, or the respect owed to its Constitution and its laws." And it raised the standard of the constitution as the symbol for which the battle had been fought. "After four years the Government returns to the city of Mexico with the banner of the Constitution and with our laws, which never, even for one instant, ceased to exist within the national territory."[20] Thus by 1867, after a complete decade of civil war and foreign intervention, after a decade of forcing Mexicans to choose between the forces of tradition and the new politics as represented by the Constitution of 1857 and the Reform Laws, the liberals had won and their constitution was the most revered, the most venerated document in Mexican history. It is significant to note that when men revolted, as Porfirio Díaz would do unsuccessfully in 1871 and again—this time successfully—in 1876, they would do so in favor of the Constitution of 1857, a dramatic change from the age of caudillos, when men always revolted against the prevailing constitution.

If the first consequence of the Reform War and the French intervention was to solidify the position of the Constitution of 1857 as the national symbol, the second was to convince the men of the Reform that they could not rule with it. Throughout the decade between 1857 and 1867 the liberal elite became increasingly aware that the constitution, written to ensure a compromise among political factions, made a strong national government impossible. The constitution had been written in reaction to the centralized and absolute dictatorship of Santa Anna and as such made certain that the presidential office would never be able to exercise the kind of aggressive leadership Santa Anna had displayed. Yet this was exactly the kind of leadership Juárez came to regard as essential for the survival of the nation. In this way, the Reform War and the French intervention heightened the paradox that confined the Reform: on the one hand the reaction against dictatorial caudillo politics, on the other the need for strong, dynamic leadership to complete the work of nation-building.

The central question, then, was the authority of the president, his ability to make decisions and compel the nation to accept them. Prior to the Reform War, the liberals felt the most dangerous element in the political system was a strong president. Yet during the war Juárez, as a president unchecked by legislature and judiciary, had by decree carried the reform process to new levels. The separation of church and state, the nationalization of church property, the secularization of cemeteries, the creation of the civil registry—all these had been accomplished without the legislature or the consent of the people. They had been the acts of the president in consultation with his advisers. Juárez had, in effect, become a dictator while the constitution remained suspended during a time of crisis. He justified his actions in vigorous terms: "Neither liberty, nor constitutional order, nor progress, nor peace, nor the independence of the Nation would have been possible without the Reform."[21] But the time had come to return power to Congress, where according to the constitution it belonged. To do otherwise would have been hypocritical, especially after fighting the Reform War in the name of the constitution.

The return to experimental democracy was, however, only a temporary break in the growing concentration of power in the office of the presidency. Francisco Zarco, in his circular to the nation of January 20, 1861, gave clear indications of the policy the government was going to pursue. Even though the constitution has been restored, he said, and even though the state of siege has been lifted and all the laws restored, "the Executive, without becoming a dictator . . . will not paralyze his actions, and in those cases that demand it he will not sit back before these difficulties in the name of legal formalities." He assured the nation that the constitution would be respected, that there would be no dictatorship, that the government would abide by the laws. "But," he warned, "the government will be reorganized, legislative measures will be dictated, and the government will accept the responsibilities of being active and of vigorously attacking national problems." Sounding a theme that would become the motto of the dictatorship of Porfirio Díaz a decade and a half later, Zarco declared: "the Government will try to combine order with liberty."[22]

It soon became clear that the emphasis would increasingly be on the former. On February 2, 1861, Juárez, still invested with dictatorial powers, issued a law on freedom of the press. It declared that the right to write and publish freely was inviolable and that the expression of ideas was not subject to any judicial or administrative inquest "except in the case of an attack on morality, an infringement of the rights of others, the provocation of some crime, or the disturbance of public order."[23] The law left vague what exactly a disturbance of public order was, and this vagueness would come in handy in later presidential battles with the press. Then on May 28, 1861, the government proposed to the new Congress that certain guarantees contained in the constitution be suspended so that the government could more forcefully prosecute the battle against the remaining conservative bands and the bandits that infested most Mexican roads. In particular, the government wanted Congress to remove the constitutional prohibition against "political crimes." Although the debate got sidetracked on the question of presidential responsibility for the McLane-Ocampo treaty, the assassination of Melchor Ocampo on June 3, 1861, stunned the Congress into action. The next day Congress decreed that the "hateful assassins"—Félix Zuloaga, Leonardo Márquez, Tomás Mejía, José María Cobos, Juan Vicario, Lindoro Cajiga, and Manuel Lozada—had lost all protection the constitution might have given them. Three days later, on June 7, Congress fulfilled the wishes of the administration and suspended several constitutional protections. Individuals could now be forced to serve the government for just compensation, and the free press law was severely restricted. The right to assemble was limited only to those assemblies authorized by the president. Special tribunals, outlawed by article 13 of the constitution, now returned for political crimes, and the president set the rules and penalties. Almost all power in the state flowed into the hands of the president, and, as José Linárez, president of the Congress, put it: "With the end of the armed revolution, the political revolution begins."[24]

The suspension of constitutional guarantees was limited to six months, and as the period drew to an end some of the liberal elite began to think in terms of reform of the constitution itself. Such ideas, in light of the importance the constitution had achieved during the Reform War, raised serious questions of strategy and ideology. José María Mata, on November 9, 1861, proposed one such reform. In a letter to Francisco Zarco, Mata suggested three small but significant changes. The first of these focused directly on the presidency. He noted that article 84 of the constitution prohibited the president from leaving the Federal District without permission of Congress. For Mata such a restriction, though not important in itself, did limit the authority and independence of the president. Sarcastically he described a situation in which the president might want to go for a picnic in Chapultepec or for a vacation in Tacubaya, both suburbs of Mexico City. According to the constitution the president would first have to ask permission from Congress and at the same time demonstrate that there was "grave" need for this trip. Mata termed the whole thing "completely ridiculous."[25] Yet in late 1861 few were willing to tamper with the constitution. Its growth as a national symbol made any attempt to alter its provisions seem perilously close to treason. In fact, Congress, mindful of its prerogatives and fearful of the growth of presidential power, removed the suspension of constitutional guarantees on October 12, two months before the law of June 7 was supposed to expire.[26]

It was, by all accounts, a futile gesture. As the threat of foreign intervention became a reality in December 1861, there was little Congress could do in the face of the presidential drive for power and the danger Mexico faced. And on December 11, in secret session, Congress once again made the presidential office omnipotent "with no other restriction than the salvation of the independence and integrity of the Nation, the constitutional form of government, and the Reform Laws." Congress felt itself so weak that it defeated, by a vote of 51 to 47, a proposal that would maintain part of the power in the legislature.[27] Thus by December 1861 the constitution had once again been suspended and the president ruled absolutely. As Vicente Riva Palacio explained at the last session of Congress on December 14: "The Congress committed to the President the salvation of the Republic" because "in these solemn moments energy and ability depend always on unity of action."[28]

The Reform War had begun the inexorable shift of power from the legislature to the presidency; the French intervention accelerated the process. Parliamentary government, that first desire of the liberals in the middle fifties, came to an end in the early sixties. As one provincial newspaper expressed it: "What is necessary now is for the government to maintain its power in order to save the nation. Later there will be time for parliamentary debates."[29] And Zarco in *El Siglo XIX:* "No one exceeds us . . . in our aversion to dictatorship, but it is necessary . . . that Mexicans and patriots think exclusively about independence, about the nationality of the Republic."[30] Juárez too echoed these sentiments; to ask the president to save the nation while enjoying democracy was, he declared, like asking him "to play a tambourine without making any noise."[31] Congress got the message and twice more before the government had to abandon Mexico City increased and reaffirmed the absolute power of the president.[32] Having done this, Congress put the burden of saving the nation exclusively on the president. His failure would mean the end of Mexico; his success, on the other hand, would have important consequences, not the least of which would be the linking of the office of the president with the health of the nation itself. The stronger the president, the stronger the nation.

Thus when Juárez's term of office expired in 1865, he extended his tenure by simple decree. So much has been written about the decrees of November 8, 1865, and so much of what has been written has been polemical, that the significance of Juárez's action has been lost in the dust of historical controversy. The crucial point about his "coup d'etat" was that with the prorogation of his tenure in office Juárez emancipated the office of the president from all legal fictions and limitations. The constitution may have been a national symbol, but real power resided in the presidency. As Guillermo Prieto, a caustic critic of the prorogation, put it: "Living with his cause, [Juárez] believed that he alone could keep the Mexican flag aloft. And to this fanaticism, to this exaltation that has the fire and intensity of religious passion, he sacrificed all scruples."[33] Prieto was not entirely correct, because Juárez did not sacrifice all his scruples. In fact, great care was taken to put the prorogation within the constitutional context. In the circular that accompanied the decrees of November 8, Sebastián Lerdo de Tejada, as Juárez's chief adviser and cabinet minister, went to great lengths to put the action within the framework of the constitution. He argued carefully that the constitution intended the vice-president to become president only in cases where it was possible for elections to be held and for some reason they

were not. But the present situation, Lerdo argued, bears no relationship to
the situation the constituents had in mind in 1856 and 1857. "In such a case
as the present war," Lerdo wrote, "the supreme necessity of conserving the
government makes the prorogation just and necessary." Not satisfied with
this argument, Lerdo went on to use the omnipotent powers of the president
as further justification. He pointed out that under the Constitution of 1857
the legislative power had the authority to decide the propriety of presidential
action. And at this moment the law of December 11, 1861, granted the president legislative power with, in the words of the law, "no other restrictions
than the salvation of the independence and the integrity of the Nation, the
constitutional form of government, and the Reform Laws."[34] The words of
the 1861 law had come back four years later to haunt those who fought the
trend toward omnipotent presidential power.

By 1866 it was becoming increasingly clear to the liberals that the concentration of power in the office of the president was a necessity, even after
victory over the French. Francisco Zarco, writing to Juárez in July 1866, as
the war was beginning to turn in favor of the Mexicans, called for the institu-
tionalization of this process. "You and with you the Republic," he wrote,
"will triumph over the Empire and the Intervention, and now is the time to
begin thinking about reorganizing the country." He urged Juárez to take
advantage of the situation and move vigorously, although he left vague how
Juárez ought to proceed.[35] Five months later, as the Mexican forces swept
southward, defeating the remnants of the imperial army, Ignacio Vallarta
struck the same theme. "No government since Independence," he declared,
"has had such a favorable situation. National sentiment, so profoundly
wounded by the Intervention, is today completely with the Constitutional
Government." Nothing is left of the reactionary forces, and "all the Republic
wants a strong national government." Vallarta argued that all Juárez had to
do is command and all Mexico would obey. "I believe," he concluded, "that
you have all the elements of authority necessary to command universal
respect."[36]

Such urgings were hardly necessary. If the Reform War had raised doubts
about the viability of the political structure established by the Constitution
of 1857, the French intervention did little to dispel them. When the government returned to Mexico in July 1867, it had ruled for an entire decade
without the constitution, and although the constitution had become a symbol
of veneration and respect throughout the country, for the liberals it now
required significant reform and modification. Clearly one of the major
legacies of the decade of civil war and foreign intervention was a tradition
of unrestricted presidential power and a desire for swift and unchecked
decision-making. All the major reforms that the single Chamber of Deputies

had been set up to perform had, in fact, been accomplished by an omnipotent president. Authority had become centered in the presidency, even though officially it resided in Congress. The politics of the Restored Republic was designed to resolve this paradox.

Juárez and his advisers believed that the revolution was over for Mexico and that the hour of reconstruction had begun. They were convinced that the victory over the empire marked a radical new course for Mexican history, and during July and August they debated the best means of signifying the transition. On August 14 the results of their work became public. It came in an unusual form, the *convocatoria*. Although the main purpose of the document was to establish the dates for the elections of president, Supreme Court, and Congress, it also contained the program for the concentration of power in the hands of the president. Article 9 of the *convocatoria* called for a referendum on five constitutional amendments. The five reforms were: (1) establishment of a Senate, (2) granting to the president the veto, (3) prohibiting cabinet ministers from making personal appearances before Congress to deliver their yearly reports, (4) limiting the power of the Permanent Deputation, which wielded congressional authority when Congress was not in session, to call special sessions of Congress, and (5) fixing exactly the line of succession to the presidency.[37]

In asking for this referendum, the government went over the head of Congress, which had the official responsibility to amend the constitution, and appealed directly to the people. Obviously Juárez and Lerdo, the authors of the *convocatoria,* took Prieto's and Vallarta's suggestions to heart and believed that the moment to strike was at hand. Lerdo gave some indication of the reasoning behind the strategy of the *convocatoria* in the circular he issued to explain and defend the process. He noted that "the Constitution of 1857 has been the banner of the people," who have shed their blood to defend Mexican independence and save the Republic. For Mexicans the constitution was the source of all the principles of progress, of all civil rights, and of the best form of government for the Mexican people. But it was a human work and to want to reform it was not to want to destroy it—"the change in circumstances alone requires additions and reforms." Lerdo, having justified in general terms the need for reform, then moved on to discuss the central issue: power. Under the Constitution of 1857, he declared, "the Legislature is everything and the Executive lacks proper authority," yet "Mexican society needed essential reforms . . . and by means of the dictatorship they have been accomplished." The need for a radical single-body legislature was over because the revolution was over. Normal times had returned and "in normal times the despotism of a convention can be as bad as or worse than the despotism of a dictator." Thus the constitutional reforms were essential to redress the imbalance of power and assure the nation of continued vigorous leadership. Lerdo then went on to explain why the government appealed directly to the people for the reforms. The normal process would be too slow in these critical moments, and besides, "the free will of the people, being the source of all authority, is superior to any law."[38]

It was a strong statement of the liberal principles at work in 1867. Whereas a decade earlier the liberals had seen a divided Congress as the major obstacle to restructuring Mexico along modern lines, now they considered a weak executive the chief hindrance to continued modernization. The division of Congress would change the legislature from a radical convention to a deliberative body; the veto would give the president the authority he needed to override Congress; the prohibition of personal presentations by the cabinet would prevent Congress from harassing the executive power; and the limiting of the authority of the Permanent Deputation to call special sessions of Congress meant that Congress would meet less often and the president could act more freely. Given the assumptions of the liberal group, it was a logical and dramatic move in the direction of modern politics; given the strength of the Constitution of 1857 as a national symbol, however, it was doomed to failure. From all sides the *convocatoria* was assailed, and the bitterness and intensity of the assault prompted Juárez to issue his own defense on August 22, 1867. He lamented the tone the debate had taken and assured his countrymen that his only purpose was to ensure peace in the future and the consolidation of national institutions. "I will be happy," he pathetically concluded, "if before I die I can see a permanent consolidation."[39]

He never got his wish. The reforms proposed in the *convocatoria* were never ratified by the people, and in his welcoming address to the newly reestablished Congress in December, Juárez admitted his defeat. He pointed out that although many voted for the reforms, the great majority either voted against or did not vote at all—a move that signified opposition, not to the reforms themselves, but to the manner in which the *convocatoria* proceeded. Thus, concluded Juárez, "the Government will submit to the wisdom of Congress the proposed reforms so that it can act on them in accordance with the rules established in the Constitution."[40] The attempt at radical democracy had failed; the strength of the constitution as a national symbol prevailed over the desire for a strong president.

Yet the reformers were not finished, and ultimately—although their victory would not be as clear-cut as the *convocatoria* envisioned—they would win. The press of those changed circumstances that Lerdo referred to eventually drove even the most ardent constitutionalists into the arms of the presidency. The government may have returned to the capital, but remnants of the imperial army remained in the field. In Yucatán, for example, the conservative forces had enough strength to capture and kill the governor of the state, General Manuel Cepeda. Throughout the country discharged soldiers became bandits and ready arms for would-be caudillos. There was no longer a French intervention, but there was no peace either. Into this situation the government moved quickly. On December 18 the government asked Congress for the suspension of several constitutional guarantees so that the war against the conservatives could be pressed without limits. The opposition to the request was vigorous; Mata, Prieto, Zamacona, and Montes led the denunciations, accusing the government of asking Congress to vote itself out of existence. Montes argued that the president should be given all the money and equipment necessary to finish the job but that the constitution should not be touched. After long and ardent debate Congress voted the suspension of constitutional guarantees for bandits by a vote of 67 to 53.[41]

This was the first suspension of constitutional guarantees in the Restored Republic and it lasted until April 1868. At the same time, in Sinaloa, several caudillos, led by Trinidad García de la Cadena, Jesús Toledo, and Lic. Irenio Paz, revolted against the government. In response, the administration requested the restitution of the Ley Doblado of January 25, 1862, which gave the military the right to try and execute rebels. Clearly unconstitutional, the Ley Doblado received a hostile reception in Congress. The opposition pointed out that the law was designed for use against bandits and kidnappers, not for political movements. They emphasized that article 23 of the Constitution outlawed the death penalty for political crimes. Only the worsening situation in the north held the government's case together, and after five months of debate Congress authorized an extension of the Ley Doblado—but by the close vote of 66 to 59.[42]

Slowly but surely the president chipped away at congressional authority, each time using local difficulties to enhance national power. When revolts in Zacatecas and San Luis Potosí threatened to cut off the north from the central authority in Mexico City in early 1870, once again the administration petitioned Congress to suspend constitutional guarantees of civil liberties. In particular, Lerdo asked Congress to extend for six months the law of December 11, 1861, which was actually an extension of the original suspension of June 7, 1861. When Congress finally passed the request on January 17 it suspended the following constitutional articles: 11 (the right of free travel without passport), 27 (guaranteeing the sanctity of private property), 7 (freedom of the press), 13 (abolition of special tribunals), 19 (limiting detention in jail to three days), 21 (restricting the application of judicial penalties exclusively to the secular courts), and 9 (freedom of association). Moreover, the law rewrote three articles. Article 5 was rewritten to read: "In case of national emergency all individuals can be obliged to render personal services with payment of just compensation." Article 16 was altered to give government authorities the right to search and seize individual property, and article 26 was modified to allow military commanders to demand personal services and housing without judicial approval.[43] In short, the law of January 17 created a perfect police state, one in which the president had the power to pursue order at the expense of liberty.

In December 1871 the Revolt of La Noria, led by Porfirio and Félix Díaz, produced the fourth suspension of constitutional guarantees. Actually, this suspension was little more than an extension of the previous decree, and Juárez continued to act as if the suspension was in force, even when it expired. Nor did his death, on July 18, 1872, retard the process of concentrating power in the hands of the president. No sooner had Lerdo legally assumed the office than he asked for and received a law to be applied directly against bandits (Ley de Plagiarios) that extended the suspension of the constitutional guarantees of civil liberties. What is significant about this fifth suspension is the size of the vote in favor of the bill: 110 in favor to 21 against.[44] It was one of the largest majorities the president had ever received and demonstrates the weakening of congressional resolution to defend itself against the creeping despotism of the presidency.

The Restored Republic lasted 120 months. Of these at least fifty saw the suspension of the constitutional guarantees of civil rights. In the remaining seventy the president often ruled as if the suspension was in force. What this meant for the political structure of Mexico was not that the constitution had been destroyed or even ignored. Far from it; the Constitution of 1857 continued to command powerful forces of respect and even adulation. The elaborate efforts the executive undertook in order to suspend the constitution bear witness to its continuing influence. Instead of a destruction of the constitution, Mexico experienced a process of shifting power away from Congress and to the presidency. The process had begun during the Reform War, accelerated during the French intervention, and continued throughout the Restored Republic. By 1876, when the last successful coup d'etat of the nineteenth century would take place, power was formally concentrated in the hands of the president.

More than any other event of the Restored Republic, the creation of the Senate in 1874 signified the end of weak presidential rule. It will be recalled that Juárez had requested the creation of a second legislative body in the *convocatoria* of 1867, and that the resulting plebiscite was so inconclusive that he abandoned the project. Juárez never completely gave up on formally concentrating power in the office of the president, however, and in 1869 again requested the formation of a Senate. Again, Congress moved slowly and the request was denied. Yet by 1874 Lerdo felt the time was ripe for another try.

This time it worked; on October 30, 1874, the committee on constitutional rules certified that since enough state legislatures had ratified the proposed reform of the constitution, the Senate would go into existence on September 16, 1875.[45] Legislative authority, once the hope of the revolutionaries of the 1850s, was now irrevocably divided, and power rested almost completely in the hands of the president.

Two massive and bloody wars—the Reform War and the French intervention—converted the Constitution of 1857 from the banner of one political faction into a truly national symbol, an almost sacred document that all Mexicans recognized as the law of the land. Such was the prestige of the constitution that, unlike the situation before the Reform, there would be no calls for a new constitution with each change of government; nor would it be until the Díaz regime had become an obviously unrestricted dictatorship that men like Emilio Rabasa would begin to question its utility.

Yet for all its strength as a national symbol and as the source of legitimacy for the reform movement, the Constitution of 1857 experienced radical alterations. Nation-building, in its early stages, involves the concentration of power in the hands of a recognized, legitimate national authority. The delegates to the Constitutional Congress had hoped that this authority would rest in the unicameral legislature as a protection against the abuses of presidential power experienced under Santa Anna. The realities of having to defend the Reform against both Mexican and foreign opponents forced the liberal leadership to abandon its early ideals and seek a new solution to the dilemma of attempting reform within a juridical framework of law and order. The result was a unique solution to the paradox of liberalism that had plagued Mexico since independence: the constitutional dictatorship. Before the Reform, Mexico had been torn by tendencies toward legislative dominance and caudillo politics; now these had been reconciled into one system. By 1876 Mexico had the formal trappings of democracy and a balance of power, but in reality power rested almost exclusively with the president. When Porfirio Díaz seized the presidency in 1876, the ensuing dictatorship was a logical extension of the political restructuring that had taken place since the Reform War.

Structuring power and exercising power are, however, two different processes. Once the Reform had been legitimized and power formally concentrated in the office of the president, the next task was to make that power a reality.

6. Arms, Politics, and Caudillos

Insurrections such as that carried out by the Ayutla group in 1855 are often referred to as seizures of power. Successful rebellions do not, however, result in the seizure of power; they destroy power. As Ignacio Altamirano observed, the Ayutla movement was "little more than pure destruction, but this destruction was necessary before we could build a just society."[1]

Once destroyed, power does not immediately reappear at the same level but tends to diffuse itself from abstract "national" centers to more concrete local levels. Power—influence or control over the actions of others—can exist in two dimensions: it can be expanded or contracted, and it can be concentrated or dispersed. The problem for the Ayutlans was not to seize power, for almost none existed in 1855, but instead to make power, to mobilize old institutions and create new ones for the effective expansion and concentration of power. In the language of nation-building theory, this is the penetration crisis.

The expansion and the concentration of power mark the first stage of political modernization. As David Apter put it, the breakdown of the old order leads to "an exaggerated emphasis on power." Apter sees power in the early stages of modernization as both compensation for weakness and disintegration and potentiality leading to fulfillment of modernizing nationalist yearnings.[2] Samuel Huntington identifies a similar process. "Modernization," he writes, "is associated with a marked redistribution of power within the political system: the breakdown of local, religious, ethnic, and other power centers and the centralization of power in the national political institutions." Huntington argues that policy innovations vary directly with the concentration of power within the political system; the more power is concentrated, the more possibility that innovation and reform can occur. Since fundamental changes in society and politics come from the purposeful actions of men, modernization requires authority to make the changes operative. Thus the success of carrying out a nation-building program hinges on the ability of the new elites to reassemble and reinstitutionalize at the abstract national level enough power to enforce public policy.[3]

The preceding chapter traced the formal concentration of power in the hands of a single innovating authority, the president. Prior to the Revolution of Ayutla others had attempted such a concentration of power. For example, the last dictatorship of Santa Anna in 1853 represents the culmination of the process during the age of caudillos. Yet Santa Anna failed; localism, as represented by the Ayutla movement at its inception, brought him down. The crucial question remains: Why did Santa Anna's attempt at centralization collapse? And why did the Reform concentration succeed? The answer lies in the nature of legitimacy. Santa Anna could claim no legitimate right to authority. On the other hand, as we have seen, the Constitution of 1857 became the source of legitimacy, a symbol of the nation for a large number of Mexicans. By 1867 the constitution and the Reform had become inseparably linked, and both were ultimately tied to the very existence of Mexico as a nation-state.

The Reform War and the French intervention were critical elements in the legitimization process. They were the result of two world views in conflict, views that were irreconcilable and therefore destined to meet on the field of battle. Yet these momentous struggles raised not only the issue of legitimacy but also the question of force. The battles had been a test of strength, army against army, weapon against weapon, power against power. For ten years the liberal elite learned first-hand the difficulties of carrying out its reforms; it also learned the need to monopolize force. As Max Weber has pointed out, one of the hallmarks of the modern state is a legitimate monopoly of the ability to use force. The state, in order to make itself the ultimate arbiter of human affairs, must prevent private or local entities from employing force to settle disputes.

Prior to the Reform almost all power had been in the hands of local political bosses, the caudillos, who, because of their monopoly of force, determined the outcome of political struggles.[4] After independence, power diffused from the "national" viceregal level, where it had rested for almost three hundred years, to the local centers of authority and prestige. Creole hacendados like Santa Anna developed a political system, *caudillaje,* characterized by four interlocking elements: (1) political groupings formed of patron-client sets held together by personal relations between leader and follower and a universal desire for wealth; (2) the lack of institutionalized means for succession to office; (3) the solving of political disputes by violence on the local level; and (4) the consistent failure of national caudillos to secure their hold on political office.[5]

Although usually looked upon as a period of total anarchy, the post-independence politics of Mexico merely shifted the locus of power from the center to the periphery. Richard Morse has argued that post-independence Mexico (and much of the rest of Latin America) resembled the nucleated city-states of the Italian renaissance. The masses were passive and inarticulate; there were no institutions to mediate between local power and national politics; armies were under local control. "For lack of a politico-spiritual commonalty," Morse writes, "sources and directions of leadership were wholly fortuitous. The consequent emergence of opportunist caudillos—as of Italy's city tyrants—deranged the predictable interplay of hierarchical class interests."[6]

With power dispersed to the local levels after 1823, the ultimate source of caudillo authority was the hacienda. Here the creole aristocracy—the hacendados—reigned, surrounded by retainers who formed the nucleus of their private armies. The strength of each hacendado depended on two factors: the production of the hacienda and the strength of the private army. Both of these elements required large amounts of human labor. Thus each hacienda was potentially the enemy of its neighbor, since each was striving to maximize the number of men in its command and the amount of land under its control. In many parts of Mexico the haciendas fought not only with each other but also over Indian land, which supplied both land and labor for the growing great estates. In this atmosphere of competition and conflict, the lack of a unified creole political elite becomes understandable; out of it grew the vehement opposition to any form of centralized government. Such a government would inevitably seek to concentrate and expand power at the expense of regional political entities.

The goal of the creole caudillo was to obtain wealth. To do this he needed a band of retainers—clients—who formed his private army. But just as the caudillo needed the clients, the clients needed the patron; from him they received sustenance and protection. These close interpersonal relationships between patron and clients made two skills essential in the maintenance of the band: charisma on the part of the leader, and his ability to distribute correctly the accumulated wealth. The charisma of the caudillo is usually expressed as *machismo* or masculinity, and it is invariably related to domination of both women and men. *Machismo* also implies a ready willingness to use violence to accomplish this domination. It was within this psychological matrix that the game of politics was played out. Each group depended exclusively on the magnetism of the leader; the death of the patron meant the instant dissolution of the band.[7]

The caudillo held his band together and even increased its size not only by the force of his personality but also by the amount of his wealth and his acumen in distributing it wisely. In an age when the range of economic activities was extremely limited, the possibilities of borrowing from banks non-existent, and

land an essential prerequisite for most financial dealings, men with money
became magnets for those willing to trade loyalty for sustenance. These
hombres de confianza—as the retainers were called—gave their loyalty to a
patron as long as the caudillo continued to supply largess; when funds from
government treasuries or customs houses ran dry, so did support from clients.[8]
When, for example, Santa Anna could no longer supply enough money to his
military followers in 1854 and 1855, many deserted him and joined the
Ayutla rebellion.

Such a political system had obvious weaknesses. First of all, the bonds
that held groups together were tenuous at best. Charisma can be fleeting, and
the chronic lack of money and prizes made the rule of the caudillo short-lived.
Thus the coup d'etat was a built-in ingredient of *caudillaje* and not surprisingly
it was often led by the closest followers of the caudillo. Juan Alvarez, who had
supported Santa Anna in 1853, turned on him in 1854 when the informal pact
of non-interference was violated. Such rapid fluctuations of loyalty go a long
way to explain the political turnover in Mexico prior to the Reform. In the
thirty-five years from the Plan of Iguala declaring Mexico independent to the
Plan of Ayutla, Mexico had forty-four changes of government. In 1833 the
presidential chair changed hands seven times; in 1847 it had five occupants;
and in numerous years three changes were normal. The average life-span of a
Mexican government in the years 1821 to 1855 was nine months. Yet this
rapid turnover does not indicate equally rapid political mobility. On the
contrary, the same men tended to return to office. Nicolás Bravo was president three times, Anastasio Bustamante three times, José Joaquín Herrera
three times, and Santa Anna eleven. Twenty of the forty-four changes
involved four men.

The sparse number of participants in caudillismo indicates that a praetorian
oligarchy (in the words of Samuel Huntington) ruled Mexico prior to the
Reform. Politics was a struggle not between parties and ideologies but between
personal and family cliques. In this political environment there were no effective political institutions capable of mediating or moderating conflict. "In
oligarchical praetorianism," Huntington writes, "the dominant social forces
are the great landowners, the leading clergy, the wielders of the sword. . . .
Politics assumes an individualistic Hobbesian pattern. No consensus exists
on the means of resolving disputes; few, if any, political organizations or
institutions exist."[9] For the men of the Reform such a political system had
meant the frequent occurrence of violence and limited access to high political
office.

The dictatorship of Santa Anna in 1853 and the subsequent exile and
imprisonment of all opponents to caudillismo had taught the liberals the
dangers inherent in the system. Where they had once been willing to cooperate

in the process, they now sought its total destruction. Juan Alvarez, the leader of the Ayutla movement and a caudillo himself, described the presidency as "the target of all potshots . . . the field of personal battles." Under the caudillo system, the highest office of the land was little more than "a rich mine whose treasure has to supply the all-consuming thirst for gold."[10] Others argued that the only hope for national unity lay in the total abolition of the traditional political system.[11] José María Lafragua launched the most bitter attack on the caudillo system. He accused the creole oligarchy of creating anarchy and chaos: "They want to stop progress and make government impossible." They do this because "this incessant anarchy supplies fortunes . . . and wealth that satisfy 'bastard' interests; because they hope the boredom of some, the egoism of others, and the disgust of all will force the people to succumb to the oligarchy."[12]

The liberals also objected to the personalistic aspects of caudillismo. They saw in the traditional system devices for keeping new elites out of power, particularly in the creole emphasis on the man rather than the nation. Once in office the Reform group tried to create an effective nation-state that would transcend individual considerations. As one author expressed it: "Individuals may die . . . governments can disappear or give way to another, but the nation always exists."[13] It was Lafragua, as usual, who summed up the nationalist feeling on the matter. He argued that "the preservation of the nation is undoubtedly greater than any personal considerations." And he went on to declare: "The nation is the patrimony of no one. No man, however great he might be, no class, however important it might appear, has the right to decide arbitrarily the fate of the nation." Recalling the disaster of the Mexican-American War, Lafragua predicted that, if the personalistic caudillo system continued, "anarchy will reappear, the nation will break up, and our nationality will be lost."[14]

As a result of the political system that existed in Mexico before the Revolution of Ayutla, local caudillos controlled the military. Each caudillo rewarded his retainers with positions in the army. The obvious consequence of this procedure was the rapid increase in the number of military men—in particular officers, since who rewards friends with menial positions?—and the expenditures to keep the army fed, clothed, housed, and armed. Under Iturbide the army numbered 16,136 men; by the end of the last Santa Anna dictatorship the number had climbed to 64,316—a 400-percent increase in thirty-five years.[15] To pay for this force, the government had to allocate increasingly more money to the military. By 1855 almost 80 percent of the federal budget was spent on the army, with the rest spent on administrative costs and payments on the national debt. In this way, the military (along with the hacienda) became the basis of support for the caudillo structure of Mexican politics.

The liberals deeply distrusted the military. They had seen military incompetence cost Mexico half her territory in 1848; they had been exiled or imprisoned by a military dictator; they had witnessed the incessant political activity of the army associated with caudillo politics. Above all, they knew that no major changes would take place in the political structure of the country until the military had been reformed and subordinated to the state. Lafragua asserted that "every nation has a crucial moment in which it can move forward to form a modern state or slip backward into civil war and disintegration." The Reform had now provided such a moment, and Lafragua saw as the first step in that direction the reduction of military power because "the army has abandoned the flag out of self-love and personal ambition."[16] Even more bitter attacks assailed the military in the years immediately after Ayutla. One newspaper feared "the complete destruction of the patria," which it blamed on the military. It described the army as "corrupt, immoral, and dishonored" and said "all they care about is their own preservation, forgetting there is a nation to which they owe all obedience." The paper blamed the army for "the destruction of the Mexican nationality [and] the death of our beloved patria."[17] Juan Antonio de la Fuente stated that "the aristocracy . . . has always used the army against the people, even in times of peace," and called for extensive reform of the military structure.[18] Throughout Mexico the military establishment came under severe attack, and it became increasingly evident that the liberal group was not going to allow the army to play its traditional role in Mexican caudillo politics.

The liberals were careful to make clear, however, that the reforms would not destroy the military but only "reform and moralize" it. Moralization of the military meant its removal from political activities. They wanted to reverse the belief that "the nation is for the soldiers and not the soldiers for the nation."[19] The first step the reformers took to moralize the army was to limit the military *fuero*. The *fuero* had been granted to the military late in the eighteenth century, partly in response to increasing foreign incursion into the Spanish colonial empire. Men who fell under the *fuero* were exempt from certain taxes and could not be tried in non-military courts. These privileges extended not only to the soldier but also to his family in its broadest sense—father, mother, brothers, and even servants.[20] As the number of men in the army steadily increased during the first half of the nineteenth century, the control of the secular state over them decreased dramatically. Since the *fuero* was the most visible and vulnerable of the military prerogatives, it was the first to come under attack.

On November 23, 1855, Benito Juárez, the minister of justice in the new government, issued a law on the military and ecclesiastical *fuero*. Known as the Ley Juárez, the law was designed to reorganize and modernize the judicial system. To do this the military (and also ecclesiastical) *fueros* were limited in the range of their application. Military courts were allowed to hear only cases that involved military crimes or "mixed" crimes, that is, cases that might be only partly military in nature. At the same time, the civil cases then pending in military courts were to be removed from military jurisdiction and transferred to civilian courts, and military commanding generals were prohibited from hearing any cases whatsoever.[21] Through this judicial reform the modernizers hoped to strike at the heart of military privileges, thus reducing the political independence and power of the army. The idea was to cleanse the army so that "soldiers might become good citizens." Besides, as *El Siglo XIX* argued, the army could not complain because "the military *fuero* was a concession by the nation-state granted as much for the convenience of the courts as of the soldiers."[22] What was evident in 1855 was that the *fuero* was no longer convenient for a nation-building program.

Nor was a large standing army. Its outlandish size and cost had been a constant source of irritation to the liberals, who saw in the large army "one of the principal causes of our misfortunes." They argued that there were too many soldiers for a bankrupt state, too many officers, poor training, and too much favoritism in promotions. They wanted an immediate reduction in its size because "men of good will instinctively feel a certain aversion to the military." Its size had made it a "monster" and an "insatiable sponge."[23]

But reducing the size of the military establishment was not an easy task, primarily because the Reform group spent the first ten years of their rule in constant warfare. First they had to fight the conservatives who had been ousted in the Revolution of Ayutla. Then, immediately after beating the traditionalists in the Three Years War, the constitutionalists had to fight the French for five years. Nevertheless, even in the midst of recurrent military struggles, the liberal group worked to reduce the political activities of the army. No sooner had they ousted Santa Anna than they began to reduce its size. On August 16, 1855, all the auxiliary troops were disbanded with the hope they would return to "honest occupations." Then active battalions were dismantled, the draft *(leva)* was annulled, military pay was cut, and commanders were restricted in their ability to extract taxes from citizens.[24] Striking a blow at Santa Anna's massive army, Ignacio Comonfort, as minister of war under Juan Alvarez, prohibited prosecution of all soldiers who left their units. This law was also aimed at the draft, which nineteenth-century liberals abhorred because "to recruit fathers of families and laboring men left their dependents in poverty and exposed to immorality."[25] To signify the coming reduction and reform of the army, the first budget proposed by the liberal elite reduced federal expenditure on the military. Whereas Santa Anna had allocated almost 80 percent of his 1854-1855 budget of 39 million pesos,

Comonfort's 1856 budget of 14.2 million pesos specified only 31 percent for the military. The absolute projected reduction was a whopping 700 percent—from 31 million pesos in 1854 to 4.4 million in 1856.[26]

These reforms, limited as they may have been, had major and unforeseen consequences. The dramatic reduction in the military budget required equally drastic cuts in the ranks of enlisted men. Many had become soldiers as a last resort when work in other areas was not available. The army at least offered the comforts of semi-regular pay, clothes, food, and housing. Military life was not ideal, to be sure, but better than poverty, hunger, and village huts. The pay cuts, reductions in size, and end of the draft for the army in 1855 and 1856 threw many out of work and into a job market that simply did not exist. And these jobless men became the cannon fodder for the conservative rebellion that blossomed into the Reform War. Fighting offered surer rewards than highway robbery, kidnapping, and plundering haciendas.[27]

The Reform War from 1858 to 1860 delayed further military reform because both sides were completely dependent on the army for survival. But the army that supported the constitutional government was not the same army that defended the traditional order. On the contrary, a new military structure was being created during the war. The leaders of the new army—men such as Jesús González Ortega, Vicente Riva Palacio, Santos Degollado, and Manuel Doblado—were civilians who had to command armies because the regular army supported the conservatives. Thus although the Reform War may have delayed significant military reform, it did lay the basis for the creation of a new military structure that would remain loyal to the new nation-state.[28]

The victorious liberal army had barely recaptured Mexico City in December 1860 when González Ortega, the commander-in-chief of the constitutionalist army, ordered the abolition of the old standing army. "The Mexican army," he argued, "has been the obstacle to all social progress in the nation since our independence from Spain." He denounced the traditional military as "viciously structured and guided only by personal interest" and accused it of "constantly disturbing public order."[29] But González Ortega did not get rid of all army units. He left a small permanent army consisting only of those who had fought on the side of the constitutional cause. In this way the Ayutla group not only removed the old military aristocracy but also created one of its own. It is significant that the men who rose to military prominence in the constitutional army were later the staunchest defenders of the Mexican nation against the French-conservative invasion. Without the creation of this new military structure it is doubtful that the liberal group could have resisted the French intervention.

As a safeguard against a rebirth of militarism in Mexican politics, the reformers hoped to occupy the new military in useful activities. Francisco

Zarco, among others, vigorously proposed that the army be given significant, non-political tasks to perform. The favorite project was fighting the marauding Indians who crossed into Mexico from the United States. Recalling that the United States agreed in the Treaty of Guadalupe-Hidalgo to preserve the sanctity of Mexican territory, Zarco noted that this part of the agreement had been ignored. He argued that involving the army in such activity would make it "a national war on whose success depends the integrity of our territory, our honor as a civilized nation, and the future of our race." "The war against the barbarians," Zarco concluded, "is nationalistic, it is highly patriotic, and it offers a glorious future for our army."[30] It had one other major advantage: while fighting the Indians on the northern frontier the army would have little time for politics.

But this was only a first step in the depoliticalization of the military. The new leadership realized that their reform left only a small, though loyal, military force for the defense of the nation. It was clear that in times of emergency few soldiers were available to the new government and equally clear that the reform group could hardly depend on their enemies, the traditional military. Thus they had to reestablish a strong military posture without creating a large standing army. The solution to the dilemma was the traditional institution of the citizen army or national guard. *El Siglo XIX* first called for a national guard to supplement the small standing army. The newspaper proposed that it be used to provide police protection in addition to its military duties, and assuaged any fears of its becoming a tool of dictatorship by arguing that because it was a citizens army it could not be corrupted. *El Siglo* also proposed that all Mexican men be required to enlist, thereby making the national guard an instrument for creating and integrating a national consciousness among all Mexicans. This view of the national guard led liberals to call it the "people's army."[31]

On December 29, 1855, three months after the victorious Ayutlan army had marched into Mexico City, the new minister of gobernación, José María Lafragua, issued a circular to the governors of the states requiring them to begin forming a national guard. Using the unwillingness of the conservatives to accept the new rulers as a justification, Lafragua wanted the national guard to be an "armed people ready to defend the liberty they have just won."[32]

In the Constitutional Congress, Isidoro Olvera pushed through a reorganization and strengthening of the national guard. Presenting his arguments to the convention, Olvera noted that Mexico was a country of such widespread apathy in political affairs that "we fear that the country is condemned to tyranny or absorption by a more aggressive and vigorous race than our own." Obviously and unsubtly referring to the North American menace, he argued that one way to prevent these twin traumas was to force Mexicans to participate in civil affairs by arming them for defense, training them in physical fitness, and above all educating them. The best way to achieve these lofty goals was through the institution of the national guard. Olvera recognized that past attempts to institute similar programs had foundered on the rocks of too many commanders too well dressed trying to order hungry, poorly equipped, and miserably trained guardsmen into battle. This sharp dichotomy between officer rank and guardsman was, in the opinion of Olvera, antithetical to the whole purpose of a national guard: to establish the "reality of popular sovereignty." In his proposals Olvera envisioned a national guard that was educated and concerned with maintaining law and order while cutting across class lines. Its duties would be to defend the republic and maintain law and order in the absence of a sufficient police force. Olvera's proposals were eventually included in the final draft of the constitution.[33]

But the national guard, useful as it may have been for the development of a nationalist sentiment among all Mexicans, could not provide the police protection required in Mexico in the middle of the nineteenth century. Bands of marauding bandits plagued the highways and terrorized traveling businessmen and farmers bringing their produce to market. Banditry had always been a problem in rural Mexico, and previous governments had tried unsuccessfully to cope with it. Under Santa Anna, hacendados were allowed to form their own vigilante groups to police the roads. These private armies met vigorous resistance from state and local officials, who correctly feared that the hacendados would quickly turn from police activities to intervention in political affairs.[34]

When the Ayutla group ousted the traditional politicians, they realized that the private armies were both insufficient for adequate police protection and too dangerous politically to continue. Obviously Mexico needed a national police force, one that the federal government would finance and—more important—control. The task of creating a rural police force fell to Minister of Gobernación José María Lafragua, and to accomplish his goal he studied the Spanish civil guard *(guardia civil)*. This recently created police force was a completely national institution, outside the control of provincial officials, in which men of one district patrolled another. This was to prevent illicit dealings between police and local officials. Lafragua, though impressed by the civil guard, proposed modifications in this procedure. In his view Mexico needed a police force that worked in home districts so as to be better able to cope with roving bandits. He also wanted the states to share in the cost of the enterprise, particularly since the federal government could barely support the now reduced standing army. Finally, after much discussion, in 1857 President Comonfort issued the formal creation of a rural Mexican guard.[35]

The new police guard had wide-ranging responsibilities: controlling small-time gambling at country fairs, fighting fires, breaking up fights, escorting money shipments and important officials, and serving with the regular army. Members of the police were volunteers or federal appointees, and they were paid according to military scales (about twenty pesos monthly, which was equal to twenty U.S. dollars of the same period). Even though the national government had hoped to be able to control the guard, in fact the states managed most of the supervision, financing, and direction of the guard's activities. And as the political situation deteriorated, the government's ability to support a police force disappeared. For three years, 1858-1860, the constitutionalist group fought for their lives; the question of a national police force remained buried under the weight of national survival.

Once victorious in 1861, the liberals were again faced with the problem of internal security. Discharged soldiers terrorized the countryside; recalcitrant conservative bands roamed with impunity; and the government appeared helpless in the rampant chaos. In response to increasing pressure for action, the reformers decided that the states were incapable of effectively controlling the situation. Juárez and his ministers—increasingly disenchanted with federalist decentralization of authority—rapidly came to the conclusion that only a national police force, centrally administered, could produce internal security. This is but one example of the growing centralization of political power and monopolization of force achieved by the liberal group. Thus, on May.5, 1861, in a move that signified the desire to gather power at the national level, the government formally created the rural police force, the rurales.[36]

The rurales were to become one of the key instruments through which the liberals began to mold a modern nation state. To make the post attractive, each recruit was paid a monthly salary of 33.75 pesos; commanding officers (there were four in the original plan) were to receive 210 pesos monthly; other officers received more than 50 pesos monthly. By comparison with the pay in the old rural guard, the rurales offered a good opportunity for adventurers—even if they did have to buy their own uniforms and supplies and furnish their own horses. The uniforms were to include grey jackets with red trim, Mexican leather pants with slits, and a sombrero. Although authorized to carry muskets, lances, and swords, the rurales quickly settled on the more efficient carbine. Yet even with the high pay and flashy uniforms the rurales did not become the elite corps they were designed to be. Instead, they were recruited from local bandits, private armies, disenchanted soldiers, and petty criminals.[37]

Local adventurers can, however, become effective police officers when the pay and working conditions suit their temperament. Apparently such was the case with the rurales. Given the job of bringing law and order to Mexican roads, the rurales pursued their task with vigor. They also had a political task: to eliminate enemies of the regime. Both jobs involved the summary execution of violators after a perfunctory trial more closely resembling a kangaroo court. President Comonfort had authorized such extra-legal activities on December 6, 1856, and this together with the "Ley Fuga"—the shooting of a prisoner on the pretext of an escape attempt—gave the rurales increasing authority over the Mexican countryside.[38]

The French intervention interrupted the activities of the rurales as it did everything else in Mexico. Pushed out of their home territories, many of the rurales became fierce guerrillas in the Mexican cause, earning themselves much glory and prestige.[39] Once the shots had rung out on the Sierra de las Campanas and Maximilian lay dead, the government faced continued upheaval in the countryside. Kidnappings, murders, rapes, and banditry were everyday occurrences. The army, which had numbered over sixty thousand men in 1867, saw its numbers cut to twenty thousand within a few months after victory. The dumping of forty thousand men onto the already glutted job market produced many able and ambitious social bandits.

The government responded with an immediate revamping and reorganization of the rurales. In July 1867, Juárez ordered the formation of a new rural police force; in 1868 three more units followed. By 1869 the government had more than a thousand rurales patrolling the states of Mexico, Puebla, Querétaro, and Morelos. Juárez requested and received from Congress permission to put the rurales under the exclusive jurisdiction of the ministry of interior. Also, Juárez requested more money for the rurales and suspension of constitutional protection to criminals caught by the police. The former caused little problem; the latter produced a furor. As we have seen, however, Congress eventually acquiesced, and by April 1869, sections of the constitution had been suspended.[40]

In the meantime, untroubled by the niceties of constitutional debates, the rurales continued to expand their influence and prestige. Mounted on horseback, armed with carbines, applying the Ley Fuga to political or social enemies, and far enough away from Mexico City to prevent truly effective central control, the rurales brought to distant villages for the first time the power of the nation-state. Although they did not recognize it, by 1876 the rurales had become agents for nation-building.[41]

The transformation of the military officer corps, the reduction of both the size and activity of the army, the creation of the national guard, and the formation of the rurales—all were designed to reassemble power at the national level. With the officer class loyal, the cost of the military within bounds, and the political clout of the army effectively reduced, the liberals had accomplished a long-standing goal. Power had been removed from the traditional army and institutionalized at the top of the political structure. The national guard and rurales provided alternative structures to divide and thus subordinate contending power cliques. Control of the army no longer provided immediate access to the presidency, as the failure of Porfirio Díaz to overthrow the government in 1871-1872 bears witness.

Yet these reforms and innovations had left one major institution untouched— the caudillo. In every state there existed powerful men who could, with the proper alliances, forge a counter-force against the governing elite. Many caudillos had supported the Ayutla movement because it promised to protect them against creeping centralization represented by the ultimate caudillo, Santa Anna. They continued to support the liberal cause in the Reform War because conservatism had traditionally linked with some form of central government. The French intervention had been a severe test of national loyalty for the state chiefs, and some, like Santiago Vidaurri of Nuevo León and Coahuila and Manuel Lozada of Nayarit, actually joined the imperial government.[42] Others, like Porfirio Díaz of Oaxaca, became national heroes for their daring exploits in the national cause.

The French intervention prevented Juárez and his government from making strides in the direction of reducing the local power of the caudillos; in fact, the national government was almost totally dependent on the good will and military expertise of these local chiefs. And once the war was over, the chiefs, who had ruled their territories for four years almost unmolested, expected to have the situation continue. There were four caudillos who had a national following: Porfirio Díaz in Oaxaca, Ramón Corona in Durango, Diego Alvarez in Guerrero, and Mariano Escobedo in San Luis Potosí. Lesser caudillos included Trinidad García de la Cadena in Zacatecas, Florencio Antillón in Guanajuato, Juan N. Méndez in Puebla, Jerónimo Treviño and Francisco Naranjo in Nuevo León, Ignacio Pesqueira in Sonora, Luis Terrazas in Chihuahua, Juan N. Cortina and Servando Canales in Tamaulipas, and Manuel Lozada in Nayarit. By 1876 all but one of these powerful local chiefs—Porfirio Díaz—would either be completely subordinate to the national government or dead.

One of the more important caudillos who did not survive the French intervention was Santiago Vidaurri of Nuevo León and Coahuila. His struggle against the growing forces of centralization is a prototype of the struggles that would occur in almost every state after the intervention. The ultimate goal of the Reform program was the destruction of the traditional caudillo system of politics. The reduction of the size of the army, the transformation of the officer class, and the formation of the national guard and the rurales were efforts to concentrate power at the national level. This is precisely what the caudillos feared, and Vidaurri's reactions to this process were typical.

The conflict began immediately after the Ayutlans overthrew Santa Anna. Vidaurri had supported the Ayutla movement for much the same reason that

Juan Alvarez led it: both men wanted to be rid of federal intervention in the internal affairs of their fiefdoms. His early support of the revolutionary movement made Vidaurri an "eminent member" of the Ayutlan group. Even though Vidaurri refused to accept the reformation of the Plan of Ayutla made in Acapulco that strengthened the hand of the executive, he still preferred the liberal federalists (as he believed the nation-building group to be) to the centralist conservatives. At the same time, the liberals needed all the help they could get and thus tolerated Vidaurri's deviant position.[43]

Vidaurri severely strained this mutual association by his first action after the new government began to consolidate national power. In the chaos that reigned after the overthrow of Santa Anna, Vidaurri, in a move to expand his territorial control, unilaterally declared the unification of the states of Coahuila and Nuevo León. Horrified by such behavior, the liberal press in Mexico City vehemently attacked Vidaurri and the illegal unification. In a long editorial, Francisco Zarco argued that the Ayutla movement's goal had been to produce national unity and the only way to achieve this elusive ideal was to have all the states support the national government, not go their separate ways. As Zarco saw it, the union of Nuevo León and Coahuila created a power outside national control and constituted a "danger to national unity." Such a union was a "criminal act producing the ruin of our nationality."[44]

As editorial pressure mounted throughout the early months of 1856, the government, which had been hesitant to alienate Vidaurri, responded by declaring the union illegal and sent the question to the Constitutional Congress for final settlement. The special committee established to look into the matter produced a report favorable to Vidaurri's actions. The committee, fearing more civil war, judged Vidaurri's support for the revolution too important to be jeopardized with hostile legislation. Nevertheless, the report stunned the nationalist Congress and it rejected the committee's posture.[45] In the midst of a law and order movement Congress was not about to allow pockets of local power to remain unchecked by the emerging nation-state. To be sure, there was little Congress could do about the situation, but it realized that it could not give legal sanction to traditional caudillismo.

In the meantime, Vidaurri strengthened his position in the north and quietly ignored the actions of the national government and Congress. While this uneasy truce lasted for two years (1856-1857), the federal government generally left Vidaurri alone, and he responded by writing courteous letters to the new cabinet ministers.[46] The inevitable crisis came, however, during the Reform War. After assuming the presidency of the country and command of the Reform government, Juárez wrote Vidaurri that he expected his full cooperation in both spiritual and material support for the long war ahead. Vidaurri responded in a carefully worded letter that clearly stated his position.

He reaffirmed his loyalty to the liberal cause and assured the government that it had "firm support on the frontier." He accepted Juárez's presidency, arguing that only in this way could Mexico achieve her destiny—"pacification and progress of the nation under the absolute rule of law." To assure Juárez of his support he announced that a thousand men had been sent to attack the conservatives in San Luis Potosí, and he hoped that two thousand more could be mustered. But he noted that he did not have enough money to pay the men and therefore the federal government must be prepared to support the army. Vidaurri concluded his letter with an undisguised warning to the new president: "I am obliged to request now and forever that you never send troops into these parts." He went on to declare that he could effectively govern the northern frontier and that federal interference would only cause "treachery."[47]

When it was evident to Vidaurri that the liberal government would barely survive the Reform War, much less make war on his independence, he decided to support the cause. Surely he remembered the intensity of Santa Anna's intervention in the internal affairs of his territory, and he feared a conservative victory would result in further centralization. Thus, in December 1858, Vidaurri marched at the head of an army into San Luis Potosí to oust the conservatives from the strategic area.[48]   In August 1859, he sent a strongly worded letter of support for the Reform Laws nationalizing church property and secularizing Mexican society.[49]   But, typically, other caudillos challenged Vidaurri's stranglehold on Nuevo León—Coahuila, and when he was off fighting the conservatives they seized control of the area. Vidaurri immediately retired from the field of battle in order to recapture his kingdom, thus badly hurting the liberal cause. By January 1860 he had successfully ousted his rivals, but his actions had left a bitter taste in the mouths of the constitutionalist group. To many, Vidaurri's retreat to regain dominance in the north looked suspiciously like rebellion against the government. In any case, his credentials as a supporter of the liberal cause suffered greatly. He had shown himself to be more interested in caudillo politics than national survival.[50]

Vidaurri's traditional caudillismo, which had survived the Reform War, became open rebellion during the French intervention. Driven from the capital by the French, Juárez and his small band of followers drifted northward, ultimately reaching the edge of Vidaurri's territory—and the inevitable violent conflict. During the interlude between the Reform War and the French intervention there had been reserved and tense communications between Vidaurri and the federal government. A rumor that Vidaurri was considering the formation of an independent nation, the Republic of Sierra Madre, hardly helped relations. While vehemently denying these rumors, Vidaurri incessantly complained to the government about federal interference in his state.[51]   To the constant pleas for money by the government, Vidaurri turned a deaf ear. Although he controlled the port of Matamoros and was probably the wealthiest governor in the country, Vidaurri pleaded poverty in his refusal to help the Reform cause.[52] So anti-liberal had Vidaurri become that he even prohibited the announcement of the Mexican victory over the French army on May 5, 1862.[53]

One of the more flagrant violations of government orders by Vidaurri was his admission back into the country of Ignacio Comonfort, the exiled former president and author of the celebrated coup d'etat of 1857. Since the liberals blamed the bloody Reform War on Comonfort's acceptance of the conservative Plan of Tacubaya, they were determined to prevent him from returning to Mexico. Branding him a traitor, the government turned down every request for permission to return. But Vidaurri, badly needing a leader to marshall his troops, granted Comonfort permission to enter the country. When the news reached the government, Juárez immediately responded with an order to Vidaurri to arrest Comonfort and remand him to the government for trial on the charges of treason. Vidaurri replied that he would not arrest his friend and threatened that, should the government try to do so, revolution might result. As the French advanced inland after their landing in Veracruz, Juárez's resolve to provoke open conflict with Vidaurri weakened. Eventually, under the pressure of foreign intervention, Comonfort was legally readmitted to the country and even made commander of the armies of the north. Yet Juárez did not forget his humiliation at Vidaurri's hands, and as he approached the outskirts of the caudillo's territory, the relationship between the two forces— one traditional, the other modern—was distinctly hostile.[54]

Nothing that occurred in the fateful meeting changed the hostility; in fact, open warfare broke out between the liberal group and the caudillo. Although the story of what happened can be found in many sources, this conflict has not been seen as a struggle between two world views, two views of Mexico that were irrevocably incompatible. In the eyes of the Reform group, Vidaurri was an anachronism, a representative of an obsolete and dangerous caudillo political system. They were determined to break his—and every other caudillo's—power. As Juárez put it, "It is necessary either to subordinate Vidaurri or eliminate him."[55]

Ostensibly the issue was money. On January 20, 1864, José María Iglesias, the minister of the treasury, informed Vidaurri that from now on the revenue of the customs house in Piedras Negras belonged to the national treasury. Iglesias soon discovered that Vidaurri had ordered the officials at the Piedras Negras customs house not to turn over the receipts. Vidaurri justified his actions with vague statements about "states' rights," to which Iglesias bluntly inquired: "Are you or are you not going to obey our orders?"[56] When it was clear that he was not, Juárez decided the time for confrontation had come.

He ordered a march on Monterrey, Vidaurri's stronghold. Bolstered by Doblado's troops, Juárez entered Monterrey on February 12, 1864. There he met briefly (most accounts agree on ten minutes) with Vidaurri. When Vidaurri's son drew a pistol on the president, Juárez and his entourage performed a hasty and ignominious retreat.[57] Juárez retaliated for this second humiliation by declaring the separation of Nuevo León and Coahuila and a state of siege in each state, thus giving himself legal authority to intervene in the internal affairs of the states. He then massed troops for an attack on the caudillo. Seeing himself vastly outnumbered, Vidaurri fled northward and sought asylum in the United States. The Mexican government declared him a traitor.[58]

Realizing that the liberals no longer tolerated traditional caudillos, Vidaurri joined the French imperial government. It was the last desperate act of a traditional caudillo whose age was coming to an end. By 1867 he had served as minister of the treasury, chief of Maximilian's cabinet, and regent of the empire. When the Mexican troops entered Mexico City, Vidaurri was captured. Porfirio Díaz, the commander of the army, was in charge of his trial (the outcome of which was a foregone conclusion) and execution. On July 10, 1867, while a military band played polkas, waltzes and *cangrejos*, Vidaurri, kneeling in a pile of excrement, was shot in the back on a main plaza in Mexico City.[59] Such was the end of the northern caudillo.

Santiago Vidaurri, like many other caudillos, had hoped to maintain independence from the growing central power personified by Juárez and the Constitutional Army. The geographical location was too strategic, the amount of territory involved too large, and the consequences in both political and economic terms too severe for the liberals to leave Vidaurri alone. Vidaurri had no choice: either submit or be eliminated. He chose to struggle and he lost.

Lesser caudillos, however, did not have to make such dramatic choices. If the lesser caudillo's territory was distant, small, and inconsequential, the reformers were more willing to compromise and adjust. The case of Manuel Lozada, the cacique of Nayarit, illustrates the treatment accorded a less potent political enemy. His ultimate demise demonstrates, however, that no matter how unimportant the challenge may have been, all threats to the growing power of the state were met and crushed.

Lozada had supported the liberals during the Reform War for much the same reason as Vidaurri: both feared conservative centralization and hoped for a better deal from the weaker liberals. During the French intervention Lozada began by supporting the Juárez government until it became clear to him that the French were going to take over most of Mexico. He then shifted ground and offered his services to the empire. No sooner had he made this transition of political loyalties than the Mexican forces began winning a few victories in the north and the tide seemed to be turning. To end all the confusion Lozada declared his neutrality—a position from which he figured he could not lose.

Lozada's shifting caused intense disgust in the liberal camp. General José López Uraga, in an 1864 manifesto, described Lozada as a national enemy, a man "without principles . . . and without any other titles than those of traitor and bandit."[60]   Others among Juárez's military advisers counseled direct action against Lozada. Ramón Corona, one of Juárez's best generals and fierce enemy of Lozada, suggested in 1866 an invasion of Tepic, Lozada's stronghold, even before the French had been beaten. His reasoning was clear. He had just received word that Lozada was now neutral in the Mexican-French struggle. Corona argued that this move had been inspired by General González Ortega, who hoped to use Tepic as a refuge from capture by federal forces. Corona contended that this was only the beginning; Tepic, in his view, would become a permanent hotbed of rebel activity, a "constant source of disorder." To prevent this from happening, a military campaign had to be launched immediately while the process of asylum was in its formative stages. In a postcript to the letter, Corona revealed that he had no plans to move into Tepic unless Juárez gave him direct orders. He did not, however, feel himself constrained should Lozada make some move against his forces. In fact, he concluded, "I would see [such a move] as a great advantage for me."[61]

Dedicated totally to the destruction of the empire and unwilling to risk civil war, Juárez did not respond to Corona's suggestions, even though Corona's predictions that Tepic would become a source of rebel activity came true only too quickly. Nevertheless, Juárez kept a distrustful eye on Lozada's activities during the last months of 1866 and early 1867. On July 22, 1867, Lozada finally recognized Juárez's as the legal government—two months after the fall of Querétaro and the capture of Maximilian. During the trial of Maximilian and his generals Mejía, Miramón, and Castillo, Lozada wrote a long and well-reasoned letter asking the government to spare their lives.[62] All of this—the delay of recognition and the plea for Maximilian's life—convinced Juárez that Lozada was an "evil man" and that the "Lozada question" had to be resolved.[63]

The first move Juárez made to resolve the Lozada question was to make the canton of Tepic, originally a part of the state of Jalisco, a separate military district under federal control. It was hoped that the authority of Lozada could be reduced through the introduction of federal authority into the district. Lozada was too strong, however, and federal officials got as far as Guadalajara and that was it. In the meantime, letters poured into Mexico City from Sinaloa, Jalisco, Colima, and other areas around Nayarit complaining bitterly of Lozada's land reform program and banditry. A good example is the diatribe written by the governor of Sinaloa, Domingo Rubí, who described

Lozada as a constant threat to peace and as a man whose continued existence "constitutes a great ignominy for the Nation." He noted that temporizing with Lozada had only strengthened his hold on the district, while at the same time troop levels were being drastically reduced. In light of Lozada's attacks on government officials and his breakup of various haciendas in the territory of Tepic, Rubí concluded with a bit of exaggeration that Lozada "is the greatest criminal not of the Republic but of the entire world."[64] So threatening had the position of Lozada come to be by the end of 1867 that Corona, now military governor of Jalisco, asked to be transferred to another post if Juárez continued to prevent him from wiping out the Tepic stronghold.[65]

Corona's fear that Tepic would become a hideout for rebels was quickly realized. The first notorious rebel to seek Lozada's asylum was Plácido Vega, the former liberal chieftain who turned against Juárez and the liberal program in 1869. Vega obtained Lozada's support by promising him an independent state should his revolt be successful—a promise Porfirio Díaz would repeat a few years later. Vega stirred up dissidents in all the surrounding states. Again reports from Sinaloa, Jalisco, Colima, and even Baja California flowed into the capital detailing the raids, burnings, robberies, and other Vega-inspired atrocities. Everyone blamed Lozada for the situation. Domingo Rubí once again, and in tones of total exasperation at the government's failure to allow an all-out campaign against Tepic, described Lozada's activities. For Rubí and many of the liberals Lozada did not form part of the modern world. "He holds himself," wrote Rubí, "outside obedience to the federal government, the government of Jalisco, and all laws, thus forming in the midst of the country a separate entity as if it were a different Nation."[66]

The second most important political rebel against Juárez was Porfirio Díaz, who sought refuge in Tepic during the abortive revolt of La Noria in 1871-1872. Although the death of Juárez in July 1872 removed Díaz's pretext for revolt, Lozada was once again blamed for having provided protection for political outlaws. At the same time, Ramón Corona sent agents into Tepic to try to tempt Lozada into open revolt. The scheme worked, and no sooner had Lerdo taken over the presidency than Lozada announced his personal revolution in October 1872. Lerdo responded by removing the special status granted the district of Tepic, ordering federal troops into Nayarit and prohibiting further land reform in the area. Believing that the best defense is a good offense, Lozada began a military campaign that brought him to the gates of Guadalajara in January 1873. Before his march, however, he issued a Plan Libertador explaining his actions. Lozada pointed out that although he had allowed rebels into his territory, he personally had never joined those revolts. In spite of Díaz's promises of independent statehood, Lozada had never supported La Noria, nor had he actively supported Vega's activities.

The plan went on to say that Lozada had kept neutrality only because the federal government had left him alone—perhaps also explaining why Juárez and Lerdo were reluctant to accede to their commanders' demands for military action against Lozada. But now, the plan concluded, the time had come for a show of force to achieve Lozada's main goal—"absolute independence and sovereignty in the areas of government and finances." Ignacio Vallarta, the governor of Jalisco, took one look at the plan and termed it a "monstrosity." And as a government report on the incident put it, "Everyone [in Nayarit] knows that a government in Mexico exists, but they consider themselves as independent of it as a foreign nation. . . . Lozada governs as if [Nayarit] were a separate nation."[67]

Ramón Corona now had the fight he had so long wanted. Lozada had come out of his lair and invaded Corona's territory of Jalisco. For Lozada it was a tragic mistake; for Corona it was a moment of glory. Lozada's lines of communication and supply were overextended; his army was not a military machine but instead a folk migration of women and children. And they were cut to shreds by Corona's artillery. Seeing all was lost, Lozada's closest advisers *(hombres de confianza)*, Domingo Nava and Praxedis Núñez, betrayed their leader. While bathing in a stream with his escort on a sultry August afternoon, Lozada was captured and shortly thereafter shot.[68] The execution was illegal since Corona used the Ley de Plagiarios (Anti-Kidnapper Law) in what was essentially a political case.[69] But legal niceties did not count for much in the process of concentrating and centralizing power at the expense of local political bosses. Even the two betrayers, Nava and Núñez, fell before the onslaught of centralized power. Nava, who had hoped to replace Lozada as the caudillo of Nayarit, found his position increasingly circumscribed, and Núñez was shot "while trying to escape."[70] The Ley Fuga solved many a political problem.

The destruction of Vidaurri and Lozada was the ultimate result of the conflict between the growth of national power and the traditions of local autonomy. Each man had been a classic caudillo. They had been the political bosses of limited territories; they had depended on geographical isolation for protection; they had raised private armies in which personal ties were the sole bonds; they had both been deserted by their *hombres de confianza* in the end. Above all, their politics had become an anachronism in the midst of a liberal nation-building movement. The Reform demanded that every individual, no matter how isolated or independent, grant his ultimate loyalty to the nation-state. This Lozada and Vidaurri could not do, and their inability to adjust to centralization decreed their elimination. With the growth of technology and the reform of the army, the centrifugal forces of caudillismo gave way before the strength of the central government. All the powerful local chiefs—

Méndez in Puebla, Treviño and Naranjo in Nuevo León, García de la Cadena in Zacatecas—either had to accommodate growing national power or face the military might of the state. Most preferred the former, and *pan o palo,* the Porfirian technique of carrot or stick, was well established long before Díaz seized office. As one observer put it, in front of this nationalist movement "personalities are little more than grains of sand dragged about by the wind." [71]

7. Church and State: Search for Compromise

Nation-building theory concentrates on the creation of new structures or the adaptation of old ones to enforce compliance with the policy decisions of the state. The effort to create a powerful nation-state produces a crisis within the traditional or deeply institutionalized organizations. This penetration crisis must be resolved in favor of the state for the nation-building program to be successful. Both the reforms within the army and the attempt to reduce and subordinate local caudillo power were efforts to adapt long-standing institutions to the new situation. The formation of the rurales was the creation of a new institution to cope with the crisis of law and order in the countryside. Through these endeavors at reform and adaptation, the liberals hoped to remove the vestiges of Mexico's colonial past and ensure the nation's survival in the future.

For the men of the Reform no institution better represented the failed legacy of colonialism than the Catholic Church. It was the only national institution that had survived independence relatively unscathed; it commanded the loyalty of vast numbers of citizens; it wielded critical political power; and it controlled huge economic resources. Not only was it the single most powerful economic and political entity in nineteenth-century Mexico, but also it subscribed to a world view at all points opposed to the liberal Reform. Clearly, the liberals had to hammer out a fundamental transformation of church-state relations, preferably one that stopped short of violent confrontations.

The most serious difficulty was differing world views. The Mexican cleric saw the natural order of the world far differently from the Mexican liberal. In the ecclesiastical world view, men did not advance on their own merits and talents, with all having equal opportunities. On the contrary, the traditional church perception was that the individual's social position was ascribed at birth and fixed for life. In this ascriptive society social status and power were ordained conditions, not subject to change. Individual loyalties were rendered first and foremost to the church and then to the family, the corporation, and the social class. The state came last in the list of institutions to which one owed loyalty, and it was to be obeyed only so long as it acted in accordance with divine laws as these were interpreted by the clergy. All attempts to alter the fixed social and political structure were, in the church view, anti-religious and anti-social violations of divine laws.

This viewpoint was mirrored in the caste-like structure of the Mexican clergy. Throughout its history the Mexican church had discriminated against the lower classes with respect to ordination. The council of 1585 prohibited Indians from entering the priesthood, although in later years of colonial rule the prohibition was dropped. For the mestizo, however, there was never any question; he was prohibited from entering a clerical career. By papal bull mestizos had been excluded because they were considered children of illegitimate alliances between Spaniards and Indians. For the few mestizos who managed to slip into the clergy, the possibilities for reaching the upper levels were non-existent. The Mexican clergy, predominantly creole in origin, looked with disdain at Mexico's native sons.[1]

Just as the church could not accept the mestizo as a social equal, so it could not accept the state as a political equal. In the view of the ecclesiastical authority all efforts to widen the realm of secular powers were anti-religious and heretical. To each reform the clergy replied with declarations of exclusive loyalty to spiritual authority, reducing the state to little more than a secular agent for the church. When the Juárez Law of 1855 attempted to limit the ecclesiastical *fuero* the archbishop of Mexico, Lázaro de la Garza y Ballesteros, asserted that the church was not subject to secular authority because it was a universal institution above any particular nation.[2] In condemning the Lerdo Law, forcing the sale of ecclesiastical property held in mortmain, the archbishop's position was: "As much as I love my country, I must obey the will of God."[3] And to a government order seizing church property in Puebla, the bishop of Puebla summed up the clergy's view of temporal power with the pronouncement: "In a choice between obeying Caesar and God, we must choose God."[4]

An important reflection of the theocratic view of political power was the post-independence struggle over patronage. Prior to independence the right to appoint high ecclesiastical officials in New Spain had by papal consent rested with the Spanish crown. Once independence from Spain became a reality the question arose, Who has the power to appoint the upper clergy, the papacy or the new nation? The ecclesiastical position was that the Mexican state did not have the right to make these appointments and argued for complete freedom from any forms of temporal control. The state's position was that once independence from Spain had been accomplished, the authority of patronage reverted to the secular government—a view the church categorically refused to accept. One result of the unwillingness of the clergy to grant patronage rights to the new nation was that by 1830 the number of Mexican clergy had been reduced to one-third the pre-independence level and there was not a single archbishop or bishop in Mexico.[5] It seems evident that the determination of the church to maintain its domination over the secular state was so strong that it was willing to sacrifice its own leadership rather than allow the nation-state to expand its realm of authority.

At the same time, the clergy reduced the state to the role of an agent of the church. The state was, for example, charged with the onerous duty of collecting the parochial fees demanded by the clergy for performing sacraments.[6] Should an individual refuse to pay after receiving a sacrament, it was the state that prosecuted him. If a member of one of the holy orders broke his monastic vow he too was prosecuted by the secular authorities, who thereby functioned as a police force for the clergy.

The church's wealth bolstered and maintained the dominant ecclesiastical ideology. Unlike the state, the church survived independence relatively intact, despite the loss in leadership, and in the chaos following the separation from Spain it emerged as the only national institution in Mexico.[7] The church maintained this position in part because it "was incontestably richer than the state."[8] Even in 1861, after six years of anti-clerical reforms, the church still received more income than the national government.[9] Originally much of the ecclesiastical income had come from the tithe, a tax on agricultural production, but as crops were destroyed during the multitudinous independence campaigns, the church increasingly depended for revenue on its income-producing investments.[10] A major source of ecclesiastical income was the rents from church-owned property. Throughout the history of the Mexican church the readiness of believers to will parts of their estates to ecclesiastical corporations had been used by the clergy to accumulate vast tracts of urban real estate. Practically every ecclesiastical corporation owned some rural and much urban property. As a result, during the three decades before the Revolution of Ayutla the church had been the largest single landowner in the country.[11]

Precisely how much property the church owned has been a subject of intense speculation. Though contemporary estimates may have been influenced by political considerations and must now be used with extreme caution, they still provide the best evidence. Miguel Lerdo de Tejada, minister of hacienda in 1857, made the most thorough study of ecclesiastical property, calculating that the total property of Mexico had an aggregate value of 1.3 billion pesos, of which the church owned about 275 million, or 21 percent. This included half the houses in Mexico City.[12] Although there were many other estimates— some as high as 620 million pesos or half the land in all Mexico—the Lerdo percentages (but not his absolute figures) seem the most reasonable and have been supported by recent research.[13] Thus by 1855 the ecclesiastical corporation owned approximately a fifth of all property in Mexico.

Several observations should be made about the importance of church wealth to the Reform movement. Despite Lerdo's calculations, many liberals believed that the church was much wealthier than it actually was. They pointed out that Lerdo's figures referred only to land and mortgaged property and did not include the valuable gold and silver trappings or the priceless art objects. As the liberals found out later, there was in fact little gold and silver and hardly any market for works of art. In addition, much of the liberal attitude and policy toward the church assumed immense wealth simply because no other corporation was as rich or as visible politically as the Catholic Church. Here, then, is a classic case in which the perceptions of the situation were more important than the realities.

Moreover, property that the church did not own outright was often mortgaged to it. The church-operated Juzgado de Testamentos, Capellanías y Obras Pías was the major banking and lending institution in Mexico.[14] Loans by the Juzgado required land as security, with the result that only landowners could borrow. Reasonable terms, long time periods for repayment, and almost automatic renewals made Juzgado loans attractive to landowners. Consequently the church progressively gained control over much of the land it did not own. The Juzgado also controlled most of the available capital in Mexico, and there were no secular lending institutions to compete with it. All attempts to establish competing lending institutions, such as the Banco de Avío, met with failure.[15]

To administer this financial empire the church needed both capable men and a bureaucratic structure equal to the task. The clergy were numerically insignificant, but they made up for it with energy and ability. In 1850 the Mexican clergy numbered 4,375, of whom 3,182 were secular and 1,193 regular.[16] Thus in the total population of around eight million people, the clergy represented only .05 percent—a dangerously small number to control so much wealth. But church wealth was even more concentrated than these figures would suggest, for the clergy, like the rest of Mexican society, was divided into two classes: the rich elite and the extreme poor. Of the 4,375 clergy in 1850, only 166 were classified in the top echelons—meaning archbishops, bishops, capitulars, canons, and provincials—and usually only they enjoyed the benefits of the church's economic power.[17] Poverty drove the vast majority of the lower clergy into unscrupulous and dishonest practices, and often it was this clerical rabble that the liberals had encountered in their early years.[18] The fact that some of the lower clergy supported social reform may be explained by their feeling that they had nothing to lose.

They were getting nothing as it was.[19]

The church knew how to use the favorable imbalance in the distribution of economic power, and of course this had political consequences. In the first place, with the state chronically destitute and the church relatively rich, the government often found itself forced to borrow from the church. Not unexpectedly the state was reduced to the status of another debtor to the ecclesiastical corporation, with the result that the government's decision were influenced by its dependence on the church.[20] A similar effect took place among the landowners, who, hoping to extend their loans or acquire new ones, were unwilling to attack the clergy's financial empire or support those who did. Fear of having to pay off extended loans, or of being denied new ones, also kept the landowners from opposing the church, and only after the reform movement succeeded were the landowners willing to support it in the hopes of freeing themselves from debt. Through their all-embracing economic web the clergy dominated both the state and the individual, forcing each to depend on the church for financial well-being. But at the same time they were also creating a large debtor class that eagerly awaited the destruction of the ecclesiastical financial empire.

The ability of the church to maintain its dominance in Mexican society came from both its economic and its political power. Under the colonial distribution of authority, the church was in charge of the life cycles of society: birth was registered in church records, marriage was an ecclesiastical contract enforced by the state, civil rights derived from baptism, death occurred under the absolutions and prayers of the priests, and burial took place in church cemeteries. No marriage, no baptism, no burial took place without clerical approval, and in a country where proper marriage, baptism, and burial were an important part of every person's life, the power of the clergy to refuse them was indeed a potent weapon. One can only imagine the effects on the people when the church refused to bury Valentín Gómez Farías because of his outspoken liberal political views.[21] Through its control of the life cycle the church, and not the state, was the ultimate arbiter of human affairs.

The political and social powers of the clergy were further enhanced by the legal privileges that freed them from coercion by the state and made the ecclesiastical corporation a secular power competing for men's loyalties. Church buildings were havens where criminals fleeing from secular authorities received sanctuary. When a cleric committed a crime or broke a civil contract, the ecclesiastical *fuero* protected him from secular justice. Stemming from colonial policy and written into the Constitution of 1824, the *fuero* established separate courts for the clergy with their own regulations and legal codes.[22] As with the military *fuero*, the church was considered a privileged corporation, a state within the state, completely independent of secular control or restraint. Through its favored position and its control over the life cycle, the church demanded the loyalty of each Mexican from the moment he was born. At every major juncture in his life the Mexican was required to pledge once again his obedience to the church. At the same time the state seemed to most liberal Mexicans little more than a toady, collecting parochial fees, enforcing ecclesiastical rules, and impotent before the might of the clergy. It is no wonder that before 1855 the institution to which the vast majority of Mexicans gave their highest allegiance was the Roman Catholic Church.

This enormous ecclesiastical power spelled defeat for all pre-1855 reform efforts. Each attempt to readjust the balance of power in favor of secular authority had been met with stern resistance. Most of these reforms were on the state level and were extremely limited in their goals. In 1826, motivated by the dire poverty of the local government in contrast to the opulent church, the state of Durango confiscated some clerical funds to finance an irrigation project. Similarly the congress of Zacatecas proposed the seizure of clerical revenues to establish an agricultural credit bank.[23] Such limited measures with limited goals were met with unlimited ecclesiastical intransigence. Denouncing the proposals as heretical, the church rallied public opinion and marshaled its political and economic resources to crush the plans. When the conflict reached national levels, as in the reforms proposed by Gómez Farías in 1833, the church became still more rigid and uncompromising. Influenced by the liberal, anti-corporate ideas of José María Luis Mora, Gómez Farías planned to secularize the California missions, close the church-dominated University of Mexico, abolish the tithe, and remove the government from the jobs of collecting parochial fees and enforcing monastic vows. Though the reform was designed to modify and somewhat reduce the power of the church, the clergy responded to it as if it were a full-scale attack on religion. Their absolutistic world view did not permit them to distinguish between reform and revolution—all reform was revolution, and revolution was heresy. As a result, they toppled the government and removed Gómez Farías from office. Mora left Mexico, never to return. Ecclesiastical domination continued for another quarter century.[24]

Prior to 1855 only one event shook the impenetrable fortifications of the church. It coincided with the American invasion of Mexico. In 1847, with the state bankrupt and American troops rapidly approaching Mexico City, Gómez Farías, again in office, ordered the expropriation of fifteen million pesos worth of church property to meet the urgent fiscal needs of the beleaguered nation. Believing the survival of ecclesiastical independence to be at stake, the church called on its military friends for protection. Proclerical army units—the Polkos—revolted against the government and once again Gómez Farías was removed from office. Subsequently, Mexico lost the war and half its territory.[25] Even though the Polkos revolt jeopardized the existence of Mexico, the church felt it more important to protect its privileged position.

There is no doubt that "the clergy were . . . the main planners and financial power behind the rebels."[26] Nor can there be any doubt that the Polkos revolt profoundly affected the liberals. Time and again, afterward, they referred back to the revolt in an effort to prove that the church had betrayed the nation. *El Siglo XIX,* an organ of the Reform group, wrote that clerical actions during the American War proved the clergy's desire for "the death of the country" because "they hate everything Mexican."[27] Another liberal newspaper accused the church of high treason in the Polkos revolt. "Why isn't the clergy full of shame and confusion," it asked, "when the Nation remembers their lack of patriotism, their sordid greediness, and their criminal egotism?"[28] Finally, the French intervention provided superb opportunities to draw analogies with the American invasion. Francisco Zarco, editor of *El Siglo,* asserted that the clergy had been disloyal in both cases. "They wear on their foreheads the stain of traitors to their country and fight in the ranks of the invaders."[29] Thus in winning the Polkos battle the church planted the seed of its defeat; it irrevocably alienated the liberals and linked itself with treason.

Such attitudes were not part of the liberal ideology of the reformers in 1833. Partly because of their different social, political, and economic experiences, the Reform leadership and the liberals of two decades earlier carried with them distinct sets of ideological assumptions. It is true that each group saw the privileged church as detrimental to economic development and that each sought to reduce ecclesiastical power and autonomy. It is also true that both reform groups, influenced by the individualism and egalitarianism of nineteenth-century liberalism, called for equality before the law and the limitation of corporate privilege. The ecclesiastical *fuero* thus figured prominently in the reform programs of both eras, as did the reduction of clerical wealth and political power.[30] And yet for all these similarities there were striking differences between the two groups, particularly in their attitude toward the church. Throughout the 1833 reform the church was attacked within the framework of the anti-corporate liberalism formulated by José María Luis Mora, but it was not attacked as an enemy of the state or as an anti-national element in Mexican society. Mora, the intellectual leader of the 1833 reformers, desired the separation of church and state, with Catholicism remaining the official religion of Mexico. He also wanted the state to support the church and pay all ecclesiastical expenses. Mora's strong conviction was that the Catholic religion was the principal source of national unity, and he advocated reform, not destruction, of its privileged position.[31]

The Reform group, on the other hand, came to power in 1855 deeply imbued with anti-clerical sentiments. They were agitated, as we have seen, by the treasonous behavior of the clergy during the American invasion, and during their political careers they had felt the sting of the church's social discrimination. In a revealing pamphlet issued after the success of the Ayutla revolt, an anonymous liberal demanded revenge on the church for its discriminatory policies. The author reminded Mexicans that mestizos had been singled out for special taxes and that they had been refused admission into the priesthood, all because "ecclesiastical lawyers said they were illegitimate." The whole system amounted to "another enormous injustice sanctioned by clerical laws."[32] It is evident that the rigid class system and the hierarchical society sanctioned by the church created a deep sense of class consciousness among the liberal elite, something that was entirely lacking among the creole reformers in 1833. And these differences meant that a more dramatic and intense attack on ecclesiastical power was to begin as the liberals began their reforms.

But the full implications of this struggle were not immediately recognized. The Mexican Reform had a dynamic to it; it did not develop at one moment but came out of a historical process. The liberals did not come to power in 1855 with their solutions to the problems of nation-building clearly defined. They knew that the traditional economic and political structure had severely restricted the possibilities of national survival, and they believed that to change this situation two things were necessary: equality and the secularization of society. To achieve these goals the church had to be reduced to its proper sphere, but the liberals in the years 1855-1857 did not delineate what that sphere should be. Members of the Ayutla group wrote to each other that they did not want to see "the sacred alliance between man and God" ruptured, and the new government prohibited all direct attacks on the church.[33] The liberals hoped to establish juridical equality and secularize society without openly attacking the church. It was their failure to understand the rigidity of the ecclesiastical position that led the Reform group into a moderate stance on the ecclesiastical corporation. The result was an experimentation with reform that was to have tragic consequences.

The liberals also accepted the basic corporate structure of Mexican society at the same time that they hoped to restrict corporate power. This seeming contradiction permeated the first Reform laws aimed at the church as a corporation and gave these laws a marked lack of direction. The liberals, long aware of the abuses of the special courts established through the *fuero* system, realized that equality was an essential part of the creation of a modern nation state. Benito Juárez, as early as 1840, had come to the conclusion that as long as juridical inequality existed there would be no allegiance to the state or its legal system. He voiced his concern during a patriotic celebration, declaring that "the nation must protect each man, freeing him from the duties that oppress, removing every obstacle that hinders the free

exercise of his rights."[34] He later called for judicial reform "with all men
equal . . . before the law."[35] It was clear to many people that as the new
minister of justice in 1855 Juárez would sooner or later turn his attention
toward the problem of ecclesiastical *fueros*. One observer correctly predicted
that "there will be great reforms, particularly in regard to the clergy," and
just as incorrectly forecast that such reforms would lead to "national
unity."[36]

The resulting Juárez Law in November 1855 suppressed all special tribunals
except the military and ecclesiastical courts, and these were prohibited from
hearing civil cases. The most radical aspect of the law was the provision that
allowed any individual to renounce his *fuero* and seek justice in the secular
courts.[37] The purpose behind the abolition of special tribunals was to substitute the secular state as the dispenser of all justice in the nation. Juárez
argued that as long as individuals and classes had special privileges there could
be no equality and the power of the state was diminished. Individual loyalty
under the *fuero* system was to one's corporation, not to the nation. In reply
to ecclesiastical attacks on the law, Juárez summed up the liberal position: the
only privilege retained in Mexico, he asserted, would be "the *fueros* of the
supreme authority of the Nation."[38] In other words, corporations as privileged, independent entities interfered with the development of a sense of
nationalism. Only their abolition would make the state the supreme power
in the nation.

The Reform, through the Juárez Law, had made equality before the law a
fundamental tenet of liberal ideology, and yet, when examined critically, the
law clearly accepted the basic corporate structure of Mexican society. The
failure to abolish the entire *fuero* system by leaving the church its right to
hear criminal cases meant that in 1855 Mexican liberalism had only partially
defined its idea of the proper relationship between church and state. The
desire to limit special privileges was a necessary step in the direction of equality before the law, but, by permitting the corporate structure to remain intact,
the reformers only reinforced individual loyalties to intermediate, not national,
institutions.

A few liberals recognized the significance of allowing corporate privilege to
persist. Ponciano Arriaga asserted the law did not go far enough, and Pedro
Escudero argued that not suppressing all *fueros* at once only delayed a necessary action. Antonio Aguado made the most telling criticism. He observed
that by granting the clergy their *fuero* in criminal cases the state was in effect
sanctioning clerical arguments that the *fuero* was of divine origin. Though
claiming that it established true equality under the law, the Juárez Law
actually strengthened the ecclesiastical corporation and weakened the sovereignty of the nation in judicial matters. Aguado was correct when he observed

that the ecclesiastical corporation's position as a state within the state was unchanged by the Juárez Law.[39]

A similar contradiction appeared in the second Reform measure of the post-Ayutla years, the Lerdo Law. It was hoped that the secularization of society, one of the primary goals of the liberal movement, would lead to the economic independence of the state, a large, propertied middle class, and a clergy administering to souls rather than pesos. The obstacle that most visibly stood in the way of secularization was the economic resources of the church. The liberals reasoned that until the economic base of clerical power was restricted, little could be done to weaken the political power of the church and to fill the resulting vacuum with the secular nation-state. Thus some move was necessary against church property and wealth, and that was the purpose of the Lerdo Law.

The principle of secular interference in the economic affairs of the church was well established by 1855. Under the Bourbon kings Spain had expelled the Jesuits and confiscated their large property holdings, and, as we saw in chapter 2, in 1804 the Spanish crown had called for all ecclesiastical investments to be withdrawn and placed at the disposal of the monarch. Within Mexico there were such precedents as the nationalization plan of Lorenzo de Zavala and the reforms of Gómez Farías and Mora in 1833 and 1847. Most recently, in 1854, the Spanish crown had forced the church in Spain to sell ecclesiastical property. All these provided important examples for the Mexican liberals.[40]

The Lerdo Law was a complex decree ordering the sale or disamortization of all corporate property except that used directly by the corporation. The sales were to be taxed by the government to provide funds for the chronically impoverished state. In the future no corporation would be allowed to administer or own real estate.[41] This meant that the church had to sell all property held in mortmain, that the clergy could no longer receive donations and gifts in the form of real estate, and that the church would lose its income from rented property. The church was to be reimbursed for its lost income, since the purchasers of disamortized ecclesiastical property had to pay interest to the church on the purchase price, interest equivalent to the rent previously paid. In this way the Lerdo Law attacked church property ownership while it left church wealth undiminished—only the form of the wealth was changed.

The official justifications stressed the economic consequences of disamortization and ignored almost completely the political and social—or noneconomic—considerations. The law itself stated that its purpose was to put into "free circulation a large part of the real property [which is] the fundamental base of public wealth." The lack of mobile real estate, the preamble to the law concluded, was "one of the greatest obstacles to the prosperity and

growth of the Nation."[42]   Lerdo, in his circular issued in explanation of the
law, stated that it had two objectives: to free immobilized property and to
create a tax system based on circulating real estate. The results he hoped for
were improved living conditions for the renting middle class and poor,
increased output from the land, and an improved and equitable tax system.
Only at the very end of his long circular did Lerdo consider political motivations for the disamortization law. Such a law, he said, "was the only path
toward the well-being and happiness that daily seems more distant because
of the combined action of the mistakes that remain . . . from the colonial
epoch and of the miserable and sterile revolts that have kept [the nation] in
perpetual agitation since political emancipation."[43]   But this was the merest
hint at non-economic considerations, and the overwhelming thrust of Lerdo's
argument was on the financial aspects of the law. It is significant that he
hardly mentioned the church in his circular. As Manuel Payno put it some
years later, the Lerdo Law, like all early Reform measures, was a compromise
designed to "consolidate peace between Church and State."[44]   Ezequiel
Montes, minister of justice, adviser to Comonfort, and a moderate on church-
state matters, wrote to the more radical Joaquín Moreno that prudence was
necessary in dealing with the church and that though radicals might be unhappy
with both the Juárez and Lerdo laws, "they are enough to change Mexican
society profoundly."[45]

Others, however, saw the law differently. José María Lafragua, another
moderate cabinet minister in the Comonfort government, minced no words in
a letter to Santiago Vidaurri. "That law," he wrote of the disamortization
measure, "is our reply to so much calumny that has been spread by mali-
ciousness and ignorance. The present question is the truly social question."[46]
Later, in another private letter, Lafragua expanded on the goals of the Lerdo
Law. After summarizing the economic aims of the law—increased agricultural
production, division of property, mobilization of land held in mortmain, and
the general betterment of society—he argued that the basic purpose was to
make sure "that there is no power in the nation greater than the nation
itself."[47]   And to prove that no powers or persons could put themselves above
the nation, the government summarily exiled the bishop of Puebla, who had
bitterly complained about the Lerdo Law.[48] Thus the law had more to it than
a change in the form of church wealth; it had political and social implications
that the reformers hid behind a cloak of economic syllogisms.

Pressured by clerical intransigence, the liberal position eventually altered,
as seen in the lengthy published correspondence between Montes and Lázaro
de la Garza y Ballesteros, the archbishop of Mexico. Here was a head-on
conflict that demonstrated clearly to the liberals that the hoped-for compromise between secular nationalism and traditional ecclesiastical authority was

unraveling. Garza y Ballesteros argued vigorously that the church was not bound to obey secular authority when that authority ran counter to divine law as the church interpreted it. Nor was ecclesiastical property subject to secular control. All attempts to tamper with the church, its *fueros,* or its property were heretical, anti-religious, and anti-social. This was the crux of the conflict. The Reform group had already identified their best interest with the well-being of the nation-state. The task before them was to create a situation in which all other Mexicans, including the clergy, would make the same choice. Montes ultimately saw the problem and in growing frustration and anger at clerical obstinance burst out, "Never have I been able to understand how the supreme authority of the Republic, independent of other nations, could submit the control of a huge portion of its territory and the loyalty of its subjects to any other power."[49] With this the question of sovereignty, the question of who was to rule Mexico, was out in the open. At its core the Lerdo Law provoked the problem of where ultimate authority resided in the Mexican political, social, and economic structure: in the traditional, theocratically oriented church or in the modern, secular nation-state.

And yet, like the Juárez Law, the Lerdo Law did not answer the question of who was to rule Mexico. Just as the Juárez Law sanctioned the ecclesiastical *fuero* and thereby maintained the ecclesiastical corporation in its privileged position, so the Lerdo Law guaranteed that the church would remain the dominant economic power in the state. Though the church was prohibited from owning and administering property, the disamortization law confiscated no ecclesiastical real estate; instead, the law promised the church full value for its land and minor economic hardships. Ignacio Ramírez, a member of the Reform leadership but a tireless critic of the attempt to compromise with the church, saw the inherent dangers of leaving the church's formidable economic power relatively untouched. He argued that the stated purpose of the disamortization law was to make land available to the poor who were now renting, but that, in fact, the law was a sham because the poor would never have enough money to buy the land, pay the *alcabala,* and then maintain the property. Ramírez saw the law helping only the rich and middle classes, making more land available to the already well-landed hacendado and supplying land for the first time to the landless middle classes—all at the expense of the Indians and the poorer classes.[50]

In his analysis Ramírez was correct: the people who benefited most from the disamortization of church property were the new professionals, those who were forming the backbone of the liberal movement. As a result of the Lerdo Law they became landowners for the first time, and, since owning property is an important symbol of status and position in Hispanic culture, the arrival of a new group of landowners had significant consequences for Mexican liberal politics. For its making the land available to them, the new landowners now owed a debt to the nation-state. What Ramírez, in his exclusive focus on the poor, did not see was that disamortization was structured to shift both land and loyalty only in relation to the powerful groups—land from the clergy to the emerging professionals and loyalty of the landowners from the church to the nation-state. The poor simply did not enter into the liberal equation.

Ramírez criticized the disamortization law with respect to its economic consequences but said little about the church. Not so Melchor Ocampo, who, after closely watching the disamortization operation and clerical intransigence, leveled a stinging attack on the Lerdo Law for its effects on the church. In a long letter to Juárez written in 1859 Ocampo denounced the disamortization law because it strengthened the ecclesiastical corporation rather than the nation-state. He pointed out that the Lerdo Law had made the church the owner of land it only administered and made the clergy even more the masters of Mexican society than they had been previously. According to Ocampo, the church, when forced to sell land, seized the opportunity to make it seem as if the ecclesiastical corporation, rather than the nation, had made the land available for purchase—with the result that purchasers felt they owed a debt to clerical generosity. Ocampo showed how the law left the church better off than before, since the ecclesiastical corporation now received the same rents but was relieved of the upkeep costs on the property. He also criticized the law for taxing the buyer instead of the church, thereby making purchase difficult if not impossible for those who did not have the cash on hand. And, finally, he argued that "if their insolence and spirit of domination had not been superior to all economic consideration, the clergy would have accepted without a murmur the decrees that so benefited them." Ocampo went on to suggest that had the church been more observant it would have "blessed and raised statues to those who, with so much damage to civil society, assured and guaranteed them . . . the possession of property often illegally gotten and always badly administered."[51] Although bitter in the extreme, Ocampo's criticism went to the heart of the liberal failure in the post-Ayutla years: the failure to recognize that secular nationalism and the traditional church had no common ground, that compromise between the two was impossible.

Although it has generally gone unnoticed, the acceptance of the church as a privileged corporation found other forms of expression in the years prior to the War of the Reform. In each case a law was issued with the express purpose of promoting the power of the nation-state and in each case the church came out ahead. An 1857 law ordered all citizens to register with the government and removed civil rights from those who did not comply. Under the law, birth, matrimony, adoption, death, and religious vows were to be registered by secular officials. There was much debate within government circles on the issue, and Lafragua added a personal note to his copy of the law, commenting that although the measure was modeled on the effective French codes it would fail in its purpose.[52] He was particularly worried about civil registration of marriage, arguing that clerical control over Mexican women and Indians would force them to circumvent the law. What Lafragua did not mention, however, was that the registration law once again put the state in the position of a church agent, for the state was required to register religious vows and then enforce them at the command of the clergy.

The unwillingness of the Reform to attack openly the corporate privileges of the church also dominated the Constitutional Congress. The issue that best displayed the attempt by the liberals to fuse secular nation-building and the traditional ecclesiastical position was the debate over religious toleration. The Constitution of 1824 had made Catholicism the official religion of Mexico, but article 15 of the proposed constitution abolished that provision and declared that men could worship as they pleased, with all religions receiving official protection. The clergy vigorously opposed the article and poured out hundreds of pamphlets denouncing the idea of religious toleration.[53] The law, said Archbishop Garza y Ballesteros, would destroy society because man lives in a Catholic world where persons are not free to worship as they please. Garza argued that no one in Mexico believed in the false religions; to introduce them could only result in social disintegration.[54] Both Garza and Pedro Barajas, bishop of San Luis Potosí, argued that the church was the only truly national institution to which Mexicans were loyal and to destroy it would mean not only social but political destruction as well.[55] And, as the debates reached their climax, one thousand women signed a clerical petition charging that article 15 would destroy the Mexican family.[56]

Many of the delegates still believed it possible to establish a secular nation-state while at the same time maintaining the church in its privileged position. Lafragua summed up the moderate position in his attack on article 15. He was deeply troubled, as we have seen, by the specter of social disintegration. Religious intolerance was "in the public interest," according to Lafragua, because worship by alien religions would be violently resisted by five million Indians and a million and a half women—"both enemies of the Reform." He predicted that freedom of worship would produce riots and civil wars that would require the government to react with arrests and trials, alienating many fellow citizens from their loyalty to the nation. He also predicted that with toleration the Indians would return to their ancient cults, and he played on the modernizers' fear of Indians by reminding the deputies of the vicious and bloody caste war in Yucatán. In reply to those who argued that toleration would promote immigration and badly needed economic development, Lafragua argued that it was not intolerance but instability that kept foreigners

away; cure the causes of caudillismo and instability and the immigration problem would disappear. In conclusion, he asked that the new constitution make
Catholicism the official religion of the state as the old Constitution of 1824
had done.[57]

Lafragua implicitly accepted the pro-clerical arguments that Catholicism
was in fact the binding tie among Mexicans, and like many liberals he feared
that the destruction of the ecclesiastical corporation would bring down the
entire social and political edifice. Assuring the church its privileged position
was one sure way of preventing a breakdown of law and order, social disintegration, and anarchy.

Matching Lafragua's fear of social disintegration was his pronounced fear
of the masses. Mexican liberalism in the middle of the nineteenth century
was not a mass movement, nor did it conceive of a popular democracy.
Throughout his speech Lafragua referred to the masses as "ignorant,"
"intolerant," "fanatic," and "superstitious." As he saw it: "Unfortunately,
the condition of our society is far from what it ought to be. . . . We cannot
deny that a great majority of our population is very far from becoming a
people." His fear of the masses in general was carried over into disgust with
the Indians in particular. Many Indians, according to Lafragua, wanted to
return to the age of Cuauhtémoc, others wanted caste wars against whites,
and some just wanted land and were willing to fight for it. Whatever the
case, the Indians were "agitated" and "very dangerous."[58] Fear of social
disintegration, elitism, dissociation from the masses, distrust of the Indian—
these were the elements that frightened the Reform leaders. So they attacked
the church's political power, but they wanted to maintain the church's privileged corporate position as a bulwark against social dissolution.

Some of the liberals, however, believed such a compromise would never
work. They slowly realized that two uncompromising views were edging
closer to open conflict precisely because neither could accept the basic
assumptions of the other. José Antonio Gamboa, a deputy from Oaxaca, put
the matter squarely before the Congress.[59] Gamboa asserted that Mexico
could not survive as long as the clergy continued to dominate the secular
powers; it was a question of national "life or death." The clergy were
responsible for the ills that plagued the nation: the small population spread
out over vast distances, no feeling of community, no sense of national unity,
localism and isolation, no national markets, no investments in agricultural
production, and, above all, the national weakness that tempted the American
"colossus" to absorb Mexico in the name of civilization. All the clergy cared
for, Gamboa emphasized, was the center of the nation; they could not care
less about the plight of the provinces—where the majority of the liberals had
come from—or what happened to the people who lived there. What was

called Catholic unity by opponents of toleration was little more than mass
ignorance and superstition. Thus to end the misery of the people, to reduce
the power of the clergy over the lives of Mexicans, to bring industry, commerce, and entrepreneurs to Mexico, to protect the provinces, and to prevent
absorption by foreign invaders, toleration was a necessity.

Though opposing the Lafragua position on toleration, Gamboa adopted
many of the same liberal attitudes and values. His distrust and dislike of the
Indians ran just as deep as Lafragua's, and at one point he proposed large-
scale immigration and inter-marriage as a means of destroying the Indian
population of Mexico. In that way, he argued, "the threat of being absorbed
by the Indian race" would disappear and "the Indians would be absorbed into
our race." He called for "a human barrier: for five million Indians, ten million
whites." Both Gamboa and Lafragua made constant references to caste wars,
suggesting a fear of social and political disintegration that transcended their
positions on the church. And, finally, both men stressed their concern for
the provinces as opposed to the central core orientation of the clerical party.

That in spite of their similar concerns Lafragua and Gamboa could reach
entirely different attitudes on religious toleration reflects the transitional
nature of the years between the Revolution of Ayutla and the 1857 Tacubaya
revolt. The Mexican Reform movement in these years sought to find some
compromise between the rigid, theocratic world view of the church and the
newly developed secular attitudes. In the process, freedom of worship was
defeated. The church, however, did not regain its former status as the official
religion of state. Instead, a compromise measure, article 123, was proposed
for the new constitution; it called for the state to interfere in religious activities as the laws required. This action was the result of the forceful secularism
of Ponciano Arriaga, who argued that to omit all mention of the sovereignty
of the secular nation-state meant "the sovereign power of the nation . . .
could do nothing about ecclesiastical problems." Mexico, according to
Arriaga, was a new nation creating itself by casting off the old, alien systems
and adopting laws relevant to the Mexican situation. To omit a statement
on national sovereignty in ecclesiastical affairs would, in Arriaga's opinion,
result in the establishment of a sovereign and independent church. If the
new constitution failed to act, he concluded, "then not only would the
being and life of Mexico disappear, but even the shadow and name of
'nation.'"[60] Arriaga's dire warnings were heeded and article 123 was included
in the final version of the Constitution of 1857. Once again the church had
weathered a major challenge to its privileged position, and once again the
liberals had reinforced the corporate structure they wanted to destroy.

The search for compromise with the ecclesiastical corporation was a fundamental part of the liberal Reform. It is also consistent with nation-building

perceptions about the process of modifying and adapting traditional institutions to new situations. This modifying procedure—the penetration crisis—applies not only to official structures like armies, local political chiefs, or police forces, but also to independent, non-governmental institutions like religious organizations. The personal history of the Reform leaders, the behavior of the church during past national crises, the exigencies of the creation of the secular nation-state—all dictated substantial reform of the basic church-state relationship. The Juárez Law, the Lerdo Law, the laws on civil registration, the votes on religious toleration—all indicate a cautious and curiously ambivalent approach to altering the position of the church in the new political order. The evidence suggests that the liberals had hoped to achieve a smooth blending of the traditional and the new in their relationship with the Catholic Church. Yet the profound division between two irreconcilable world views made the search for compromise a tragic failure.

8. Secularizing the State

At the heart of the ten years of violence from 1857 to 1867 was the Catholic Church's desire to destroy the Reform. The church stimulated, financed, and sometimes even directed anti-Reform armies. The Ayutla government had barely begun to function when prominent clerics organized popular rebellions against the liberal program. The first, and one of the most serious, of the rebellions occurred in the strategic city of Puebla in 1856. President Comonfort took command of the federal army himself when his general defected to the conservative cause. The pro-clerical rebellion had swiftly captured the entire state of Puebla and was menacing the national capital. With lightning strikes, Comonfort managed to crush the rebellion and reestablish governmental control over the territory.

In a move that astounded both liberals and conservatives, Comonfort ordered the governors of Veracruz and Puebla as well as the *jefe político* of the territory of Tlaxcala to seize church property from the diocese of Puebla in the name of the nation. The funds from the sale of the property were to be used to reimburse the government for the expenses involved in putting down the Puebla revolt. Despite clerical cries of outrage and anathemas, the government pursued its plan while justifying its actions in strongly nationalistic terms. Ezequiel Montes, minister of justice and ecclesiastical affairs, said the seizure of church property had violated no laws nor had it injured the church's spiritual power. In the realm of dogma, morality, and administration of the sacraments the church was still supreme, but in the areas of temporal property and public wealth the secular state was to be the ultimate authority. Moreover, he asserted that "it would be absurd to suppose that in the nation there was one class that enjoyed all the comforts this association produces but did not suffer the responsibilities that come with it." Montes concluded with an ironic lament: "How sad would be the condition of the supreme government if it lacked full power to put an end to the excesses of individuals and corporations that abuse their power or their wealth in order to disturb with impunity the tranquility of the nation!"[1] Ezequiel Montes, a moderate who had sought accommodation between church and state, now found himself unexpectedly radicalized by the inflexible and rebellious behavior of the clergy.

Other liberals experienced similar changes in attitude toward the church. One principal repercussion of the Puebla revolt was to heighten the feeling among the liberal group that the clergy were disloyal to Mexico and out to destroy all secular authority. From his governor's chair in Oaxaca Benito Juárez wrote that the conduct of the clergy in Puebla only proved "they care nothing for the progress and happiness of the country."[2] Lafragua grumbled that priests "have exchanged the shepherd's stick for the rebel's saber," and he began to question seriously for the first time the patriotism of the clergy as citizens of Mexico. As minister of gobernación he issued a circular in which he referred to the Puebla revolt as an example of the unwillingness of the clergy "to recognize the supreme power of the nation," and he went on to assert that the church had now become "an enemy of the nation."[3] Francisco Zarco supported the seizure of clerical property because the church had become "an enemy of the people." He wanted ecclesiastical property from Puebla to be used to rebuild Mexican society because "it is time the national government stop being a huge joke [rey de burlas]."[4] Such was the effect of the clergy's rigid position when confronted with limited secular reform. The radicalization of the more moderate members of the Reform group was to have profound consequences in later years.

The clerical response to the Constitution of 1857 further extended the radicalization pattern and produced a severe crisis in the Mexican political structure. Because the new constitution contained the Juárez Law and the Lerdo Law, and because it provided for freedom of speech, education, press, and assembly, secular interference in ecclesiastical affairs, and, above all, the required oath of loyalty, the high clergy issued a decree declaring that anyone taking the loyalty oath to the nation and its new code of laws could no longer receive the sacraments.[5] Every Mexican was obliged to take the oath, and many were now placed in the impossible position of having to choose between God and country. In the meantime, the clergy played on the deeply rooted faith of most Mexicans with great success. Some priests declared that those supporting the secular authorities would be dragged off at night by Satan.[6] The prefects of various villages resigned out of fear of clerical reprisals against their families, and in at least one case all the local village officials resigned rather than swear allegiance to the secular nation-state. There were also cases in which fanatical mobs attacked those who openly supported the constitution.[7] On the local level the effects of the clerical effort to undermine and destroy the Constitution of 1857 were confusion, chaos, and despair.

Within the Reform group the actions of the clergy produced a reaction of intense anger. When Juan José Baz, governor of the Federal District, went to the National Cathedral during Holy Week as a representative of the president in a symbolic act to demonstrate the patronage of the nation over the church, he was met by a choir boy who informed him that he could not enter. Furious, Baz demanded stern action against the clergy because "it appears that there is a strong desire to provoke sedition and revolt, perhaps to have public victims whose blood would fertilize such profound and ruinous hatreds."[8] Liberal newspapers echoed Baz's resentment, calling the religious question a "matter of life or death for the country." As *El Siglo* put it: "Until now, through criminal neglect, Mexico had two powers: one temporal, weak and subordinate, the other spiritual, potent and arrogant. These two powers have struggled for control of the nation. . . . By lamentable disgrace, the spiritual power has won these fratricidal battles."[9] *El Siglo* argued that the clergy refused to accept the constitution because "they want to control Mexico's destiny, they want to be the only temporal sovereign, they want to be absolute masters of our society."[10] Even the government joined the fray and in highly nationalistic language referred to the clergy as "anti-national interests" with "illegitimate and anti-national" goals. The government circular referred to the clergy as "enemies of the State."[11] Thus ecclesiastical opposition to the reconstitution of the secular nation-state produced two results: it furthered the process of identifying the church as an enemy of the modern nation and radicalized many of the liberals who had hoped for conciliation and accommodation between church and state.

By the end of 1857 the Reform group could see more clearly that compromise between the theocratic and secular positions was becoming an impossibility. It had been a difficult three years, full of secular action and clerical reaction, and each year had brought the conciliatory policy closer to the brink of disaster. The overwhelming desire of the liberal movement during these transitional years had been to create a secular nation-state while at the same time maintaining the traditional corporate structure of Mexican society. For this reason the Juárez Law confirmed the ecclesiastical *fuero,* the Lerdo Law assured the church that its wealth remained intact, and the constitution, though not making Catholicism the official religion of state, did not permit religious toleration to interfere with the predominance of the church. To each measure the church responded with anathemas, excommunications, and finally rebellion. As the clerical response to limited reform became more intense, so did the anticlerical feelings of the liberal group; the church increasingly was labeled "anti-national," "disloyal," and "unpatriotic." With the outbreak of the Tacubaya revolt in December of 1857, the search for moderation was completely discredited, and partial solutions to the problem of the privileged ecclesiastical

corporation were abruptly terminated.[12] From that moment the radical
elements in the Reform movement were in charge of Mexico's national destiny.

More than any other event in the Mexican national experience the Tacubaya
revolt altered forever the course of church-state relations. As a corporation the
church had maintained enough power to thwart the reform intentions of the
secularization movement as well as enlist the support of the entrenched traditional factions in Mexican politics. Their combined might drove the liberal
reformers out of Mexico City and into a Veracruz enclave. Once in command,
the clerical party annulled those reform laws that touched on the church; the
Juárez and Lerdo laws were struck down and the church got back its *fuero* and
property. The constitution and its oath were abolished, while salutations
poured in from bishops, archbishops, and even Pope Pius IX.[13]

To all appearances the church had won a magnificent victory; secularization
appeared doomed to the fate of previous reform movements, crushed beneath
the political, economic, and spiritual omnipotence of the Catholic Church. The
forces of traditionalism had prevailed; or so it seemed. Underneath the appear-
ance of victory, however, forces were at work to undermine the theocratic
victory. In the conservative camp the demands of prosecuting the war against
the recalcitrant liberals forced the church to sell land, submit to taxes, and
even part with precious ceremonial silver to meet the demands of the state—all
of which suggests that the church was going to be reduced in economic might
by whichever group, liberal or conservative, held control of the developing
nation-state.[14]

But it was within the Reform movement that the violence and disloyalty of
the clergy had its greatest impact. The two world views that had been fencing
with each other, seeking out weak points for fatal jabs, were now locked in a
deadly battle for survival. Moderates who had previously sought reconciliation
between the newly emerging secular state and the traditional corporate structure now turned in a rage on the church. José María Lafragua, a former leader
of the anti-toleration forces in the Constitutional Congress, called for the
complete destruction of the clergy because "for them the nation [is] nothing."
He asserted: "As long as there is a class in the Republic that has more power
than the government, then that government will be ephemeral and even
ridiculous."[15] By the summer of 1859 Lafragua was calling for the nationalization of church property.[16]

A similar shift can be detected in the attitudes of Guillermo Prieto, another
moderate who became a strident anti-clerical. It was Prieto who had written
to Comonfort in 1855 that he hoped "the sacred alliance between man and
God" would not be ruptured.[17] But by 1858 Prieto had changed his tune,
and in a long, revealing letter to Ocampo he reviewed the aims of the Mora
program in 1833, contrasting them with the results of the Lerdo plan in

1856. Mora, in Prieto's view, wanted to make each renter a landowner and based his reform on the principle "that [church] property is national, on the subordination of the clergy to the government, on the distribution of [property], and on the abolition of clerical clientele who gave to it the prestige of a political power." According to Prieto, Lerdo's program, as representative of all the reforms in the immediate post-Ayutla years, had left the church both its power and its hold on the loyalties of most Mexicans; the obvious solution was to nationalize church property and destroy its corporate structure.[18] This was a dramatic turnabout for the moderates within the Reform group, one that held the promise of intense anti-church measures.

Prior to the Tacubaya revolt there were few who saw the clergy and the church as "anti-Mexican," but afterwards Santos Degollado summed up the growing anticlerical feelings: the clergy "are indifferent to the loss of Mexican nationality because their nationality is Roman."[19] In Degollado's perception of the new situation the clergy now represented a foreign and alien power that wanted to overrun Mexico's sovereignty. He argued that it was no longer in the national interest for a foreign monarch to own so much national territory, particularly when it was used to finance revolution against the legitimately constituted secular authorities, and Degollado, like Prieto, called for nationalization of all church property. Such feelings toward the church only added fuel to the strident anti-clerical sentiment that resulted from the Tacubaya revolt.

The Ayutla movement had come to power with strong feelings against the church for its discriminatory practices and its behavior in the Polkos affair. These sentiments had been strengthened as the post-Ayutla attempt at conciliation and compromise between secular nationalism and the theocratic world view rushed headlong toward disaster. The Tacubaya revolt, with its class warfare and ideological content, signaled the final point of departure for the liberal attitude toward the status of the church in a modern nation. In the new definition the church was to be completely separated from its secular activities and reduced to a subordinate economic and social position. In short, Mexican liberalism was going to create a "Mexican Church" loyal to the secular nation-state.

The new position on the church found its fullest expression in a circular issued on July 7, 1859, by the constitutional government in Veracruz. Although it spoke on many issues of those critical times, the first problem considered was the church-state conflict. The manifesto accused the clergy of starting and financing a civil war that could destroy Mexico just so they could keep their colonial privileges and continue abusing the power their riches had bestowed on them. In order to end once and for all the power of the church, the Reform movement adopted the following program: complete separation of church and state, suppression of all regular orders, abolition of all brotherhoods, nationalization of church property, toleration of all religions, prohibition of both the entrance of women into the convents and the use of secular authority to enforce the collection of parochial fees.[20] It was a sweeping reorientation of the Reform program and reflects an awareness on the part of the liberals that there was no room for accommodation between the traditional, theocratic world view and secular nation-building.

Under the new conception of church-state affairs, the state replaced the church as the ultimate arbiter of human affairs, and the liberals implemented the new policy with an important series of laws. The most significant was the first, that of July 12, 1859, nationalizing all church property and declaring the absolute and perfect independence of church and state. As promised by the circular, all regular orders were suppressed, habits were banned in public, new convents were prohibited, no one was allowed to enter a convent, the funds of the Juzgado de Capellanías were nationalized, and no church property could be sold.[21]

Accompanying the law was the usual justification circular, this time written by Manuel Ruiz, minister of justice and ecclesiastical affairs. Casting his eye back over Mexico's history since independence, Ruiz noted that the thirty-eight years had been marked with bloodshed and violence, all caused by the clergy. He reminded his countrymen that the clergy were solely responsible for the revolt in Puebla and the coup d'etat of 1857. Both actions were designed to destroy the modern nation-state and maintain clerical power. The clergy "has not permitted the stability of any government, they have impoverished and wrecked the nation, they have held up its progress, and more than once they have humiliated it before other nations of the world." They had been able to do this because of their wealth and power. Thus, to dry up the fountain of evil it was necessary to take away the wealth that had been so abused. History taught the nation that until it took this action there could be no peace and no viable secular nation-state. To assure that the nationalization of church property would bring peace, Ruiz argued that the complete separation of church and state was a necessity. The government was in effect giving up the claims of patronage that had previously been a source of conflict. Now the church was free to select its own officials, and the state was free of any responsibility for enforcing church rules and regulations.[22]

In one brilliant stroke the policies and practices of the past were wiped out by the force of a secular reform that had matured to full awareness of its own logic. It was the first nationalization in Mexican history, and the result was a widely broadened concept of secular political power. It was now clear to the liberal elite that the earlier reforms had left the church's power unchecked. As Juan Antonio de la Fuente put it at a patriotic celebration: "In vain the '55 [Juárez] law left the clerical *fuero* more extensive than the famous [viceroys] would have believed possible; in vain the disamortization law preserved church rents intact; in vain the laws maintained parochial fees. . . . The clergy responded to the *fuero* law with sedition, to the mortmain law with more sedition, to humanity in taxation with unlimited scandals and riots."[23]

For many, the most important part of the nationalization law was not nationalization itself, though this was hardly ignored, but rather the separation of the secular and spiritual powers. Juárez expressed the sense of liberation that came from separation: "The most important [aspect of the law] is the absolute independence of the civil power and religious liberty . . . and if we triumph I will have the satisfaction of having done something good for my country and humanity."[24]

Not only did the nationalization law mean an extension of secular authority through a reduction of clerical political and economic power, but it also implied that the state would increasingly take over the civil functions performed by the clergy, particularly those affecting the everyday life of Mexicans. One by one, new laws removed ecclesiastical control over the individual life cycle. The first of these was a law making marriage a civil contract, thereby effectively limiting the power of the clergy to withhold the sacrament for political reasons. It was decreed that no marriage would be recognized by the state unless it was registered with the proper officials, and women were given equal rights in the marriage contract.[25] The latter provision had two goals: to advance the cause of equality before the law for all citizens and to reduce ecclesiastical domination of Mexican women. It was well remembered that thousands of women under the direction of the clergy had successfully blocked passage of religious toleration in 1856. The constitutionalists hoped that by giving women greater civil rights female loyalty to the church would be weakened and allegiance to the secular nation-state encouraged.[26]

The work of secularizing the life cycle required a civil registration law. Such a law was put into effect, and it differed markedly from previous registration laws.[27] The registration of birth, marriage, death, and burial was included, but baptisms and religious vows, which had been a part of earlier attempts at civil registration, were now absent. Their exclusion reflects the fuller liberal vision of a secular society. With the separation of church and state, the legal obligation to register baptisms and enforce obedience to religious vows immediately ceased. In this manner the state removed itself from religious activities while at the same time eliminating the ecclesiastical threat of withholding registration of birth, marriage, and death for political reasons. With the civil registration law the Mexican life cycle was for the first time in the hands of the secular nation-state.

Since the clergy had been eliminated from the burial process, there was no longer need for the church to control the cemeteries. In fact, to have left the clergy in charge of the cemeteries would have prevented the operation of the civil registration, for the church could still close its crypts to anyone out of ecclesiastical favor. Thus the Veracruz government secularized all cemeteries in Mexico, bringing them under the aegis of the state.[28] Not only did the measure enhance the process of secularizing the life cycle, it also forced a reorientation of individual loyalties; no longer was it so important to secure the good graces of the church, for an individual's destiny was now determined by the state.

Melchor Ocampo summed up the motives behind the secularization laws in a circular that demonstrated that the Reform Laws returned to the secular government only what it had originally possessed: the right to dominate civil society. Ocampo bitterly denounced the clergy because "the ministers of the church in Mexico say it is illicit to obey Mexico, the temporal sovereign." Good men had had to choose between submitting to the clergy in matters of patriotism, liberty, order, independence, and human dignity and living a life of sin and prostitution. Such were, in Ocampo's opinion, the consequences of clerical control over the life cycle, and they would remain until the civilian power began to lead the people once again "down the path of tolerance and order, of morality and justice."[29]

To dramatize the new alignment of power, the Juárez government permitted only three religious festivals: Thursday and Friday of Holy Week, the Thursday of Corpus Christi, and Christmas. Perhaps remembering the humiliation of Governor Baz on the cathedral steps, the same decree prohibited all government officials from participating in religious functions in their official capacity.[30] Meanwhile, the Mexican delegation to the Vatican was recalled; the new separation of church and state signified that there was no longer a need for representatives of the secular nation-state to have diplomatic negotiations with a religious power.[31] It was a purely symbolic act, since the papacy had refused to recognize the Juárez government, but symbols played an important role in the Reform movement. In 1860 Juárez, for example, always cognizant of the importance of symbolic action, made sure a civil judge publicly registered his newly born daughter in compliance with the Reform Laws.[32] Similarly, Jesús González Ortega renamed the main streets in Zacatecas City "Calle de la Reforma," "Calle de la Esclaustración," and "Calle de la Tolerancia de Cultos."[33] Such symbolic action demonstrated an understanding on the part of the liberals of the power of social communication to further their cause.

The complete reorientation of the Reform movement was accomplished with the last of the Reform Laws: the establishment in 1860 of religious toleration throughout the Mexican nation. Although article 3 of the nationalization law declared that the state would protect the Catholic Church "as it would any other," there had not been an outright declaration of toleration. It was not until eighteen days before the final triumph of the liberals that the Juárez government thought it had the strength and popular backing to complete the secularization process. In a sweeping measure the government guaranteed the "natural right" to worship in any form. It was now law that the state could not interfere in spiritual affairs, but, even more important, religious bodies could no longer interfere with the workings of the secular authorities. At the same time, the law completely abolished the clerical *fuero,* which the Juárez Law had left intact in the thwarted hope of achieving peace in Mexico. To assure that priests no longer assumed political roles, the new law abolished the practice of using church buildings as asylums for criminals, required any cleric ordering a member of his congregation to commit a crime to be tried for that crime, prohibited religious celebrations in public without approval of the secular authorities, and denied public officials the right to discuss religious affairs in their capacity as public servants. Churches were obliged to support the state financially whenever called upon, though individual clerics maintained their tax exemption. And, finally, the law prohibited public religious oaths and declared that the oath on the constitution violated the separation of church and state and was abolished.[34]

The law on religious toleration reflects the end of the earlier attempts to fuse the traditional church with the secular nation. Fittingly, it was accompanied by a circular written by Juan Antonio de la Fuente, minister of justice and public instruction, who had strenuously opposed religious toleration in the Constituent Congress four years earlier. Now, as the liberal elite were about to terminate the civil war and reestablish their power, de la Fuente declared that the nation had been on the brink of destruction solely because of the disloyalty of the "privileged classes," who had never had the interest of the nation at heart. The new banner of Mexican nationalism was "liberty, equality, and progress": liberty for all to participate in the political system, equality with the end of privilege, and progress through the elimination of the traditional dominant elements and the substitution of a new ruling group. To de la Fuente, theocratic despotism—"that evil alliance of church and state"—had meant little more for Mexico than civil war, injustice, and a lack of civil, political, and religious liberty; it was "an ominous system destroyed by the Reform." Now both church and state were confined to their proper spheres of authority because "the state will not mix in religious matters, nor will it permit the slightest trace of competition in society." De la Fuente stressed the desire of the constitutionalist group to secularize all civil functions so that the clergy could never again coerce political opinion and actions, and he admitted that the oath on the constitution was a mistake because it mixed political and religious actions. As he put it: "From now on the sovereignty of Mexico and her republican institutions will have impotent enemies because the state has reassumed all its power and will never permit a private will to dominate it."[35] The message of modernization was clear: no individual, corporation, class, or faction was to have power superior to that of the secular nation-state. From that moment on, the ultimate arbiter of human affairs in Mexico was to be the nation.

Secular liberalism, at least in law, had triumphed over the conservative-ecclesiastical alliance. Juárez, in his first address to the new Congress after the reestablishment of the constitutional government in the capital in 1861, summed up the changes that had taken place in Mexico since the Ayutlans had first seized office five years earlier. Referring to the Juárez and Lerdo laws, he pointed out that the constitution had permitted the ecclesiastical corporation to dominate Mexico at the cost of equality, justice, and progress. "From this the laws of the Reform were born: the nationalization of property in mortmain, freedom of worship, the absolute independence of spiritual and civil powers, the secularization, so to speak, of society."[36] Manuel Payno, another who had sought the reconciliation of secular nationalism and the corporate church, now called the Reform "the springtime of the nation" and argued that only with the secularization of the state could Mexico take its place in the ranks of modern nations.[37] Others, particularly liberal newspapers, urged strict enforcement of the Reform Laws so that "the Church would never again be as it was before the [Ayutla] revolution, a state within the State."[38] Even textbooks carried the message; one taught that for centuries the church had prevented nations from governing themselves and argued that the very definition of "nation" was the process of eliminating the political power of the church.[39]

The Reform Laws permanently fixed the juridical position of the church in Mexican society; future laws and decrees only modified the fundamental creation of a secular nation-state with supreme power over the clergy. Exercising these newly won powers, the government ordered all governors to seize one-third of all fees, tithes, donations, and other payments to the church in order to pay off debts incurred by the state during the three years of civil war, of which "the clergy had been the principal promoter, financer, and instigator."[40] With a terse note the government expelled the papal delegate to Mexico; his presence in Mexico, the note said, was "by no means suitable" and he was ordered out immediately. At the same time the government expelled Archbishop Garza and four other bishops, adding to the rapidly growing contingent of former Mexican clergy living abroad.[41] A new press law allowed attacks on the church, and laws were issued secularizing hospitals, abolishing the Juzgado de Capellanías, and extinguishing religious communities throughout the nation.[42] But, for all this, the fundamental characteristics of Mexican liberal attitudes toward the church were not altered. The Reform Laws of the years 1857 to 1860 had molded the dominant ideology of anti-clericalism. With its demands for the loyalty of all individuals, the church was seen as a danger to Mexican patriotism. In its opulence the church had dominated the economic structure of Mexico. As a vestige of colonial rule the church had supported the aristocratic classes and their privileges against the ambitious newcomers and equality. As a universal institution the church was seen as alien to Mexico, a foreign power out to conquer the nation. All of this the Reform sought to destroy by taking from the church its lands and wealth, by eliminating its *fueros* and special privileges, and by creating a "Mexican Church" answerable to the state for its actions.

The success of the Reform in secularizing the state was reflected in the failure of the French intervention to disturb the newly established power relationships. The intervention was an act of desperation by the Mexican clergy, a vain attempt to recapture a lost age and reestablish clerical domination. From the beginning, however, things went wrong in the clerical plan to reverse the secularization process. Even as the clergy sang Te Deums for the advancing French and conservative forces, the authority of the state was upheld. Napoleon III had already ordered his representative in Mexico not to tamper with property sold under the disamortization and nationalization laws. Labastida, the former bishop of Puebla and now archbishop of Mexico, was forced from the Regency because of his inflexible demands; and when he retaliated by closing the cathedral doors to French troops, the French commander threatened to blow them open if necessary. Labastida ultimately capitulated.

Clerical hopes that things would improve with the arrival of Maximilian in 1864 were also in vain. Desperate for money, Maximilian sped up the process of selling nationalized property instead of returning it to the church. As a principle of state he enforced the Reform Laws on civil marriage and registration and demanded that the clergy stop intervening in secular affairs. Since negotiations with the papal nuncio got nowhere, Maximilian upheld religious toleration, reaffirmed the right of the state to nationalize church property, opened cemeteries to all creeds, and reserved for the state the right of publishing papal decrees.[43] Thus rather than undoing the secular Reform, Maximilian strengthened its provisions and firmly established secular domination of the church in Mexico.

Once again the clergy failed to understand the lessons of the past few years. During the Three Years War the church had suffered at the hands of both liberals and conservatives in the ideological struggle between two world views. Similarly the church found both French and Mexicans determined to uphold the secular thrust of the Reform movement. The Mexican clergy failed to comprehend the nature of the modern nation-state with its demands for undiluted individual loyalty, secular society, and the subordination of traditional corporations. Nor did the clergy realize that the form of government was inconsequential, that both republic and monarch, Mexican and foreign, would make the same demands on the church; its past privileges, authority, and political power could never be fully recovered.

The French intervention did not fundamentally alter the liberals' attitudes toward the church, but rather strengthened the view that the church was a foreign agent and that the clergy were disloyal to Mexico. Liberal newspapers accused the clergy of being "the true enemy of the people" because "since Independence they had worked to bring to their true patria, Rome, the sweat of the people."[44] Guillermo Prieto wrote that "the clergy has sold our nationality to foreigners for a handful of gold."[45] Others blasted away at the clergy as foreign agents, accusing them of murdering such national heroes as Hidalgo, Morelos, and Matamoros while betraying Mexico to Spain. Now they had betrayed Mexico once again, only this time to France. As one author put it, "The Catholic clergy is everywhere and always first the son of the Mother Church and afterwards, although not always, the son of the mother patria. Rome is their capital, the Pope their sovereign. Between two contradictory orders, one emanating from their country and the other from the Apostolic Chair, a cleric never hesitates to obey the second."[46] Ignacio Ramírez declared that the church was little more than any other "foreign speculator" and saw the intervention as an attempt by the clergy to wage war against the Mexican nation in the interests of foreign powers.[47] Clerical support for the intervention thus confirmed already-held opinions that the clergy were disloyal to the nation and were subversive agents of foreign powers wishing to recolonize Mexico.

Even after the victory of the Mexicans in 1867 over the shattered French empire, the church-state issue maintained its fixed quality. Juárez generally ignored the church on the assumption that the problems had been satisfactorily settled, but his attempt to give the clergy the right to vote was met with such strident attacks that it was abandoned.[48] Sebastián Lerdo de Tejada, on becoming president at the death of Juárez in 1872, raised the Reform Laws to the position of constitutional provisions, expelled foreign Jesuits, and abolished the last remaining religious order, the Sisters of Charity. Although these actions did reopen old wounds, the church was completely impotent to prevent Lerdo from carrying out his plans; no longer could the clergy raise rebellious armies against the secular nation-state.[49]

It has often been argued that the church recovered its power during the long reign of Porfirio Díaz, but it is the thesis here that the basic power relationships were determined during the Three Years War and remain essentially unchanged today. Though the clergy supported the Díaz rebellion against Lerdo in the expectation of receiving better treatment, their hopes were once again squashed. Díaz knew how to keep the church under the secular thumb while making it appear to the church that it was better off. His method was to alternate between Lerdo's hard-nosed enforcement of the Reform Laws and great laxity in applying them, thus keeping the church politically off-balance and in his debt at the same time. The church may have regained some of its economic power but it never exercised the political domination it had known prior to the Reform movement.[50] The Reform Laws and the intensely nationalistic feelings that grew out of twelve years of civil and foreign war had drained the blood from the political veins of the church, leaving it an anemic shadow of its former power.

9. Nationalism in a World of Nations

Few students of Mexican history consider nationalism a vital issue for the nineteenth century. Indeed, the one scholar who has attempted a systematic analysis of Mexican nationalism, Frederick Turner, openly states that "nationalism is most conspicuous by its absence in nineteenth-century Mexico." Similarly, John Johnson declares flatly that there was no nationalism in Latin America until 1925. He cites strong class distinctions, a European orientation on the part of elite groups, separatist tendencies, and weak and uninspiring governments as the reasons for the lack of nationalist feelings in Latin America prior to the twentieth century.[1] Yet both Turner and Johnson seem to relate nationalism solely to the type experienced by much of the western world in the twentieth century with its mass tendencies, sophisticated symbolic manipulation, and high levels of communication. They fail to make an important distinction between the elite political culture and mass political culture.[2] As has been argued throughout this book, Mexico experienced at mid-century a profound ideological crisis that questioned traditional values and offered changes in the political structure. This legitimacy crisis was accompanied by an equally far-reaching identity crisis within the political elite. The central argument of this chapter is that the identity crisis within the political elite produced the beginnings of modern Mexican nationalism. In addition, Mexican nationalism seems to have sprung neither from internal ethnic divisions nor from class conflict but rather from two interrelated sources: a deep and abiding concern for territorial integrity and a heightened sense of uniqueness, of difference from other cultures. In both of these areas foreigners and foreign powers played the crucial roles.

In fact, the liberals came to power in 1855 already keenly aware of Mexico's unhappy relationships with foreign powers. And no event more colored their view than the Mexican-American War and the peace treaty signed at Guadalupe Hidalgo. The Ayutla elite had uniformly opposed the Treaty of Guadalupe

Hidalgo, painting it a treasonous act.[3] Manuel Doblado, as governor of Guanajuato, had called for active rebellion against the "cowardly government" so
that the war would not end. Doblado asserted that by not accepting the "law
of the victor" Mexico would begin to see the "marvels of patriotism."[4] Like
Doblado, many liberals fought the signing of the treaty because it violated
Mexico's national sovereignty by alienating Mexican territory to foreigners.

This attitude carried over into the Revolution of Ayutla. As the new political elite prepared to seize power and modernize the nation-state, their spokesman, Juan Alvarez, justified the rebellion on nationalist grounds. Alvarez said
his revolt was against Santa Anna because the one-legged general had sold or
given away much of Mexico. As Alvarez put it:

> Because of [Santa Anna] the territory of Texas was lost; by his ineptitude
> or malice California was lost; to satisfy his ambition he sold the Valley of
> La Mesilla for ten million; and because, even after these robberies, he needs
> still more money, he is at present concluding secret contracts with the
> Americans to sell them Baja California and other lands that add up to half
> of what remains of Mexico.[5]

Pursuing this line of attack, Alvarez issued a manifesto to the Mexican
people reminding them of the "sad history of what took place in the last two
years of [Santa Anna's reign]. The nation saw her territory dismembered by
an infamous deal that served only to fill the coffers of Santa Anna and his
accomplices."[6] And once Alvarez was in power the focus on loss of national
territory as an integral part of Mexican nationalism did not cease. The new
cabinet in 1855 issued a manifesto laying down the guidelines of the new government. The first principle of the new government, the manifesto said, was
"to preserve as inviolable the national unity." To do this the new government
promised "to crush at all cost any plan of separation or dismemberment of
national territory."[7] That the new government made territorial integrity one
of its principal concerns suggests the importance of nationalism for Mexican
liberalism at mid-century.

The emphasis on territorial integrity gave Mexican nationalism a mild character; it expressed a distrust of foreigners rather than a hatred of them. Many
of the Reform elite actually hoped for better relations with foreigners and
lamented the fear that pervaded the nationalism of these early post-Ayutlan
years. José María Iglesias, for one, called for Mexicans not to adopt the Roman
attitude of viewing all foreigners as "barbarians" and hoped for a day when
such distinctions would disappear and there would be world peace.[8] On the
other hand, others like Benito Juárez knew that the ideals of Iglesias would
be crushed in a world of national power politics and urged the government to

end the civil strife so that Mexico could prepare for the eventual foreign struggle.[9] José María Lafragua, prophetic as usual, argued that continued civil war
would surely bring on foreign intervention. Because more money would have
to be spent on the military, eventually Mexico would be unable to pay her
foreign debts. Lafragua predicted that commerce would collapse, agriculture
would decline, "international relations will change and friendly nations will
demand reclamation: then will come intervention, then . . . forgive me for not
finishing such a horrible picture."[10] Eight years later the French finished the
painting.

While Iglesias continued to hope for an age without foreign conflict, minor–
but influential–events further stimulated Mexican nationalism. One incident
involved the American and British consuls in Tepic, who had made personal
fortunes smuggling contraband goods into Mexico. When Santos Degollado,
the governor of Jalisco, removed from office their Mexican cohorts in corruption, the two consuls fomented revolution. Eustaquio Barron, the British
member of the guilty twosome, managed to convince England that Mexico's
behavior threatened her national sovereignty, and Great Britain broke off relations. When England threatened war the Mexicans were at a loss. Some suggested an alliance with the United States, but Matías Romero, in a confidential
letter to Benito Juárez, argued that "an alliance with the United States would
be even more dangerous, and unfortunately we are not in any condition to
fight a colossus." After much British pressure, Comonfort gave in to Barron's
demands, reinstated him as consul, paid him damages, and subjected Degollado
to trial for his behavior.[11] Mexico had been humiliated and the Ayutlans
knew it.

A second incident developed when, in December 1856, thirty armed men
invaded the Hacienda of San Vicente and murdered the owner, his family, and
servants. This everyday occurrence in Mexico would not have turned into an
international incident except that the hacendado had been a wealthy Spaniard.
The Spanish ambassador responded to the news of the massacre by delivering
an ultimatum to the Comonfort government: the killers had to be caught and
punished and Spain paid proper damages within eight days. Needless to say,
the Mexican government could not apprehend the culprits, and, true to its word,
Spain withdrew diplomatic recognition of the government. In response the
Mexican newspapers bitterly attacked the Spanish actions. *El Siglo XIX*
claimed that the assassins were actually Spaniards hired by reactionary elements to promote discord between the new government and Spain. And
besides, *El Siglo* asked, why should Mexico pay Spain damages for a private
tragedy?[12] As a result of the San Vicente incident Spain once again occupied
a prominent position in Mexican nationalism.

Even before the San Vicente assassinations, however, anti-Spanish feeling had run strong in the Reform movement. Juárez constantly expressed fear of another Spanish reconquest. His concerns became more generalized when *El Siglo* ran a document written by a group of anti-government conservatives that called for a Spanish invasion of Mexico to oust the new government and establish a member of the Spanish royal house on a Mexican throne. This throwback to the days of Iturbide's Plan of Iguala was branded "conservative treason" by Zarco, who wrote that the conservatives consistently "give proof that they care little for the nation."[13]

These incidents, though not major in themselves, set the tone of Mexican nationalism as the delegates to the Constitutional Congress began their deliberations. And yet the Constitution of 1857 is notable for its mildness when dealing with foreigners in Mexico. The only provision of the new constitution that has anti-foreign overtones is article 32, which in part says: "In equal circumstances, Mexicans will be preferred to foreigners for all employment, offices, and commissions named by the authorities in which citizenship is not required." When this section of the article came before the delegates for ratification, it was adopted unanimously and without debate. The rest of the article, requiring the government to set up schools to train Mexicans in the art of working, received careful scrutiny. Guillermo Prieto attacked the provision on the grounds that it implied government protection for workers at a time when active government interference in public affairs was being reduced. To this argument Ponciano Arriaga replied that there was substantial inequality between Mexicans and foreigners in the arts and crafts and that the government had a responsibility to correct that imbalance. Arriaga's persuasion carried the day and Congress adopted the second part of article 32.[14]

Other provisions of the new constitution established the usual limitations on foreigners within the nation-state. Article 33 stated that all foreigners in Mexico had to pay taxes, obey the laws, and submit to judicial procedures "without calling on resources other than those conceded to Mexicans." Obviously the authors of this provision had in mind the calling of outside forces, as had been done during the San Vicente affair by the Spanish. This same article 33 gave the government the right to expel from the country any "pernicious foreigner." But attempts by Arriaga and the drafting committee to include even further restrictions on foreigners in Mexico were unsuccessful. As part of article 33 Arriaga wanted a specific statement limiting the rights of foreigners to make claims against the government and to demand the firing of government officials. Perhaps he had in mind the Barron-Forbes incident and the subsequent trial of Degollado. Nevertheless, the proposal aroused vigorous opposition. Zarco, while denouncing the "groundlessness, injustice, and excessiveness of the majority of foreign reclamations that have annihilated the treasury and enriched a few audacious adventurers and insolent smugglers," argued that the provision had no place in the national constitution since it referred strictly to international treaties. Arriaga responded that the Barron incident demonstrated the need for such restrictions but agreed to retire the article from debate.[15] Thus, even in the face of direct foreign interference in Mexican internal affairs, few Mexicans were willing to carry an anti-foreign bias beyond mild expression.

When the government made its appeal to the nation to support the new constitution, it made it on the grounds that further civil strife would cause immediate foreign intervention and the "disappearance of Mexico as a sovereign nation." Furthermore, Mexico found itself generally in good relations with foreign nations both in Europe and America, and the new government wanted that situation to continue. But Comonfort issued a strong warning to foreigners that the new government felt that its "first duty—and most burning desire—is to preserve national independence and integrity. It also has the most firm and indestructible conviction not to enter into or sign any agreement that will endanger either."[16] For the Ayutlans the fear of foreign intervention was never far away; the optimism and hope engendered by the Constitution of 1857 did not dispel the nervousness. Many still believed that although the constitution treated foreigners well, Mexicans opposed to the new rule would entice foreign powers to intervene in national politics. As Francisco Zarco expressed it only nine days after the promulgation of the constitution: "Some still dream of establishing a throne for a foreign prince, while others seek the intervention of foreign powers."[17] When the Reform War began in December 1857, Zarco's fears received a terrible confirmation.

The war came as no shock to the Reform group. Comonfort's fears of civil strife were grounded in the long tradition of solving political differences on the battlefield. Now, however, instead of one caudillo fighting to oust another, two opposing ideologies, two irreconcilable world views, struggled for the mastery of Mexico. For the liberals the civil war revived the recent fears of foreign intervention. Melchor Ocampo, from the constitutionalist stronghold in Veracruz, summarized these feelings. He predicted that the civil war would make it impossible to make payments on Mexico's foreign debt. The world would then conclude, if it had not done so already, that Mexico was incapable of governing itself and that the only way to make that poor nation stable would be through foreign intervention.[18] Meanwhile, some conservatives were already calling for foreign intervention and were using precisely the arguments Ocampo feared. Most of the pamphlets urging European intervention argued that only in this way could American expansionism be halted. Also, most hoped that when the intervention came it would be led by the Spanish and French because these two nations were Latin and Catholic—necessary prerequisites for successful intervention.[19]

Such arguments, coming as they did at a time of great national crisis, infuriated the liberal leadership. Benito Juárez, already stunned by the speed with which the European powers had recognized the Zuloaga government, denounced any intervention. When news reached Veracruz that Spanish troops were on their way to aid the conservatives, Juárez reacted sharply; he fired off a protest to Spain, fortified Veracruz for the attack, and branded the conservatives "false Mexicans in whose hearts national sentiment is nothing." And the liberal press in Mexico naively expressed shock that Mexicans would actually seek foreign troops as allies.[20]

In terms of Mexican nationalism the conservative flirtation with intervention opened the door for the liberals to co-opt the nationalistic rhetoric. The liberals quickly pointed out that the conservatives could hardly be motivated by true nationalism if they sought foreign help to win the struggle. As *El Siglo* phrased it: "The liberal party hopes to achieve its political ideas without foreign assistance and will sacrifice its principles before compromising the independence of the Republic." Although in the conservative view the only way to prevent the absorption of Mexico into the United States was through foreign, in particular Spanish or French, intervention, such a position left the nationalist field completely open for the liberals. And they did not miss their opportunity. *El Siglo* once again: "The first of [the liberal party's] goals has been and always will be the real and active conservation of the nationality and independence of the Republic, rejecting both the American yoke and that of every other nation."[21] The conservative position of supporting foreign intervention left the liberals in sole possession of the nationalist label.

Seeing their advantage in the psychological warfare that accompanied the Reform War, the liberals played on the themes of liberal nationalism and conservative collaboration with foreigners. From Veracruz flowed denunciation after denunciation, all emphasizing the anti-national character of conservative policy. The liberals accused the Zuloaga government of trying to sell territory to the rapacious Americans as a means of financing the war effort. Returning to the propaganda themes developed by Alvarez a few years earlier, they carefully pointed out that the major losses of national territory had taken place when the conservatives had been in power.[22] But it was the Mon-Almonte Treaty that stirred the liberal propaganda mills to a feverish pitch. Negotiated between the conservative General Juan N. Almonte and the Spanish minister to Mexico, Alejandro Mon, the treaty pledged Mexico to pay Spain for damages to Spanish property and citizens injured during the Reform War. Moreover, the treaty seemed to approve the coming of Spanish troops to Mexico to aid the conservative cause. Though in fact the treaty contained little that was opprobrious, José María Lafragua sent a barrage of letters to Ocampo protesting the treaty and demanding that the government condemn it vigorously. Not only did the treaty compromise Mexican independence and national honor, Lafragua argued, but it also forced Mexico to pay private damages. And, he concluded, "Nations are not like individuals"—whereas individuals are bound to pay damages, nations must be completely independent of outside interference and coercion.[23] Even before Lafragua's outburst, Ocampo had issued a circular from the Ministry of Foreign Affairs that condemned the conservative government: "They speak of Mexican national interests and sovereignty, those cowardly and impotent traitors who have offered their land to foreign nations."[24] The Veracruz government could hardly ignore Lafragua's logic and Ocampo's fuming, and in January 1860 it roundly condemned the Mon-Almonte Treaty, claiming that it violated all rules of international law and justice. The government decree denied the responsibility of the Mexican government to pay private claims and castigated the Spanish government for making treaties with usurpers who had no authority to negotiate treaties anyway.[25]

If the liberals uniformly rejected the thought of European intervention in Mexican affairs during the Reform War, their relationship with the United States was more complex. Letters from American filibusterers poured into the liberal camp with offers to bring American troops to help in the war. Juárez politely rejected such offers, arguing that foreign troops should not be involved in the internal affairs of Mexico and that all money the liberals raised had to be used to pay for its own army.[26] Nevertheless, as the military and political situation of the liberals worsened throughout 1859, desperation characterized the Veracruz group. Santos Degollado, the minister of foreign affairs, sent Melchor Ocampo on a mission to the United States with the purpose of ascertaining how many troops might be available to the Juárez government should victory with purely Mexican soldiers elude it. Degollado did, however, order Ocampo to influence the United States government in any way possible to prevent volunteers from coming into Mexico.[27] Even though flirting with the idea of using American troops, Mexican liberals maintained a cautious and fearful attitude toward having any foreign troops on Mexican soil.

Of all the events in the years 1855-1876, none more seriously calls into question the strength of nationalist sentiment on the part of the liberals than the McLane-Ocampo Treaty signed on December 14, 1859. This treaty, which has been severely criticized by some Mexican historians, gave to the United States rights of transit over the Isthmus of Tehuantepec and from Matamoros to Mazatlán, provided for the passage of goods over these routes without taxes, permitted the United States to send in troops in case of threats to American goods and citizens in these areas, and established the payment of four million dollars to Mexico.[28] On the surface it looks as if the liberals had given as much away to foreigners as the conservatives had done in the Mon-Almonte Treaty, and conservative historians have carefully pointed this out.[29]

And yet others have meticulously studied the documentation surrounding the treaty and have concluded otherwise.[30] The debate still rages and it will be a long time, if ever, before it is settled. Nevertheless, for our purposes the treaty provides an interesting case for studying the role of nationalism in the development of the Mexican Reform.

The background to the McLane-Ocampo treaty is a long and complex story involving American desires for passage through the Isthmus of Tehuantepec, the acquisition of territory under the guise of Manifest Destiny, and claims by both Mexicans and Americans for damages to property. The most pressing of these issues was the American desire for passage rights over the Isthmus of Tehuantepec. Although in 1847 the concession had been granted to a Mexican company, the director, José de Garay, had sold it to the British company of Manning, Mackintosh, and Schneider. After the defeat of Mexico by the Americans, the Treaty of Guadalupe Hidalgo turned the right over to the victorious Yankees. Santa Anna was required to confirm the privilege in the Treaty of La Mesilla (the Gadsden Purchase).[31] By the time the men of Ayutla faced the issue of Tehuantepec, American claims to passage rights were well established. In this sense, the McLane-Ocampo treaty gave to the United States only what it already had through other treaties.

But Americans in the age of Manifest Destiny wanted much more; passage rights over the Isthmus of Tehuantepec were one spoke in the ever-expanding wheel of American territorial acquisition. No sooner had the reins of power been turned over to Comonfort in 1856 than the United States minister, John Forsyth, proposed that the new government sell Mexican territory to the United States. Although Forsyth himself had little confidence in any move to acquire Mexican territory, he nonetheless faithfully followed the directions of President Buchanan's secretary of state, Lewis Cass. For Baja California, most of Sonora, and the top part of Chihuahua, Forsyth offered Mexico twelve to fifteen million dollars. At the same time he tried to negotiate another treaty confirming American sovereignty (not just passage rights) over the Isthmus of Tehuantepec.[32] When the proposed treaties were submitted to the Mexican government, Sebastián Lerdo de Tejada, the minister of foreign affairs, rejected them outright. Forsyth wrote to Cass that "the present government of Mexico has firmly sworn before the Nation not to cede an inch of national territory," and Lerdo's reply confirmed that judgment. In it Lerdo stated that the Mexican government "considers inadmissible any plan that is based on the surrender of any part of the national territory." He also rejected the American terms for Tehuantepec on the-grounds that they "curtailed the rights of sovereignty in this land."[33] And Comonfort, recalling that the Organic Law prohibited the alienation of national territory, said to Forsyth: "Each president has his own style, Mr. Forsyth; Don Antonio's [Santa Anna] consisted in selling his country and mine in conserving it."[34] Hard-pressed though it may have been, the liberal elite had made the conservation of Mexican territory a fundamental aspect of Mexican nationalism.

The test of the nationalist doctrine of no alienation of Mexican territory came during the Reform War. Desperate for money, isolated from the international community by the rapid European and American recognition of the Zuloaga government, and faced with recurrent military defeat at the hands of the conservative army, the liberals were in an extremely vulnerable position. American recognition of the conservatives was short-lived, however; it was withdrawn when attempts to acquire land concessions from Zuloaga were rebuffed in June 1858. Still in the first blush of success, the conservatives had little to gain from selling off territory and well remembered the fate of Santa Anna at the hands of the Ayutlan propagandists only four years earlier.[35] Then the United States turned hungry eyes toward the defeated and disconsolate Veracruz government with the hope that out of that situation American expansion could be salvaged.

In December 1858, an American secret agent, William Churchwell, arrived in Veracruz dangling the tantalizing promise of United States recognition—if certain concessions were made. There is little doubt that Ocampo and Lerdo de Tejada concluded that the only way to get American recognition was to convince Churchwell that the Juárez government was willing to make concessions on the subjects of Tehuantepec and the sale of national territory, particularly Baja California. To this effect Churchwell and Ocampo drew up (but did not sign) a memorandum that held out the promise of Mexican concessions. On the basis of this memorandum Churchwell recommended to Buchanan that American recognition be granted the liberal government in Veracruz.[36] Accordingly, Buchanan sent Robert McLane, a senator from Maryland, as minister to Mexico with the right to grant diplomatic recognition. When McLane arrived in Veracruz he expected that his job of obtaining Mexican territory would be relatively easy and conveyed this impression to both American and Mexican officials. But McLane found himself in the surprising situation of encountering stiff Mexican resistance to the sale of any territory. José María Mata articulated the Mexican position: "Although we are prepared to make just and acceptable concessions to assure the development and security of American interests, in no way and for no reason will we alienate a single inch of territory."[37] Hoping to force the Mexican hand, McLane wrote Secretary of State Cass advising him that the mission recently undertaken by Miguel Lerdo de Tejada to secure an American loan should fail. The American government, understanding perfectly McLane's intentions, refused to lend the liberal government money. Thus Mexico, at a time of severe crisis, found herself pressured on all sides for concession of territory.[38]

This, then, was the climate within which the McLane-Ocampo Treaty was negotiated and signed. By the end of 1858 the liberal position was singularly difficult. Through accepted treaties, the United States had a long-standing claim to passage rights over the Isthmus of Tehuantepec, and these rights could not be ignored. Furthermore, the Veracruz group was faced with the hard reality of European support for the conservative government in Mexico City, a support confirmed by the Mon-Almonte Treaty concluded in September 1859. Thus the United States represented the only major Western power not actively supporting the Zuloaga-Miramón government and the only hope for the liberals in the game of seeking diplomatic recognition. Obviously, for its badly needed recognition certain concessions had to be made, and the concession most wanted by the American government was land. By threatening military intervention and refusing loans to the money-starved liberals, the United States hoped to badger the Mexicans into violating nationalist sentiments and selling Baja California and northern Mexico.

To back up its financial and diplomatic pressure, the United States used a little saber-rattling to force the liberals into giving up land to American expansionism. As early as 1856 Forsyth had suggested to the American government that military intervention would be necessary in Mexico. "The prevalent and growing conviction of intelligent Mexicans," he wrote, "is that without the intervention . . . of the United States . . . no government can maintain itself in this country."[39] Buchanan, in 1859, echoed Forsyth's opinion. He recommended to Congress that the legislature authorize him to send troops at his discretion into Mexico for the purpose of "obtaining indemnization for the past and security for the future."[40] The pretext for such an invasion was Mexican inability to pay the reclamation claims that Americans had lodged against Mexico. Since Mexico had no money, land was to be the form of payment.

When analyzed in this context, the McLane-Ocampo Treaty takes on great significance for Mexican nationalism. The treaty gave up no land to the Americans, but instead pledged the Americans to defend the territorial integrity of Mexico; it granted the United States rights of passage across the Isthmus of Tehuantepec—rights it already had—as well as two rail routes in northern Mexico; and it gave the Americans the right to defend these routes with troops in the case of dire emergency. This last provision was the major concession that the Mexicans had to make, but it seems minor in comparison to what the Americans had demanded at the beginning and to what they could have done with a full-scale military intervention. For this reason, Ocampo could say with much accuracy after the signing of the treaty: "With this treaty the rights and sovereignty of Mexico remain untouched, nothing has been conceded which reduces her dignity, and . . . far from endangering

our nationality, it has assured it."[41] José Fuentes Mares, highly critical of the
treaty, has written that, had the American senate not rejected it, "Juárez
would be today the blackest figure in Mexican history."[42] On the other hand,
Agustín Cué Cánovas expressed a more favorable view: "With the McLane-
Ocampo Treaty liberal diplomacy saved Mexico from both military interven-
tion and territorial dismemberment."[43] Cué Cánovas's position seems to be
closer to the truth: rather than being a defeat for Mexico the McLane-Ocampo
Treaty represents a significant step forward in Mexican nationalism. It made
Mexicans aware of the imperative necessity for every government to preserve
Mexico's territorial integrity in the face of foreign expansion. As Manuel
María de Zamacona put it, "National sovereignty must be inviolable," and the
liberal defense of Mexico during the Reform War proved that "we love our
patria."[44]

When the Reform achieved its victory and returned to Mexico City in 1860,
it immediately set about purging the country of unwelcome foreigners. The
foreign ministers of Spain and Guatemala were expelled for having supported
the conservative government. Juárez, in his address to the reestablished
Congress in May 1861, justified these expulsions. In his view, "national unity
is now a reality and we must maintain this unity in the face of foreign pressures."[45] One way to do this was to exercise the option granted by the Constitution of 1857 of expelling from the country all pernicious foreigners.
Moreover, Congress passed a law requiring all foreigners in Mexico to register
with the federal officials. In the absence of such registration no foreigner
could conduct business or expect protection from the civil courts. This action
received widespread public support.[46] Nevertheless, Mexican patriotism
remained mild in character and expression; foreigners, especially Europeans,
were suspect and distrusted, but not loathed. That would come later. For
now the government planned to cultivate Mexico's foreign relations while
signing treaties "that abandon forever this system of frauds that has done
so much damage to the nation."[47]

When the liberals won the Reform War in December 1860, the conservatives
sought military aid abroad among the European powers who had supported
their cause. Viewed in this way, the French intervention becomes an extension of the civil war just completed, only this time the cast of characters
dramatically expanded. As we have seen, the coming of the French army
and the court of Archduke Maximilian had profound consequences for Mexican liberalism in the nineteenth century, but in no area was that effect so
pronounced as in the area of nationalist attitudes. What during the period
of the Reform had been mild antagonism, centered on the preservation of
Mexican national territory, now became strong anti-foreign hatreds involving
an expanded concept of national sovereignty.

A sense of euphoria pervaded Mexico after the Reform War. Ignacio Ramírez, one of the most articulate of the Reform group, declared that in the last fifty-one years Mexico had seen Spanish, French, and American flags fly on her shores, had lost half her territory to the Yankee imperialists, had been forced into humiliating foreign treaties, and had bowed down to a "petty king" in Rome. But now, Ramírez concluded, with the triumph over the partisans of tradition, Mexico had reached true independence.[48] His analysis could not have been more accurate but his conclusion could not have been more wrong.

Almost as soon as the Reform War reached its dramatic climax at the battle of Calpulalpan, word reached the victorious liberals that European powers were considering intervention. Throughout the year 1861 liberal newspapers stridently denounced such plans and urged the government into vigorous action. *El Progreso* in Veracruz wrote: "Nations are entirely free and independent; of all the rights a nation can have, its sovereignty is without a doubt the most precious." *La Libertad*, holding forth in Durango, expressed the fear that with yet another foreign intervention Mexico "will disappear as a nation in the catalogue of the civilized peoples of the world." Less pessimistically *El Monitor Republicano* voiced its concern over Mexico's future but proclaimed its confidence in the national leadership "because this generation of leaders is more imbued with a nationalist spirit." For these new nationalists, *El Monitor* concluded, "it is better to die than to live enslaved."[49]

The intensity of the newspaper campaign to drum up patriotic sentiments matched the intensity of nationalist feeling within official circles. Ignacio Zaragoza, on the eve of his victory over the French on the fifth of May, 1862, wrote that "a nation, no matter how weak it may appear, should never allow a foreign master to violate her honor and destroy her rights." And José María Arteaga, close friend of Zaragoza and governor of Querétaro, issued an official proclamation calling for "eternal hatred for those that dare profane our soil."[50] Manuel Payno best expressed the frustration of the liberals as the intervention became a reality. "Even if we have revolutions, if our roads are unsafe, if we are uncivilized barbarians, we say, leave us alone!" He invoked international law as protection, saying that Mexicans were the masters of their ancestral lands and that "no one has the right or should even try to make us happy."[51]

Another reaction was congressional rejection of the Wyke-Zamacona Treaty negotiated with Britain in an attempt to head off British participation. Because the treaty gave Britain more control over Mexican customs houses, it was soundly defeated in Congress. "No nation in the world would have accepted such humiliation," Vicente Riva Palacio, president of Congress, explained. "The sovereignty of the nation disappears when it no longer has absolute independence in its smallest actions . . . because a nation, unlike an individual, depends on no one and can have no other master than Providence."

Riva Palacio concluded by affirming Mexico's desire for peace but "never at
the cost of national honor or the sovereignty and independence of Mexico."[52]
Unlike the attitude that prevailed during the American intervention, when to
save Mexico the government had sought a humiliating truce, the new response
of the mid-1860s was to prefer total destruction to humiliation. As Manuel
Ruiz summed up the nationalist attitude: the government is firmly resolved to
meet force with force since it embraces the "firm conviction that the ruin of
the nation is preferable to the humiliation and unjust abuse to which it will
become a victim."[53] The French would find a much different attitude in
Mexico during their intervention than had the Americans during theirs. Because
of the earlier experiences with foreign intervention, Mexican liberals were determined to maintain territorial integrity and national dignity, even at the cost of
the nation itself.

Intervention not only made Mexicans willing to sacrifice themselves, their
property, and their nation but also reinforced a growing Mexican sense of
cultural separation. One of the most crucial developments in any nationalist
movement is the increasing awareness on the part of participants that their
identity is their own and not part of another culture. Without this, nationalism becomes little more than imitation of cultural and political patterns of
other nations. Where independence had begun the process of cultural separation and the American intervention in the 1840s had encouraged it, the French
intervention in the 1860s confirmed it. As *El Monitor Republicano* put it
during the early stages of the allied invasion: Mexico is a country in which
patriotism has finally come alive; it is now "a nation that knows how to make
itself respected." And the paper concluded with the affirmation, "We are
proud to be Mexicans."[54] Each affirmation, such as the one made by *El
Monitor,* also involves a denial. When Mexicans affirmed their Mexican identity,
they simultaneously denied any other cultural affinities. Thus it is not surprising to find Mexicans, faced with the might of the strongest European
armies on their soil, denying attachments to these powers. Francisco Zarco,
surely one of the most perceptive observers of the national scene, reacted
strongly to the allied invasion, affirming his nationalism in editorial after
editorial in his newspaper, *El Siglo XIX*, while denying foreign influences
in Mexico. In one essay, for example, he denied that the Mexican Reform
was influenced by the French, stating categorically: "The Mexican Reform
is not an offshoot of the French Revolution."[55] Although obviously untrue—
the reform of the church was clearly modeled on the French pattern—Zarco's
denial represents a significant movement toward cultural separation.

The failure of France to join England and Spain in withdrawing from the
allied invasion shocked the liberals. France, in spite of Zarco's passionate
rejection, had always been a model for Mexican liberals. French philosophical

rationalism, French music, French art, French literature—all had influenced Mexican thought and culture. Now France, as the Americans had done earlier, seemed bent on an irrational and unjustified attack on a helpless nation. Ignacio Altamirano, waxing eloquent on the disgust that the intervention caused patriotic Mexicans, argued that Napoleon III had been grossly misled about the strength of Mexican national sentiment. He noted that Mexico had somehow managed to survive disaster after disaster—foreign invasions, dictators, civil wars—and was on the verge of making the Reform a reality. He criticized France for attempting to end this progress. After all, France had taught the world about patriotism and nationalism in the first place and was now violating her own traditions and legacy. As Altamirano and the liberals saw it, France was no longer the ideal. "Now," he concluded, "we are only Mexicans, we all aspire to defend our country, we obey no government except that which emanated from the people, we will die for our national sovereignty."[56]

The trilateral European intervention in Mexico proved conclusively to the liberals that there could be no compatibility between the values of the old world and those of the new. France and her allies, Spain and England, stood for monarchy, aristocracy, corporate society, and colonialism—in short, the past. Mexico—and by implication the entire new world including that old enemy, the United States—stood for democracy, progress, reform, and change— in short, the future. Between these two value systems there could be no compromise, only warfare, until one side had irrevocably won the battle.[57] Zarco saw the conflict in these terms and argued that should France be successful in Mexico, the war would expand into all the Americas. Mexico's cause, he said, "is that of all oppressed nationalities." Thus the first duty of all Mexicans is "to save the independence of the patria."[58] Perhaps an unsigned editorial in *El Siglo XIX* best expressed the growing feeling of the uniqueness of the new world: "The land of Columbus has its own soul, its own civilization, a special existence, and for this reason is called the New *World* and not the New *Continent.*"[59] The French intervention completed the process of cultural separation begun by Hidalgo a half-century earlier. After the French intervention there would never be any doubt about Mexico's national existence nor its sense of separation from the culture of the Old World.

Along with the process of cultural separation came a sense of isolation. Mexicans realized that they were alone in the struggle against the intervention. The United States, finding itself not quite as united as the name suggests, was in the midst of a bloody civil war. Europe was doing the invading; there was no one else to turn to. Manuel Payno put the matter succinctly: "We should not fool ourselves; we are alone, completely alone." As he saw it, "the only

way to save our independence is through a united effort by the sons of Mexico."
He called for "peace among Mexicans and war on the enemies of the patria."[60]
Manuel Doblado, the minister of gobernación, expressed similar views of
Mexico's isolation. "The Mexican people," he said, "won their independence
without foreign help . . . and cannot now be enslaved by any nation in the
world." He noted that Mexico was completely dependent on her own resources
and national will; should either be lacking, Mexico, as it had been known until
then, would disappear. Mexico, Doblado argued, "must fight and will fight now
and forever to prove that it has the right to be free, the intelligence to lead, and
the strength to defend the land Providence bestowed on her."[61] Mexico and
her leaders were on their own; whatever success or whatever failure occurred
would rest squarely on Mexican shoulders.

Although the all-pervasive sense of isolation and separation caused much
depression and melancholy among many of the liberals, it also produced some
positive results. In the first place, it caused them to look for the positive
aspects of Mexican culture. Juan Antonio de la Fuente, for example, argued
that independence from foreign rule had been a goal since the time of Hidalgo.
So deeply imbued was that ideal that a foreign army would control only the
territory where it marched; when it left, the people would quickly rally around
the national cause.[62] And *El Boletín de Noticias* in Tampico argued that
although the war would wreak havoc on Mexico, out of it would come a
stronger sense of Mexican nationalism. "We do not fear the loss of our nationality," the paper editorialized, and even suggested that the intervention would
be "useful and necessary" in making Europe respect the territorial integrity
and national sovereignty of Mexico. *El Boletín* also hoped that the presence
of foreigners on Mexican soil would make all citizens aware of Old World vices
so that "no longer will we model ourselves after obsolete Europeans." "The
war is a necessary evil," the paper concluded, "but the struggle with the
foreigners will have favorable results for the nation."[63] Thus some men had
great hope of salvaging a broader, more widespread sense of nationalism out
of the intervention, which in this view would bring on the kind of unity
Mexico had never enjoyed since the days of colonial rule. Love of country,
an end to apathy, expanded patriotism—these were the benefits intervention
would bring. As Guillermo Prieto, José María Iglesias, and the other editors
of the rabidly nationalist newspaper *La Chinaca* put it: "When defense of our
nationality becomes a holy cause and a religion, then Mexico will be saved."[64]

These generalized and increasingly intense attitudes of cultural separation
and isolation had their effects on the treatment of foreigners in Mexico. When
the intervention first began, Mexicans went to great lengths to point out that
foreigners had been well-treated in Mexico, had been given privileges and concessions, and had been encouraged to emigrate to Mexico under the most

favorable of circumstances. As José María Iglesias pointed out, foreigners lived in Mexico under such privileged conditions that many Mexicans tried to change their nationalities in the hopes of securing some of those benefits. Clearly, living in Mexico as a foreigner was better than living there as a Mexican.[65] As the intervention progressed, so too did anti-foreign sentiments, and the first target of Mexican nationalism was the Spanish. Given the long tradition of anti-Spanish sentiment in Mexico, it is logical and fitting that the Spanish should be singled out for vituperative attacks. In the press the Spanish were assailed as never before. *El Monitor Republicano* ridiculed the Spanish argument that they came as a "new Cortés" to liberate Mexico and free it from tyranny and anarchy. For *El Monitor* this argument was sheer nonsense; as it pointed out, the greatest national monument in Mexico at the time was the tree of the Noche Triste where Cortés rested after being routed by the Aztecs. The paper predicted that the Noche Triste would occur again because "the blood of the Mexican people is mostly Aztec and by tradition and conviction they hate the murderers of their fathers."[66] This sense of mestizo pride carried throughout the liberal propaganda during the intervention. Manuel Payno, in analyzing the reasons for Spanish participation in the invasion, pointed out with a mixture of sarcasm and pride that in 1829, during the Spanish reconquest, a handful of mestizos beat "the beautiful and handsome men of pure blood and genuine Spanish race."[67] And Carlos de Gagern, writing to explain the violent Mexican reaction to the intervention, attacked the foreigners who came to Mexico after independence. "They thought themselves superior because they had white skin and blond hair instead of swarthy skin and black hair." "In general," he concluded, "they wanted to treat the masters of the house as the servants."[68]

Such attacks in the press and pamphlet literature had its effects on the treatment of Spaniards in Mexico. Harking back to Hidalgo's 1810 grito, one of the rallying cries of the Mexican army, as it faced the combined armies of France, England, and Spain, was "Death to the Gachupines!" In Guadalajara, with great ceremony, the city council banned bullfighting because "the bullfight is one of the few remaining traces of Spanish domination in Mexico, and it is one of those barbarous and immoral vestiges of a less enlightened century than our own." At the same time, reports flowed in from the countryside telling of violence against Spaniards; in Matehuala nationalist mobs tortured and shot suspected Spaniards.[69]

When Spain and England withdrew their troops from Mexico, the focus of Mexican enmity shifted to France. *La Chinaca* carried hair-raising stories detailing the atrocities commited by the French on their march into Mexico. In particular, *La Chinaca* accused the French of raping Mexican women ("violating virgins," in its words) and labeled the French "savages of civilization." When Maximilian finally established his empire, the Juárez government came under heavy pressure to expel all foreigners, especially Frenchmen, from Mexican territory. Guillermo Prieto, editor of *La Chinaca*, opposed such extreme action but favored the immediate expulsion of any foreigner who supported the intervention and empire. As a result, foreigners were continually expelled from territory controlled by the constitutional army, although loyal foreigners were allowed to remain under government protection.[70]

If the growth of intense anti-foreign sentiment was the first result of the European intervention, an even more intense concern for the preservation of national territory was the second. In contrast to its behavior during the Reform War, the United States was no longer in a position to demand territory as the price for support. Involved in her own civil war, no longer deeply imbued with the expansionist sentiments of Manifest Destiny, the United States made only feeble attempts to secure bits of Mexican territory. These attempts met a stone wall of resistance. When, for example, the American government suggested that the island of Cozumel be sold and used as a colony for freed blacks, the Mexican government rejected the proposal without discussion. For Mexicans, an American colony on Cozumel—even a black one—smacked of Americans in Texas, and they hardly wanted another intervention to follow the one in progress. Perhaps Juárez himself best summed up the nationalist feelings in regard to the alienation of national territory. "The idea that some have," he wrote to Matías Romero, "that we might offer part of the national territory to obtain aid is not only anti-national but prejudicial to our cause. The Nation has clearly expressed its determination not to sell or alienate its territory." In Juárez's view, it was better to be conquered and robbed than to voluntarily give in to demands backed by force.[71]

Similarly, the Reform attitude toward the use of foreign troops on Mexican soil hardened considerably during the course of the intervention. At first, as the liberals lost battle after battle that forced them to retreat into the northern desert, they actively sought American support for their cause. Mexican agents in the United States energetically lined up filibustering expeditions that were to come to the aid of the Mexican side. In early March 1865, Sebastián Lerdo de Tejada, the Mexican minister of foreign affairs, issued instructions to General Gaspar Sánchez Ochoa to go to the United States to negotiate a loan, buy guns and ammunition, and recruit volunteers for an expedition to Mexico.[72] On March 29, Lerdo again turned to the United States for military aid, authorizing Matías Romero in Washington to make an agreement with the American government that would allow American troops to come to Mexico. Lerdo made sure, however, that if the troops came they would "make no attempt against the independence and autonomy of Mexico, nor against its territorial integrity, nor against its republican institutions, nor against the established government."[73] These were serious instructions that have been strongly attacked by anti-Juárez historians. It is clear, nevertheless, that neither Juárez nor his advisers were thrilled with the idea of having foreigners come and fight their battles. In a long letter to Pedro Santacilia, Juárez expressed the hope that the battle could be won without the coming of American troops. At the same time he felt that if the North in the United States won the Civil War and decided to help Mexico, he would be obliged to accept that aid provided it was done "as [by] a friend and not a master . . . without demanding humiliating conditions, without sacrificing an inch of our territory, without reducing national integrity."[74] The constitutionalists knew that inviting foreign troops onto Mexican soil entailed grave risks, yet most felt that without them the French would solidify their control over the country. It was thus a calculated gamble that could have had disastrous consequences for Mexico in the future.

Juárez soon had second thoughts about the wisdom of contracting for official American troops to come to Mexico. Perhaps these stemmed from Romero's own doubts, which he skillfully expressed in a letter to Juárez in August 1865. As a result, in late August Juárez issued instructions to Romero that he no longer negotiate with the American government but instead focus his attention on recruiting private individuals who would be willing to serve in the Mexican army under Mexican command.[75]

These attempts to obtain American assistance on either a formal or informal basis never produced results. To be sure, a few private foreigners attached themselves to the Reform cause, but their numbers never amounted to very many. Clearly, the reticence of the Juárez government in encouraging such activities discouraged large-scale foreign intervention. By the middle of 1866, as the empire of Maximilian began to collapse under the strain of internal dissension, the constitutionalist government officially prohibited the entrance into Mexico of foreigners without special permission from the government. The decree made it plain to all that foreigners would no longer be welcomed.[76] Juárez and his followers had concluded that the beginning of the end of the French intervention was at hand and to encourage further foreign participation in the constitutional cause would blunt the victory.

After the fall of the empire and the execution of Maximilian for the crime of "nationcide," Mexican attitudes toward foreign powers took on unmistakable signs of hostility.[77] Foreign policy was dramatically revised and was no longer conducted in the old fashion of granting foreign nations privileged positions within the Mexican economic system. Jesús Terán, who was serving as special envoy of the Mexican government to Italy and Spain, most forcefully enunciated the new policy even before the execution of Maximilian. Terán, in a letter to Lerdo, expressed the conviction that once the French were defeated Mexico ought to "modify the old treaties with European powers that have injured the Nation so much." He argued that since the European powers had withdrawn recognition of the legitimate national government in Mexico they had also withdrawn recognition of the treaties that the nations had signed in the past. In essence, what Terán was suggesting was that the diplomatic slate had been wiped clean by the intervention, and he urged that Mexico make no move to restore diplomatic relations with the European powers.[78]

Juárez, already leaning in this direction, picked up Terán's policy and adopted it fully. In his first address to Congress after the defeat of the empire he laid down the new "Juárez Doctrine." He noted that although foreigners had been generally well treated in Mexico, all of Europe had joined in or at least had not condemned the intervention. As far as the victorious government was concerned, the old order had been abolished and it was up to Europe to bring on a new one. Mexico, for her part, would not seek diplomatic recognition and would wait for Europe to come to her. Old commercial treaties had been abrogated by the empire, and any new treaties would have to be negotiated "under more just and equitable terms." To this Ezequiel Montes, president of the Congress, replied that all Mexicans welcomed this declaration of independence from onerous foreign treaties. Mexico had proven her right to sovereignty and did not "need any foreign government to recognize her existence as a sovereign Nation."[79] This isolationism lasted a long time, and during the reign of Sebastián Lerdo de Tejada distrust of foreign powers influenced major policy decisions. Lerdo prohibited the building of railroads in the northern provinces because he feared the loss of Mexican territory to the United States. His motto while in office was, "Between strength and weakness, the desert."[80] It was not until 1871 that Spain recognized Mexico; France followed in 1880, and England in 1885.

The new policy had significant meanings for Mexican nationalism. Above all, it demonstrated that Mexico felt herself secure internally. Most Mexicans were sure that the failure of the French intervention signified the end of foreign intervention in Mexican affairs. Many referred to it as the second war for independence, while others saw it as the beginning of a new era in Mexican development. As far as the liberals were concerned, it spelled the end of effective conservative opposition to the liberal nation-building program. And, as Daniel Cosío Villegas has summarized it, "liberals, who before the intervention were divided by ideological and personal reasons, now recognized their common nationalism."[81] For foreigners in Mexico it meant that Mexico would be following a new course in foreign affairs: no more special treaties benefiting foreign agents, sweeping changes in all commercial treaties, and negotiation of treaties along lines more favorable to Mexico.

The French intervention not only changed the way in which foreigners and foreign powers would be treated by Mexico, it also changed the way Mexicans would be treated by their government. Specifically, foreign intervention raised the issue of treason to its highest level. Prior to the French intervention there had been no working concept of treason; now treason was to be the highest crime in the land. All during the intervention the liberal government had refined the notion of treason. In 1863, prior to the evacuation of Mexico City, Congress passed a law making it a treasonous act to remain in territory held by the French. As the Mexican government fled into the desert, it declared traitors all those who served the French forces, all public officials who did not flee, and all who accepted a title from the foreign invaders. Punishment for the crime was severe: confiscation of all property and in some cases death.[82] These laws dramatically expanded the concept of nationalism, for now each Mexican was required to account to the nation-state for his behavior during the war. The state had become the ultimate arbiter of human affairs.

The treason laws were codified in the 1867 *convocatoria,* which removed citizenship from all those who recognized the empire or in any way served it. To regain the status of Mexican, each individual had to apply to the state for "rehabilitation."[83] Needless to say, this policy generated a heated debate. Even those who wanted an expanded concept of treason argued that what the country needed was not further retribution but rather amnesty, harmony, and consolidation. Others argued that only those who voluntarily joined the enemy should be considered traitors. Those who just defended their homes and farms even though in French territory were obeying natural impulses and should not be punished for it. Anti-administration tracts sustained the argument that since the government had fled before the French forces no government existed and therefore there was nothing to betray.[84] Whatever the case, many Mexicans had to wrestle with the problem of what national loyalty entailed, and in doing so they expanded their nationalist consciousness.

The consequences of the French intervention touched every aspect of Mexican life, for above all the intervention was a national experience. Mexicans everywhere—in the urban centers, in rural villages, in the deserts of Chihuahua and Sonora, in the mountains of Guerrero and Oaxaca—had faced difficult choices during those five terrible years. On the one hand, the constitutional government demanded that Mexicans leave their land, their villages, their cities and flee from the French. On the other hand, the French used intense pressure to maintain village support for the empire. Most Mexicans stayed put, instinctively unable to give up their fields and homes. Nevertheless, almost all Mexicans had to make the choice, and in this sense the French intervention brought home to Mexicans that they were Mexicans, that they belonged to a nation larger than the patria chica that had claimed individual loyalty up to that time. As Ernesto de la Torre Villar has observed, the French intervention "stimulated the cohesion of diverse groups who before were unaware that they formed a social, political, and cultural community."[85]

The second most important consequence of the French intervention for the development of nationalism was the total defeat of the partisans of tradition. The anti-Reform movement, which had tried through both civil war and foreign intervention to defeat the reform program, lost everything in the end. The turning to foreign help in this internal struggle left the nationalist field completely open to the partisans of liberalism and reform. The reactionary attempt to justify foreign intervention by arguing that it would protect Mexico from American expansionism was not convincing. More effective was the appeal by the liberal elite to the sentiments of independence and the democratic ideal, an appeal that ultimately combined liberalism and nationalism into an unbreakable combination. Never again in Mexican history would the conservative world-view successfully challenge the liberal nationalism that grew out of the French intervention.

Nation-building and nationalism have a close connection: as the process breaks down intermediary objects of individual loyalty and respect—the church, the privileged army, local political bosses—the nation-state replaces them as the ultimate arbiter of human affairs. Conflict with foreign powers heightens and sharpens the feelings of nationalism that accompany the nation-building movement. In Mexico the foreign pressures of the Reform War and direct foreign intervention in the internal affairs of the country during the empire of Maximilian both served to emphasize the development of Mexican nationalism. After the death of Maximilian in 1867 Mexico's boundaries were maintained, her place in the world of nations was secure, and Benito Juárez's dictum, "Among nations as among individuals, respect for the rights of others is peace," dominated Mexican foreign policy. Mexico took its place in a world of modern nations.

10. The Legacies of the Reform

The Reform was the crucible in which modern Mexico was formed, and it left its mark on every aspect of Mexican life. This chapter will explore the legacies of the Reform in four areas: (1) economic, (2) educational, (3) social, and (4) political. In each area the Reform movement attempted to make changes in the traditional patterns of behavior. Often the results were totally unexpected and even diametrically opposed to those intended.

In no area was this tendency toward unintended consequences more pronounced than in the area of economic development. From the moment the Ayutla group seized office, the need for profound changes in the economic structure was apparent. And yet the liberals had inherited a long tradition of economic analysis that bore little relationship to the realities of nineteenth-century Mexico. What Charles Hale calls the "doctrinaire" approach to economic development germinated with Mora and the liberals of the post-independence era. These liberal economic theorists urged the elimination of corporations and monopolies so that the free operation of a natural economic system could produce beneficial results. The basic assumption underlying the liberal economic arguments was that Mexico was primarily an agricultural and mining country and that to emphasize industrialization would be contrary to Mexico's best economic interests. As Mora put it, to do otherwise was "to try to disregard nature."[1]

Similarly, the Ayutlans envisioned a Mexico consistent with Jefferson's vision of the United States: the heart of the economy was to be found in small landowners. José María Lafragua, in his annual report written for the Ministry of Foreign Affairs in 1847, strenuously argued that agriculture should provide the basis for Mexico's economic development and urged the Mexico government to expand efforts to attract foreign immigrants to Mexican soil. Lafragua hoped that the colonization projects would create a yeoman farmer class that would produce agriculturally and provide the basis for political stability.[2]

During the Constitutional Congress some of the delegates touched on the economic questions of the day. The most famous was Arriaga's call for wholesale subdivision of large estates. Arriaga argued that until the land question was settled there would be no economic development in Mexico. And the dominant problem was that a few individuals monopolized the huge and generally unproductive haciendas while the vast majority of Mexicans "groan[ed] in the most horrendous poverty, without property, without homes, without industry, and without work." Arriaga did not attack the right of private property; in fact, he repeatedly emphasized that right as the basis of society. But he attacked the unjust distribution, the warped social relations, and the economic decay that the large estates represented. "Our people," he observed, "will never be free, or republican, or even prosperous, despite hundreds of constitutions and thousands of laws proclaiming abstract rights and beautiful theories . . . because of our absurd economic system."[3]

That the Congress, made up as it was of liberals who believed that private property was a natural and inviolable right, refused to accept Arriaga's program is hardly surprising. Besides, the reformers had other, more palatable solutions to the land question. For them, the greatest evil was not the hacienda (although many recognized it as potentially dangerous); rather, they saw in the Indian communal holdings and entailed ecclesiastical real estate the chief source of economic backwardness. During their early political careers, many of the delegates had participated in state and local attempts to break up both the traditional Indian communities and church holdings. In Jalisco, Veracruz, Zacatecas, and Michoacán—all in the liberal circle—Indian communities in particular had been subjected to forced subdivisions. These local efforts had been supported by liberal writers like Mora, particularly because the liberals saw little hope for economic development in the Indians.[4] The defeat of Arriaga's proposal was based on liberal concern for the rights of private property, not defense of concentrated landholdings.

The Ley Lerdo was the liberal solution to the problem of economic underdevelopment. As we saw in chapter 7, the principal goal of the law was to remove land from corporate control and sell it to a large number of buyers, who would then constitute the landed yeoman class. The sales would be taxed as a principal source of government revenue. Capital would begin to flow, creating more capital. Soon funds would be available for investment, and the vicious cycle of poverty and instability would be broken.

Although the law covered all corporations—including municipalities, guilds, and lay brotherhoods—its chief targets were the church and the Indian communities. And by far the largest landowner was the church. The subject of what happened to church property has been the focus of research by Jan

Bazant, and his findings suggest several important conclusions about the liberal nation-building movement. One of the most important is that the liberals themselves were prominent purchasers of ecclesiastical property. Miguel Lerdo de Tejada, the author of the law, purchased church property in Mexico City worth over 33,000 pesos. Other liberal leaders whose names appear on the lists of those adjudicating ecclesiastical property include Ignacio Comonfort, José María Iglesias, Juan Antonio de la Fuente, and Manuel Payno. All of them bought property worth more than 20,000 pesos. Payno paid over 90,000 for his real estate. Even Benito Juárez purchased a house in Oaxaca for 3,200 pesos.[5]

Several aspects of these purchases are striking. The first is that the liberals had enough capital to buy such expensive pieces of property. Although few of the liberal leadership were property owners before the Ley Lerdo, obviously many of them had used public office and their professional education to accumulate capital reserves.

A second important conclusion that comes from an examination of the buyers of ecclesiastical property is that by the end of 1857 the Ley Lerdo had created around 9,000 new landowners, most of whom had been landless prior to the Reform. Many of the buyers were merchants, professionals, and trades-men.[6] These groups became the backbone of the liberal movement. For example, the Veracruz merchants who had purchased disamortized ecclesiastical property openly welcomed the Juárez government when the Tacubaya rebellion drove it from Mexico City. And the conservatives never received support from the hacendados, who looked upon the disamortization process as a means of expanding their holdings and getting out from under heavy ecclesiastical mortgages. Thus, the liberal land program appealed to a large number of individuals who in turn supported the liberal cause when it was challenged.

The Ley Lerdo did accomplish one major liberal goal: it destroyed the economic base of ecclesiastical politics. But it did not increase the mobility of property in the long run. Those who bought the land held on to it. Moreover, because so much land was put on the market simultaneously, the values were severely depressed. The net result of both tendencies was to produce far less revenue for the government than had been expected. Nor did the disamortization establish the basis for agricultural and industrial develop-ment in Mexico. So much capital was absorbed in the purchase of ecclesias-tical real estate that little was left for investment and capital improvements. And, finally, the Ley Lerdo did not create a rural middle class. The reports of the Ministry of Hacienda indicate that the vast majority of clerical prop-erty was located in urban centers and that very few rural haciendas were sold. The Ley Lerdo, at least as applied to ecclesiastical holdings, did little to further the yeoman farmer ideal.[7]

Those rural lands that were disamortized belonged for the most part to the Indian communities. It has often been argued that the Ley Lerdo was not directed toward these unfortunate organizations and that the destruction of the Indian ejido lands occurred under Porfirio Díaz, who had altered the liberal desires for the benefit of the emerging haciendas.[8] The facts speak otherwise. The archive of Mariano Riva Palacio, long-time governor of the state of Mexico, is full of complaints, petitions, and reports of rebellions by Indians who were losing their village lands. And when Lerdo was asked to limit the scope of the law, he replied: "Unquestionably the continued existence of the Indian communities ought not to be tolerated . . . and this is exactly one of the principal goals of the law."[9] Even Comonfort added to the hard line on Indian land reform. On January 5, 1857, he issued a law on vagrancy defining a vagrant as one who was over sixteen years of age and did not work at least three days a week. Punishment was automatic conscription into the army or work at a correctional institution.[10] Had this law been enforced, its effect would have been to drive many villagers into peonage.

T. G. Powell has studied the effects of the Ley Lerdo on the villagers of central Mexico, and his conclusions present a bleak picture.[11] In general, the liberal land policy was a tragedy for much of rural Mexico. Because liberals viewed the Indian with such disrespect and saw the villages as prime obstacles to economic development, the policies adopted by the Reform government were disastrous for the communal way of life. Village after village began to find hacendados denouncing communal land before the local judge. Lands that had been farmed for centuries by the same village were suddenly sold to the highest bidder. And though the law stipulated that the former owners were to have first opportunity to buy, few Indians had the capital to pay the purchase price.

The rate of disamortization of communal lands varied according to the strength of the liberal government. During the 1856-1857 period, many villages were forced to sell off communal pastures and crop land. During the Reform War and the French intervention, however, little disamortization activity took place in the countryside. In all probability this was the result of the liberals' desire to attract support for the constitutional cause. But once the republic had been restored, the disamortization practice continued vigorously. One of the main reasons behind the energetic policy was that the states were allowed to tax the forced sale of property. With few resources at their disposal, they found the tax potential of the relatively helpless villages too tempting to overlook.[12]

An obvious result of the stringent enforcement of the Ley Lerdo in the countryside was constant rebellion. Although some villages simply disappeared quietly, many did not. Throughout central Mexico Indians rebelled, frequently joined by highway robbers. The hacendados and *jefes políticos* organized to protect themselves. Each side issued justifications, with the hacendados calling the peasants "communists."[13] The federal government found itself forced to spend huge sums to pay for the army and the rurales to put down the rebellions. During the Restored Republic, even though the conservatives had been thoroughly defeated, the military budget averaged over 36 percent of the total.[14]

A second effect of the Ley Lerdo on the rural communities was to reduce them to abject misery. All the statistics and figures that exist on rural Mexico in the aftermath of the Reform suggest the prevalence of high infant mortality, low life expectancy, low levels of food consumption, increase in peonage, and much sickness, alcoholic consumption, disorganization, and death.[15] For relief many ex-villagers sought refuge on the haciendas. There they could count on some semblance of stability, some protection from rampant exploitation, and the possibility of medical care.

A third consequence of the dissolution of the communal lands is less well documented than either rebellion or misery. Almost every observer of post-Reform Mexico has suggested that the most dramatic effect of the application of the Ley Lerdo to rural Mexico was the remarkable growth of the hacienda. As yet, there has been no systematic and quantitative study of the buyers of Indian lands or the size of the property accumulated. There is little doubt that much of the land placed on the market by the disamortization law went into the hands of the rural estates. And it is not surprising that the hacienda and not the small farmer became the dominant land-holding structure throughout Mexico during the Díaz years.[16]

Although land reform was at the heart of the liberal program, attempts were made to stimulate certain industries. José María Lafragua, in a speech opening an 1856 industrial exposition in Mexico City, urged his fellow liberals to use the state to promote industrial development in order to "spread well-being to those less well off, to pull thousands out of misery and vice, and, by increasing public wealth, to form a society that will serve as a barrier to revolution."[17] But in fact there was little industrial base on which to build. Perhaps the most important industry was the manufacture of textiles, and even in this old and well-established enterprise there was little growth and development. Constantly hampered by lack of cotton, lack of energy (in 1900 half the mills ran on human and horse power), substantial contraband, little internal market, and arbitrary taxation, the textile industry contributed little to Mexican economic development.[18]

Nothing hurt the textile industry more than the obvious lack of adequate transportation facilities. And the Juárez government during the Restored Republic actively sought funds for the construction of a railroad link between

Mexico City and Veracruz. In 1860 Mexico had only fifteen miles of usable track. Even after the Mexico City-Veracruz line was completed in 1872 Mexico still had less than two-hundred miles of serviceable roadbed. By 1876 the mileage had increased to four-hundred, but in a country as large as Mexico it was hardly sufficient to aid in the national integration of either the political system or the economy.[19]

Thus the liberal economic program of the Reform left two principal legacies to the future. The first was a land reform program that created a new group of urban landowners and an increased number of rural proletariat to provide labor for the hacienda. The second legacy was economic dependency. Because the internal efforts were directed almost exclusively at the land question, investment had to be sought abroad. And there were only two choices, Europe and the United States. For a variety of reasons—Mexico's reputation abroad, the difficulties the English had in completing the Mexico City-Veracruz line, lack of diplomatic relations, anti-European sentiments in Mexico—few European investors were willing to risk capital in Mexico. Juárez and Lerdo entered into protracted negotiations with American companies to build more railroads. The result would not appear until the 1880s, but the policies of the Restored Republic created close economic ties between Mexico and the United States, ties that many see today as the beginning of Mexico's dependency on the economic well-being of its northern neighbor.[20]

Having achieved the triumph of liberal ideology, the Reform leaders wanted to impose their victory on the rest of Mexico through education. As we saw in chapter 2, the leadership had been molded in the new secular institutes in the provinces. And liberals constantly urged an expansion of the educational system. As Juárez put it in the Veracruz decrees of 1859, "Education is the cornerstone of prosperity of a people; at the same time it is the most effective way to make abuses of power impossible."[21]

But once again, as with economic development, the press of political events limited the amount of effort or money that the liberals could put into spreading the dominant ideology. For one thing, they had little to work with: at mid-century, there were only 122 schools of all kinds in Mexico City, and of these only four were government schools. The rest were private, usually clerical. This pattern repeated itself throughout the republic.[22] Thus article 3 of the Constitution of 1857, which established free education in Mexico, was more a wish than a law.[23]

Even so, liberals continued to hope that through education the liberal vision of man could be disseminated nationwide. No sooner had the liberals won the Reform War in 1861 than Juárez issued a series of decrees on education; he created the National Preparatory School, a school for deaf-mutes, and new schools of medicine, jurisprudence, mining, and the arts.[24]

The French intervention forced a delay in the educational plans of the Reform, but once the constitutional government had been reestablished in Mexico City in 1867, Juárez created a national commission on education to draw up a plan of action. Directed by Gabino Barreda, the commission drafted an organic law on public instruction that the government issued on December 2, 1867. It decreed free, obligatory primary education, it required all cities to establish primary schools, and it established the course of study for various advanced degrees. In his annual report to Congress, the minister of public instruction, Antonio Martínez de Castro, surveyed the state of education in 1867. He found that there were only 246 schools in Mexico City, with 7,492 students (out of a total population of around 230,000).[25]

Under Barreda's guiding slogan, "Liberty, Order, and Progress," the liberal program for education came to life. Barreda made logic and positivism the basis for the new education, and emphasized that the state had the duty to force people into school. As José Díaz Covarrubias said: "We know of no right that allows a choice between education and ignorance." And the schools multiplied rapidly: in 1843 there were 1,310 primary schools in the nation; in 1857 there were 1,424; in 1870 the number had tripled to 4,570 and in 1874 had reached over 8,000. But even with this rapid growth, few children went to school; in fact, fewer than 20 percent.[26]

To accompany the emphasis on education, the liberals wrote their own textbooks. In particular, Manuel Payno's *Compendio de la historia de México* became the national history text. In it he demoted the conservative heroes like Cortés and Iturbide and emphasized the liberal tradition of Hidalgo and Juárez. He used the didactic method of question and answer (in obvious imitation of the Catholic catechism) to condemn the church, Spain, the colonial period, and the opponents of the Reform. At the same time, he stressed citizenship and nationalism. The result was to make a myth of the Reform, a myth that has dominated Mexican history and education ever since.[27]

Although the Reform succeeded in organizing a modern nation-state by 1876, its social legacy is one of failure. By destroying the charity functions of the church, by eliminating the protective legislation governing the ejido, by abolishing the *fueros* of the military, the church, and the guilds, the liberal nation-building program removed all intermediary institutions that interfered with individual loyalty to the state. At the same time, the process left the individual vulnerable to extreme exploitation both economically and politically. Within the liberal conception of the state as an essentially passive instrument of peace-keeping, nothing took up the social welfare functions of the traditional corporations. The result was a legacy of uncontrolled exploitation and an ever-increasing gulf between rich and poor.

Clearly, the most important legacy the Reform left to modern Mexico was the political solution it constructed for the crisis of national survival. The contrasts between pre- and post-Reform Mexico are striking. Prior to the liberal nation-building movement, Mexico's very existence was threatened. Constant political instability, financial insolvency, coups and counter-coups, foreign invasion and territorial dismemberment, powerful intermediary institutions of doubtful loyalty—these were the characteristics of Mexico before the Ayutla movement. With the defeat of the conservative-French alliance, the liberals were able to establish regular and orderly government. There was only one coup in the last twenty-five years of the nineteenth century, compared to forty-five in the first quarter century after independence. Indeed, what is remarkable about the post-Reform political structure is how little turnover and mobility existed as the century drew to a close. This political hardening of the arteries was to have drastic consequences when the ruling elites failed to agree on a successor to Porfirio Díaz in 1910.

Although there have been many modifications, the basic political structure created by the Reform has persisted. The constitutional dictatorship was the liberals' solution to the problem of law and order. Juárez and Lerdo both governed as dictators within the framework of the Constitution of 1857. Díaz simply extended the techniques, attitudes, and style of his liberal cohorts. He took the new technology of railroads, telegraph, guns, and even automobiles and refined a political system that received the respect and admiration of much of the western world.

This was not what the early Ayutlans had in mind. They had envisioned a Mexico ruled by a parliamentary democracy that protected individual rights. Instead, the pressure of events and the realities of nineteenth-century Mexico made the constitutional dictatorship a necessity. The result was a system that valued machine politics over democracy and order over liberty.[28] "Mucha administración, poca política." That was the catch phrase of the liberal dictatorship.

At the same time, the liberals established a pattern of subordinating powerful corporations to the will of the state. The Reform destroyed neither the Catholic Church nor the Indian community. Instead, both were subjected to severe attacks that limited their scope of action. Although the liberal nation-building movement began with the hope of a legal separation of church and state, the secularization program brought the ecclesiastical corporation under the fist of the state. The nation began to regulate almost every aspect of clerical activity, even to the point of forcing the clergy to celebrate such national holidays as the 16th of September. In this way, corporatism was fused with nation-building, a process that has continued into the multi-sector structure of the modern political system in Mexico.

The success of the liberal nation-building program permanently eliminated the appeal of the conservative ideology. All political activity after the restoration of the republic was in the name of the Constitution of 1857. For example, when Porfirio Díaz rebelled in 1871, he claimed that Juárez had violated the spirit of the constitution by having himself reelected. Similarly in 1876, Díaz launched the Revolution of Tuxtepec in the name of "effective suffrage, no reelection." And even when Venustiano Carranza saw the need for a new constitution in Mexico during the Revolution of 1910-1920, his ultimate constitutional proposal envisioned only a slight modification of the 1857 document. Political liberalism thus became the dominant ideology and has continued to be the "official" ideology today.

As part of the liberal political legacy a new set of national heroes emerged. The exploits of Benito Juárez, Melchor Ocampo, Ignacio Zaragoza, Miguel and Sebastián Lerdo de Tejada, Mariano Escobedo, José María Lafragua, Guillermo Prieto, Ignacio Ramírez, and Vicente Riva Palacio are now synonymous with Mexican nationalism. Their names grace streets, parks, plazas, and even towns and cities in Mexico. The two main streets in Mexico City are called "El Paseo de la Reforma" and "Benito Juárez." The main plaza (or *zócalo*) is "Plaza de la Constitución." In the Alameda, the wooded park near the center of the city, stands a white marble hemi-cycle in honor of Juárez. Here official celebrations take place on his birthday, on the day he issued the Reform Laws, and on the day he died. In the National Palace a room has been set aside as a museum to Juárez, and in the Museum of Anthropology in Chapultepec Park the last sign a visitor sees as he leaves the second floor contains the Juárez dictum: "Respect for the rights of others is peace."

This, then, was the Mexican Reform. The liberals of the mid-nineteenth century faced two overwhelming crises: the problem of establishing a legitimate national government and the need to forge a Mexican national identity. How they met and resolved those crises has been the subject of this book. Other crises—the question of penetration, or participation, or distribution—were left aside until much later. Indeed, the participation crisis came only at the turn of the century, when new men like Francisco Madero, Alvaro Obregón, and Plutarco Elías Calles challenged a Porfirian system whose arteries had hardened beyond repair. The penetration problem found its solution under the Sonoran dynasty in the 1920s with the formation of a single, national political party. Today it is through the modern incarnation of that mechanism, the Partido Revolucionario Institucional, that the effective control of the Mexican government takes place. The central issue still unresolved is that of distribution. Fundamentally, this question found its clearest expression in the Zapatista rebellion in south-central Mexico during the violent years 1910-1920. Since then, every government has had to struggle with the question of how to distribute the fruits of Mexican development. The degree to which the Mexican political elite can fashion a more equitable distribution system is the degree to which the authoritarian system as it has emerged from the Reform can survive.

Appendices

APPENDIX A

THE REFORM LEADERS

Name	Dates	Birthplace	Race	Education	Principal Occupation	Socio-economic Status at Birth
Ignacio Altamirano	1834-1893	Tixtla, Guerrero	Indian	Literary Institute of Toluca	Journalist, teacher	Poor
Ponciano Arriaga	1811-1863	San Luis Potosí, San Luis Potosí	Mestizo	Law Degree	Politics; exiled by Santa Anna	
Miguel María Arrioja	1807-1867	Puebla, Puebla			Bureaucrat (diplomacy); exiled by Santa Anna	
Juan José Baz	1820-1887	Guadalajara, Jalisco		Lancastrian School (Jalisco); Seminario (Mexico City)	Gov., D.F. (1846); Journalist; exiled (1853)	
Ignacio Comonfort	1812-1863	Puebla, Puebla	Creole	Colegio Militar	Military (Lt. Col.); fired from bureaucratic post by Santa Anna	Moderately wealthy
Santos Degollado	1811-1861	Guanajuato, Guanajuato	Mestizo	Law	Military lawyer, prof. of law	Poor—father's property confiscated for supporting Hidalgo
Juan Antonio de la Fuente	1814-1867	Saltillo, Coahuila	Mestizo	Law (1837)	Politics	Poor orphan
Ignacio de la Llave	1818-1863	Orizaba, Veracruz	Mestizo		Military (Lt. Col.); in 1855; gov. of Veracruz	Poor

APPENDIX A (Continued)

Name	Dates	Birthplace	Race	Education	Principal Occupation	Socio-economic Status at Birth
Porfirio Díaz	1830-1915	Oaxaca, Oaxaca	Mestizo	Institute of Sciences and Arts (Oaxaca)	Military	Poor orphan
Manuel Doblado	1818-1865	San Pedro Gorda, Guanajuato	Creole	Law degree	Politics (local caudillo)	Extreme poverty
Mariano Escobedo	1826-1902	Galena, Nuevo León			Military	
Manuel Gutiérrez Zamora	1813-1861	Veracruz, Veracruz		Primary	Merchant; exiled by Santa Anna; mayor of Veracruz	
Jesús González Ortega	1822-1881	Zacatecas, Zacatecas	Mestizo		Military; ordered shot by Santa Anna	Poor
José María Iglesias	1832-1891	Mexico City		Law	Bureaucrat; fired by Santa Anna	
Benito Juárez	1806-1872	Guelatao, Oaxaca	Indian	Institute of Sciences and Arts (Oaxaca), law degree	Politics; gov. of Oaxaca; exiled (1853)	Poor orphan
José María Lafragua	1813-1875	Puebla, Puebla	Creole	State U. of Puebla, law degree	Politics; exiled (1853)	Poor, father retired Lt. Col.
Miguel Lerdo de Tejada	1812-1861	Veracruz, Veracruz	Creole		Merchant, minor government official	Middle class
Sebastián Lerdo de Tejada	1823-1889	Jalapa, Veracruz	Creole	Minor orders; San Ildefonso	Rector, San Ildefonso	Middle class
Ignacio Mariscal	1829-1910	Oaxaca, Oaxaca		Institute of Sciences and Arts (Oaxaca), law degree	Lawyer, exiled by Santa Anna	
José María Mata	1819-1895	Jalapa, Veracruz	Mestizo	Medical degree	Medicine, exiled by Santa Anna	Middle class

APPENDIX A (Continued)

Name	Dates	Birthplace	Race	Education	Principal Occupation	Socio-economic Status at Birth
Ezequiel Montes	1820-1883	Cadereyta, Querétaro	Creole	Law degree	Lawyer, professor of law	Middle class
Melchor Ocampo	1814-1861	Pateo, Michoacán	Father unknown, mother creole	Law degree	Lawyers, gov. of Michoacán	
Pedro Ogazón	1824-1890	Guadalajara, Jalisco		Lawyer	Lawyer-soldier, joined army 1846, fought with Comonfort; gov. of Jalisco (1860); min. of war (1876)	Cousin of I. Vallarta
Manuel Payno	1810-1894	Mexico City	Creole		Bureaucrat, min. of hacienda (1850-51); journalist, author (*Los bandidos de Río Frío*)	Nephew of A. Bustamante
Guillermo Prieto	1818-1897	Mexico City	Mestizo		Journalist, poet	Poor
Ignacio Ramírez	1818-1879	San Miguel Allende, Guanajuato	Mestizo	Law degree	Lawyer, journalist, prof. of law; imprisoned by Santa Anna	Father lower gov. bureaucrat
Mariano Riva Palacio	1803-1880	Mexico City	Creole (married mestiza)		Politics; exiled by Santa Anna	

APPENDIX A (Continued)

Name	Dates	Birthplace	Race	Education	Principal Occupation	Socio-economic Status at Birth
Vicente Riva Palacio	1832-1896	Mexico City	Mestizo	Law degree	Politics, military (general)	Son of wealthy landowner
Matías Romero	1837-1898	Oaxaca, Oaxaca	Creole	Institute of Sciences and Arts (Oaxaca), law degree (1853)	Bureaucrat	
Manuel Ruiz	1822-1871	Oaxaca, Oaxaca		Institute of Sciences and Arts (Oaxaca), law degree (1845)	Politics; exiled by Santa Anna	
Jesús Terán Peredo	1821-1866	Aguascalientes, Aguascalientes		Law degree	Politics (*jefe político* of Aguascalientes)	
Ignacio Vallarta	1830-1893	Guadalajara, Jalisco		Institute of Sciences and Arts (Jalisco), law degree	Lawyer	
Leandro Valle	1833-1861	Mexico City	Mestizo	Colegio Militar	Military	Poor
José María Vigil	1829-1909	Guadalajara, Jalisco		Law degree	Journalist, prof. of Latin	
Ignacio Zaragoza	1829-1862	Bahía de Espíritu Santo, Texas		Colegio Militar	Military	Father captain in army
Francisco Zarco	1829-1869	Durango, Durango	Mestizo	College of Mines and Laws (Durango)	Journalist, bureaucrat	Poor, father in army

APPENDIX B

ROLL CALL VOTES

Variable Number	To Decide Whether	Riker Co-efficient of Significance
01	To restore the Constitution of 1824. (Moderates wanted to use it as a base for new constitution; radicals opposed.) Defeated: 38-40 *(Actas:* 39-40,* pp. 17-19)**	.3392
02	To approve the Ley Juárez abolishing *fueros* of Catholic Church and military. Passed: 70-13 *(Actas:* 71-13, p. 108; law ultimately passed 82-1)	.1344
03	To approve the decree by the government that annulled the 1853 law by Santa Anna establishing the number of generals in the army. Passed: 63-15 *(Actas:* 64-15, p. 139; approval was unanimous in final vote)	.1249
04	To prorogue the term of the Second Commission of Gobernación, which was considering President Comonfort's decree of 12 May 1856 allowing him to appoint members of the Council of State. (A negative vote was against the president. Vote in secret.) Defeated: 39-52 (p. 175)	.3943
05	To approve the motion to repeal sections 51 and 52 of the executive budget allocating funds for the *comandancias generales* (military government in the states.) Defeated: 25-54 *(Actas:* 26-55, p. 180)	.2323
06	To approve the motion to revoke the ruling of the Supreme Court declaring that Santiago Vidaurri (governor of Nuevo León) had acted illegally in joining the states of Nuevo León and Coahuila. Defeated: 36-57 (p. 187)	.3767
07	(Secret session) To annul the law of 19 September 1853 by Santa Anna allowing the Jesuits to reenter Mexico. Passed: 78-15 (p. 201)	.1891
08	To approve the Ley Lerdo prohibiting corporations from owning property, particularly the church. Passed: 77-14 (*Actas:* 78-15, p. 239)	.1891
09	To approve the commission report that declared that the government is not empowered to make objections to or observations on the decrees and resolutions of the Sovereign Constituent Congress. Passed: 63-26 *(Actas:* 64-17, p. 242)	.2817
10	To approve article 4 of the proposed constitution: No law can be made retroactive. Passed: 73-17 (p. 270)	.1977

* The vote totals have been adjusted for clerical error. The votes in parentheses are the official totals from the *Actas oficiales y minutario de decretos del Congreso Extraordinario Constituyente de 1856-1857.*

** Page where vote can be found in *Actas.*

APPENDIX B (Continued)

Variable Number	To Decide Whether	Riker Co-efficient of Significance
11	To approve article 6 of the proposed constitution: All men have the right to keep and bear arms for their security and legitimate defense. Passed: 67-21 (pp. 275-276)	.2242
12	To approve article 7 of proposed constitution: In times of peace no soldier can demand quartering, beasts of burden, or any other real or personal service without the consent of the owner. In times of war these may be requested only as the law prescribes. Passed: 71-16 (p. 277)	.1705
13	To provide for the seizure or registration of public mail in cases of "grave national interest" (Art. 8 of proposed constitution). Defeated: 25-57 (p. 278)	.2324
14	To guarantee that no one can be obliged to provide personal services without fair compensation and full consent (Art. 12). Passed: 43-37 (pp. 284-285)	.3304
15	To stipulate that no law can authorize any contract that has as its object the loss or irrevocable sacrifice of human liberty whether through occupation, education, or religious vow. Passed: 69-22 (p. 286)	.2425
16	To guarantee that the expression of ideas cannot be the object of any judicial or administrative trial except in cases that attack morality, provoke some crime or transgression, or disturb the public order. Passed: 55-29 (pp. 293-294)	.2954
17	To approve article 15: No law shall be passed that limits or prohibits the exercise of any religious cult. Defeated: 42-65 *(Actas:* 44-67, p. 308)	.5307
18	To approve freedom of education. Passed: 64-15 (pp. 319-320)	.1249
19	To limit the kinds of petitions Congress can receive. Defeated: 21-59 (pp. 323-324)	.1875
20	To stipulate that there shall be no private or government monopolies or protective tariffs for industry. Passed: 63-16 (pp. 325-326)	.1338
21	To approve trial by jury. Defeated: 40-42 (p. 334)	.3664
22	To discuss the abolition of mutilation, excessive fines, and confiscations of property as punishments for crimes. Defeated: 33-46 (p. 340)	.2857
23	(Secret) To require that each cabinet minister be expelled from the floor of Congress when matters related to his office are discussed. Passed: 50-38 *(Actas:* 51-39, p. 362)	.3942
24	To establish that all legislative power shall be deposited in one legislative body called the Congress of the Union. Passed: 44-38 (p. 373)	.3485
25	To call the question on whether to abolish the death penalty on the establishment of a penitentiary system. Passed: 46-33 *(Actas:* 47-34, p. 347)	.3038
26	To approve the abolition of the death penalty on the establishment of a penitentiary system. Passed: 65-16 (p. 347)	.1430

APPENDIX B (Continued)

Variable Number	To Decide Whether	Riker Co-efficient of Significance
27	To establish that in Congress each deputy shall represent 40,000 persons and there shall be one deputy for any fraction over 20,000. Passed: 45-35 (p. 381)	.3126
28	To limit the power of Nuevo León to annex the major municipalities of Coahuila. Passed: 44-35	.3035
29	To include as residents of a state those born in the state, thus allowing natives of a given state to serve in Congress even though they may not live there. Defeated: 38-41 (pp. 398-399)	.3303
30	To grant Congress the authority to permit two or more states to join together should the respective state legislatures request such a union. Defeated: 34-49 (p. 404)	.3129
31	To grant Congress the authority to permit parts of states with more than 80,000 inhabitants to request the formation of a separate state. Passed: 45-36 (p. 405)	.3216
32	To grant Congress the authority to establish tariffs on foreign trade. Passed: 50-32 (p. 408)	.2950
33	To grant Congress the authority to establish mints, determine the foreign exchange rate, and establish the weights and measures. Passed: 60-21 (p. 411)	.1877
34	To stipulate that the election of the president will be secret and indirect. Passed: 52-29 (p. 433)	.2591
35	To require the president to swear an oath of loyalty on taking office. Passed: 58-24 (p. 435)	.2235
36	To grant the president the authority to establish all types of ports, to fix maritime and border customs houses, and to designate their location. Passed: 67-10 *(Actas:* 68-11, p. 441)	
37	To grant the president the authority to commute the sentences of criminals sentenced by federal courts. Passed: 42-41 (p. 447)	.3755
38	To establish that federal courts have authority over cases involving: (1) laws or acts by any authority that violate individual guarantees; (2) laws or acts of the federal government that restrict the sovereignty of the states; (3) laws or acts of the states that enter the sphere of federal authority. Passed: 45-35 *(Actas:* 46-36, p. 463)	.3307
39	To stipulate that cases in federal courts will be heard before a jury composed of local citizens. Passed: 56-27 (p. 464)	.2504
40	To stipulate that the president, cabinet ministers, justices of the Supreme Court, district judges, and circuit judges shall be subject to a "juicio político" for any abuse or mistake committed while in office. Defeated: 26-53 (pp. 472-473)	.2231
41	To prohibit states from forming an alliance, signing a treaty, or forming a coalition with any other state or foreign power. Passed: 51-28 (p. 476)	.2410
42	To prohibit the states from issuing currency or "papel sellado." Passed: 64-15 (p. 477)	.1249

APPENDIX B (Continued)

Variable Number	To Decide Whether	Riker Co-efficient of Significance
43	To establish that the circuit and district courts are the federal agents responsible for issuing and forcing compliance with all federal laws. Defeated: 20-59 (p. 480)	.1696
44	To establish that the governors of the states are obliged to publish and force compliance with all federal laws. Passed: 55-24 (p. 484)	.2053
45	To stipulate that it is the obligation of the federal government to conserve the union and public order in the interior of the federation. Passed: 49-28 *(Actas:* 50-29, p. 488)	.2499
46	To limit the taxing powers of the states to direct taxes only; the federal government can levy all indirect taxes and has full authority over *terrenos baldíos.* Defeated: 24-55 (p. 491)	.2053
47	To establish that federal courts shall hear cases involving cabinet ministers, justices of the Supreme Court, and deputies of the Federal Congress but only after Congress has authorized the suit. Defeated: 14-67 (p. 495)	.1252
48	To require all public officials, without exceptions, to swear an oath to uphold the Constitution and its laws on taking office. Passed: 54-24 (*Actas:* 55-25, pp. 495-496)	.2233
49	To establish that the accused in a crime does not automatically have the right to confront his accuser but must be granted that right on request. Defeated: 38-41 (p. 499)	.3303
50	To prohibit all punishments involving shackles, chains, and irons. Defeated: 33-47 (p. 500)	.2947
51	To stipulate that in cases of grave national emergency only the president, with the approval of Congress, can suspend constitutional guarantees, with the exception of those protecting human life. Passed: 49-31 (p. 506)	.1072
52	To establish the procedure for passing laws in Congress, including presidential review before final passage. Passed: 49-31 (p. 506)	.2769
53	To permit the reform of the Constitution by a two-thirds vote of Congress and an affirmative vote by a majority of the state legislatures. Passed: 67-13 (p. 512)	.1161
54	To stipulate that a majority of state legislatures must approve the creation of any new state by Congress. Passed: 51-26 *(Actas:* 52-27, pp. 515-516)	.2321
55	To create the state of the Valley of Mexico, thus abolishing the present D.F. Passed: 60-30 (vote reconstructed from previous vote, p. 530)	.3138
56	To establish the Federal District in Querétaro. Defeated: 43-45 (p. 532)	.4207
57	To remove from the state of Mexico the districts of Cuautla and Cuernavaca and give them to the state of Guerrero. Defeated: 33-48.	.2948
58	To maintain the present boundaries of the state of Mexico. Passed: 43-38 (p. 540)	.3395

APPENDIX B (Continued)

Variable Number	To Decide Whether	Riker Co-efficient of Significance
59	To establish that the election for national political office be carried out in the electoral juntas. Passed: 51-31 (p. 572)	.2860
60	To authorize the electoral juntas to instruct their representatives as to how to vote on certain issues. Defeated: 35-44 (p. 579)	.3035
61	To exempt members of the military from the residency requirements for the Chamber of Deputies. Defeated: 15-65 (p. 584)	.1340
62	To reserve for Congress the authority to grant permission to members of Congress and justices of the Supreme Court to take leaves of absence. Passed: 65-21 (pp. 590-591)	.2151
63	To require public juries to make sure that the free education established by the Constitution does not offend public morality. Defeated: 40-41 (pp. 598-599)	.3573
64	To amend art. 33 of the Constitution (which abolished the death penalty on completion of a penitentiary system) to abolish the death penalty in five years (even if the prison system is incomplete). Defeated: 37-43 *(Actas:* 39-45, pp. 599-600).	.3666
65	To approve the request by the commission of the Constitution to retire permanently article 15 (freedom of religion). Passed: 57-22 (p. 610)	.1874
66	To abolish all judicial costs. Passed: 66-15 (p. 611)	.1341
67	To amend the Constitution by removing all residency requirements for election to the Congress (2/3 vote necessary to suspend rules). Defeated: 44-36 *(Actas:* 45-37, p. 614)	.3396
68	To give Congress the authority to name and remove the general treasurer of the nation. Passed: 41-38 (pp. 620-621)	.3303
69	To subject parochial obventions to the laws (an attempt to reform the abolition of parochial fees subject to a law indicating how the state will replace the lost funds). Defeated: 42-44 (p. 626)	.4026
70	To require that all Mexicans swear an oath of loyalty to the new Constitution; that until the Constitution goes into effect on the 16th of September, the government will continue to function as it has until now. Passed: 66-21	.2152

APPENDIX C

LOADINGS IN ROTATED FACTOR MATRIX
(Orthogonal Varimax Rotation)

Roll Calls		Factors				
No.	Name	I	II	III	IV	V
1	Rest. Con. 24	.07	-.08	.02	.03	.05
2	Ley Juárez	-.11	-.15	.00	-.12	.09
3	Army reform	-.09	-.17	.17	-.50	-.01
4	Cent.-Fed.	.18	.09	.02	.73	-.13
5	Army reform	-.12	-.02	-.06	.71	-.13
6	Cent.-Fed.	-.06	-.07	.02	-.62	.06
7	Jesuits	-.05	-.07	.02	-.15	-.09
8	Ley Lerdo	-.25	-.02	.14	-.05	-.06
9	Congress vs. president	-.23	.13	.03	-.61	-.01
10	No retroactive laws	-.08	.27	.12	-.14	-.21
11	Keep and bear arms	-.28	.21	-.01	-.20	.09
12	Limit army	.03	.14	.10	-.15	-.03
13	Mail seizure	.19	-.03	.06	.25	-.54
14	Personal servitude	-.37	.20	-.06	-.22	-.04
15	Liberty sacrifice	-.44	-.21	.11	-.09	-.29
16	Free thought	-.16	-.13	.19	.17	-.08
17	Religious freedom	-.53	-.17	.14	-.25	-.03
18	Free teaching	-.51	-.14	.47	-.00	-.14
19	Limit Cong. petitions	-.02	-.03	.04	-.06	-.08
20	Monopolies	-.40	.06	.01	-.35	.17
21	Jury trial	-.75	-.10	.11	-.10	-.04
22	Mutilation	-.66	.05	-.18	-.03	.29
23	Expulsion of cabinet ministers	.75	.04	-.08	.14	-.08
24	Unicameral legislature	-.63	-.09	.24	.12	-.04
25	Death penalty (procedure)	.08	-.04	.01	.05	-.73
26	Death penalty	-.25	.15	-.07	.19	-.60
27	Cong. representation	-.08	-.17	.58	-.08	.08
28	Cent.-Fed.	.21	-.04	-.18	.27	-.17
29	Residency requirements for Cong.	-.05	-.70	.11	-.10	-.10
30	Cent.-Fed.	-.03	.17	.46	-.08	-.07
31	Cent.-Fed.	-.15	-.06	.58	.02	-.17
32	Tariffs by Cong.	-.11	.14	.45	-.24	-.03
33	Mints by Cong.	.08	.33	.04	-.06	-.27
34	Indirect elections	.14	.37	.01	.23	-.15
35	Oath of office by pres.	.20	.46	-.40	.09	.07
36	Oath of office by pres.	-.00	-.08	-.41	-.03	-.39
37	Commute sentences by pres.	-.03	.22	-.46	.21	-.01
38	Jurisdiction of fed. courts	-.48	-.17	-.08	.14	-.06
39	Jury in fed. cases	-.63	-.07	.03	-.07	-.18
40	Juicio político	-.29	-.09	.10	.11	-.12

APPENDIX C (Continued)

No.	Name	I	II	III	IV	V
	Roll Calls			Factors		
41	No state alliances	.08	-.21	-.60	-.02	-.16
42	No local currency	-.11	.03	.02	.02	-.03
43	Laws by judges	-.44	-.22	-.00	-.03	-.12
44	Laws by governor	.41	.40	.04	.09	.02
45	Gov. intervention in states	.15	.28	-.16	-.05	.40
46	Taxes	-.30	-.53	.05	.02	-.05
47	No trial of gov. officials	-.58	-.08	-.35	.13	-.01
48	Oath by all officials	.14	.29	-.02	-.04	-.01
49	Confront accuser	.31	.25	-.25	.09	-.04
50	Shackles and chains	-.60	-.13	-.07	.00	.37
51	Suspend const.	.17	-.19	-.16	.17	-.20
52	Presidential review	-.46	.02	.38	.00	.08
53	Amend by 2/3	.01	.13	-.03	-.06	.01
54	State leg. approve new states	.15	.21	-.20	-.05	-.01
55	Valley of Mexico	-.29	-.28	.33	.12	-.23
56	DF-Querétaro	-.23	.62	-.04	-.04	-.31
57	Cuautla-Cuernavaca	-.69	.27	.08	-.07	.05
58	Maintain state of Mexico	.73	-.01	-.16	-.01	-.08
59	Juntas	-.42	.08	-.29	-.14	.08
60	Juntas instruct	-.11	-.03	-.01	-.12	-.01
61	Exempt military	-.13	.13	.08	-.04	-.15
62	Licenses by Cong.	-.55	-.01	.29	.04	.11
63	Education juries	.25	.14	-.19	-.25	-.24
64	Death penalty five years	-.09	-.11	.03	-.14	.57
65	Freedom of worship	.14	.41	.00	.06	-.06
66	Abolish judicial costs	-.33	.20	-.02	-.13	.41
67	Remove residency requirements for Cong.	.67	-.00	.76	.16	-.02
68	Treasurer by Cong.	-.02	-.33	.06	.04	.16
69	Parochial obventions	.19	.55	-.04	-.20	-.39

Notes

Abbreviations Used
AGN   Archivo General de la Nación
AHMA   Archivo Histórico del Museo de Antropología
AHRE   Archivo Histórico de la Secretaría de Relaciones Exteriores
AJ   Archivo de Benito Juárez, Biblioteca Nacional de México
AMR   Archivo de Matías Romero, Banco de México
BNRB   Biblioteca Nacional de México, Rare Book Collection
HAHR   *Hispanic American Historical Review*
LAF   Colección Lafragua, Biblioteca Nacional de México
UTLAC   The University of Texas at Austin, Nettie Lee Benson Latin
         American Collection

Chapter 1: Nation Building: The Analytical Framework

1. Walter V. Scholes, *Mexican Politics during the Juárez Regime, 1855-1872.*

2. Ibid., pp. 1 and 177. Scholes identifies equality before the law, republican institutions, and laissez-faire as the "key concepts" of "the Mexican middle-class revolution," pp. 1-2.

3. See Justo Sierra, *Juárez: Su obra y su tiempo.* Also see *La evolución política del pueblo mexicano,* which has been translated as *The Political Evolution of the Mexican People.*

4. Ralph Roeder, *Juárez and His Mexico.* Although the book does not cite its sources, I was able to verify most of Roeder's material.

5. Francisco Bulnes, *Juárez y las revoluciones de Ayutla y de Reforma.* The publication of this work stimulated Sierra into writing his defense of Juárez.

6. Wilfrid H. Callcott, *Church and State in Mexico, 1822-1857,* and *Liberalism in Mexico, 1857-1929.*

7. Carl J. Friedrich, "Nation-Building?" in *Nation-Building,* edited by

Karl W. Deutsch and William J. Foltz, p. 31.

8. Karl Deutsch, "Some Problems in the Study of Nation-Building," in ibid., pp. 11-12.

9. This definition is derived from Cyril E. Black, *The Dynamics of Modernization: A Study in Comparative History*, p. 7.

10. Henry Maine, *Ancient Law: Its Connection with the Early History of Society, and Its Relation to Modern Ideas;* Ferdinand Tönnies, *Fundamental Concepts of Sociology;* Emile Durkheim, *The Division of Labor in Society;* Max Weber, *The Theory of Social and Economic Organization* and *The Protestant Ethic and the Spirit of Capitalism;* Talcott Parsons, *The Social System.* For disciples of Parsons, see Marion Levy, *The Structure of Society;* Reinhard Bendix, *Nation-Building and Citizenship: Studies of Our Changing Social Order,* pp. 1-29.

11. The following discussion derives from Gabriel Almond and James Coleman, eds., *The Politics of the Developing Areas;* David Apter, *The Politics of Modernization;* Samuel P. Huntington, *Political Order in Changing Societies;* James Coleman, "Modernization: Political Aspects," in *International Encyclopedia of the Social Sciences,* X, 395-402; and Myron Weiner, ed., *Modernization: The Dynamics of Growth.*

12. On the rationalization of authority see Huntington, *Political Order,* especially pp. 33-39.

13. Black, *Dynamics of Modernization,* p. 14. It is important to note that these general remarks on centralization of public policy-making apply equally to the private domain, and often political modernization is accompanied by state control or regulation of certain key "infrastructure" industries—railroads, petroleum, electricity—in the desire to serve the public needs as defined by the state. On the creation of bureaucracies see Bendix, *Nation-Building,* especially ch. 4.

14. Bendix, *Nation-Building,* p. 18.

15. Black, *Dynamics of Modernization,* p. 16.

16. S. N. Eisenstadt, *Modernization: Protest and Change,* pp. 15-16.

17. On the role of ideology in modernizing societies see Apter, *The Politics of Modernization,* ch. 9. Apter defines ideology as "a generic term applying to general ideas that are potent in specific situations of conduct," p. 314.

18. Leonard Binder et al., *Crises and Sequences in Political Development,* p. 74. The following discussion of types of crises is a summary of the various chapters in this important book.

19. Eisenstadt, *Modernization,* pp. 51-82, 84-98. Eisenstadt identifies two stages of modernization: (1) a stage characterized by elites, extension of franchise, secularization, and political centralization; (2) a high level of mass participation, social communication, and mass social mobilization, accompanied by industrialization. Black notes four "phases": (1) the challenge of modernity, (2) the consolidation of modernizing leadership, (3) economic and social transformation, and (4) the integration of society. Black identifies

phase two in Mexico as taking place from 1867 to 1910 and phase three from 1910 to the present. (Black, *Dynamics of Modernization*, pp.67-94.)

20. Huntington, *Political Order*, pp. 140 ff., identifies three stages of modernization: (1) concentration of power, (2) expansion of power, and (3) dispersion of power. Other propositions are summarized in Helio Jaguaribe, *Political Development: A General Theory and a Latin American Case Study*, pp. 189-218.

21. For án analysis of other types of modernization see Black, *Dynamics of Modernization*, pp. 18-26.

22. For the "agony of modernization," see ibid., pp. 26-34.

23. For examples and analysis see Bendix, *Nation-Building*, pp. 4-15.

24. Weiner, *Modernization*, p. 7.

25. For an indictment of the traditional-modern dichotomy see Joseph R. Gusfield, "Tradition and Modernity: Misplaced Polarities in the Study of Social Order," in *Political Modernization: A Reader in Comparative Political Change*, edited by Claude E. Welch, Jr., pp. 47-62; Reinhard Bendix, "Tradition and Modernity Reconsidered," *Comparative Studies in Society and History* 9, no. 3 (April 1967): 292-346.

Chapter 2: Society and Politics: Roots of Reform

1. For general descriptions of the economic crisis, see Charles Cumberland, *Mexico: The Struggle for Modernity*, pp. 155-162; Francisco López Cámara, *La estructura económica y social de México en la época de la Reforma*, pp. 21-25; Francisco R. Calderón, *La República Restaurada: La vida económica*, vol. 2 of *Historia moderna de México*, pp. 37-222; David M. Pletcher, *Rails, Mines and Progress: Seven American Promoters in Mexico, 1867-1911*, pp. 19-27.

2. Calderón, *Vida económica*, pp. 295-306.

3. Ibid., pp. 37-39; Lucas Alamán, *Memoria sobre el estado de la agricultura e industria de la república en el año de 1844*, on p. 5 said: "The cause of our [agricultural] backwardness is the great abundance of products without consumption, and there is no remedy except the expansion of consumption."; López Cámara, *Estructura económica*, pp. 26-51; Carl Sartorius, *Mexico about 1850*, pp. 166-181; T. G. Powell, *El liberalismo y el campesino en el centro de México (1850-1876)*, pp. 32-34.

4. Stanley and Barbara Stein, *The Colonial Heritage of Latin America*, pp. 28-53; David A. Brading, *Miners and Merchants in Bourbon Mexico, 1763-1810*.

5. Marvin D. Bernstein, *The Mexican Mining Industry, 1890-1950*, pp. 8-14.

6. Romeo Flores Caballero, *Counterrevolution: The Role of the Spaniards in the Independence of Mexico, 1804-1838*, pp. 14-40.

7. Ibid., pp. 81-130; Harold D. Sims, *La expulsión de los españoles de México, 1821-1828;* Sartorius, *Mexico*, pp. 191-202; López Cámara,

Estructura económica, pp. 66-72.

8. For details of the difficulties see: Calderón, *Vida económica,* pp. 115-185; Cumberland, *Mexico,* pp. 167-169. For an example of British investment, see Robert Randall, *Real del Monte: A British Mining Venture in Mexico.*

9. Dawn Keremitsis, *La industria textil mexicana en el siglo XIX,* pp. 9-76; Robert A. Potash, *El Banco de Avío. El fomento de la industria, 1821-1846;* Calderón, *Vida económica,* pp. 85-86.

10. Calderón, *Vida económica,* pp. 185-186; Jan Bazant, *Historia de la deuda exterior de México, 1823-1946,* pp. 43-73.

11. The fundamental work on the hacienda is François Chevalier, *La Formation des grands domaines au Mexique: Terre et société aux XVIe-XVIIe siècles,* trans. by Leslie Byrd Simpson as *Land and Society in Colonial Mexico;* on land tenure see Helen Phipps, "Some Aspects of the Agrarian Question in Mexico," pp. 21-39; also see Silvio Zavala, "Orígenes coloniales del peonaje en México," *Trimestre económico* 10 (1944): 711-748; François Chevalier, "Suivances seigneuriales et présages de la revolution agraire dans le nord du Mexique, fin du XVIII^{éme} et XIX^{éme} siècles," *Revue Historique* 222 (1959): 1-18; and George M. McBride, *The Land Systems of Mexico.* On the subdivision of haciendas see Luis González, *San José de Gracia: Mexican Village in Transition,* pp. 31-39; David A. Brading, "Government and Elite in Late Colonial Mexico," *HAHR* 53, no. 3 (August 1973): 392-393.

12. Sartorius, *Mexico,* p. 166.

13. Jan Bazant, *Alienation of Church Wealth in Mexico: Social and Economic Aspects of the Liberal Revolution, 1856-1875,* pp. 32-39.

14. Powell, *El liberalismo,* pp. 37-65; Eric Wolf, *Sons of the Shaking Earth,* pp. 211-232, and "Closed Corporate Peasant Communities in Mesoamerica and Central Java," *Southwestern Journal of Anthropology* 13 (1957): 1-18; Charles Gibson, "The Transformation of the Indian Community in New Spain, 1500-1810," *Journal of World History* 2 (1955): 581-607.

15. Miguel Lerdo de Tejada, *Memoria de Hacienda,* pp. 10-15, estimated 6,859,564; *El Monitor Republicano,* 1-2 August 1857, estimated 8,283,088 with 2,656,620 creoles; Francisco Pimentel, *Memoria sobre las causas que han originado las situación actual de la raza indígena de México y medios para remediarla,* pp. 195-196, estimated 8,629,982 with two million creoles. López Cámara, *Estructura económica,* pp. 2-4. The population of Mexico City and other capitals in 1862 in Luis González et al., *La República Restaurada: La vida social,* vol. 3 of *Historia moderna de México,* pp. 112-113. Newspapers are from Mexico City unless otherwise noted.

16. Alexander von Humboldt, *Ensayo político sobre el reino de la Nueva España.*

17. Richard E. Boyer and Keith A. Davies, *Urbanization in 19th-Century Latin America: Statistics and Sources,* pp. 33-49; Antonio García Cubas, *La república mexicana en 1876,* p. 127.

18. Ministerio de Fomento, *Memoria, 1857,* Part IV, Doc. 3, pp. 11-12.

19. Brading, "Government and Elite," p. 289.

20. *Fisiología de la cosa pública . . . ,* p. 36.

21. For general comments about the position of creoles see Miguel Lerdo de Tejada, *Cuadro sinóptico de la república mexicana en 1856,* p. 28; Porfirio Parra, *Estudio histórico-sociológico sobre la Reforma en México,* pp. 27-28; Pimentel, *Memoria,* pp. 195-196; *El Monitor Republicano,* 29 July, 1-2 August, 1857; Sartorius, *Mexico,* pp. 53-61.

22. Andrés Molina Enríquez, *Juárez y la reforma,* especially pp. 110-116; C. E. Marshall, "The Birth of the Mestizo in New Spain," *HAHR* 19 (1939): 161-184.

23. *Examen racional analítico de los males públicos,* p. 14; [Mariano Otero], *Consideraciones sobre la situación política y social de la república mexicana en el año 1847;* pp. 6-7; Sartorius, *Mexico,* pp. 82-101.

24. Eric Hobsbawm, *Social Bandits and Primitive Rebels,* p. 15.

25. Paul Vanderwood, "Genesis of the Rurales: Mexico's Early Struggle for Public Security," *HAHR* 50, no. 3 (August 1970): 323-344.

26. José M. Pérez Hernández, *Estadística de la República Mexicana,* pp. 74-75, García Cubas, *México en 1876,* p.127; Sartorius, *Mexico,* pp.53, 88.

27. Woodrow Borah, "Race and Class in Mexico," *Pacific Historical Review* 23 (1954): 331-342.

28. Manuel Germán Parra, "Las grandes tendencias de la evolución histórica de la política indigenista," in *Bibliografía indigenista de México y Centro-américa, 1850-1950,* p. lxxix.

29. Charles Gibson, *The Aztecs under Spanish Rule: A History of the Indians of the Valley of Mexico, 1519-1810;* Brading, *Miners and Merchants,* pp. 227-229.

30. Eric Wolf, "The Mexican Bajío in the 18th Century: An Analysis of Cultural Integration," in *Synoptic Studies of Mexican Culture,* edited by Munro S. Edmundson; Brading, *Miners and Merchants,* p. 343; Herbert I. Priestley, *José de Gálvez, Visitor-General of New Spain, 1765-1771,* pp. 210-233.

31. The literature on the Mexican independence movements is vast. Among the best sources are Lucas Alamán, *Historia de Méjico desde los primeros movimientos que prepararon su independencia en el año de 1808 hasta la época presente;* Hugh M. Hamill, Jr., *The Hidalgo Revolt: Prelude to Mexican Independence;* Doris Ladd, *The Mexican Nobility at Independence, 1780-1826.*

32. Nelson Reed, *The Caste War of Yucatan;* Moisés González Navarro, *Raza y tierra. La guerra de castas y el henequén.*

33. Pimentel, *Memoria,* p. 218.

34. M. Lerdo de Tejada, *Cuadro sinóptico,* p. 28.

35. Torcuato S. di Tella, "The Dangerous Classes in Early Nineteenth-Century Mexico," *Journal of Latin American Studies* 5, no. 1 (May 1973): 79-105.

36. There is an enormous literature on the Mexican-American War. For basic bibliography see David Pletcher, *The Diplomacy of Annexation: Texas, Oregon, and the Mexican War.*

37. *México en 1847*, p. 30.

38. Otero, *Consideraciones*, p. 42.

39. This discussion is based on the analysis of Charles A. Hale, *Mexican Liberalism in the Age of Mora, 1821-1853*, pp. 1-38.

40. José María Luis Mora, *Méjico y sus revoluciones*, III, 15.

41. Otero, *Consideraciones;* also see *El Monitor Republicano*, 13-15, 17-21, 23-24 June 1848. For analysis see Hale, *Liberalism*, pp. 13-14; Jesús Reyes Heroles, *El liberalismo mexicano*, II, 365-401.

42. David A. Brading, "Creole Nationalism and Mexican Liberalism," *Journal of Interamerican Studies and World Affairs* 15, no. 2 (May 1973): 158-159; Reyes Heroles, *Liberalismo*, III, 337-409; Hale, *Liberalism*, pp. 39-107.

43. Brading, "Creole Nationalism," pp. 148-150; Reyes Heroles, *Liberalismo*, III, 69-245; Hale, *Liberalism*, pp. 108-147.

44. The best discussion of the Indian question is in Hale, *Liberalism*, pp. 215-247.

45. Mexican conservatism has not been analyzed thoroughly. The best summaries are in Hale, *Mexican Liberalism*, pp. 15-22; François Chevalier, "Conservateurs et libéraux au Mexique. Essai de sociologie et géographie politiques de l'indépendance a l'intervention française," *Cahiers d'Histoire Mondiale* 8 (1964): 457-474; Brading, "Creole Nationalism," pp. 139-190.

46. Alamán's life is treated by José C. Valadés, *Alamán, estadista e historiador;* Moisés González Navarro, *El pensamiento político de Lucas Alamán;* Arturo Arnáiz y Freg, "Prólogo," *Lucas Alamán, semblanzas e idearios;* Lucas Alamán, "Apuntes biográficos," in *Documentos diversos*, III, 505-522.

47. Lucas Alamán, *Disertaciones sobre la historia de la república mejicana, desde la época de la conquista que los españoles hicieron . . . hasta la independencia* and *Historia de Méjico.*

48. Alamán, *Historia*, IV, 722-724. For a systematic glorification of Iturbide, see Luis G. Cuevas, *Porvenir de México.*

49. Quoted in Francisco de Paula Arrangoiz y Berzábal, *México desde 1808 hasta 1867*, p. 442.

50. Cited in Brading, "Creole Nationalism," p. 157.

51. José María Gutiérrez de Estrada, *Carta dirigida al escmo. sr. presidente de la república sobre la necesidad de buscar en una convención el posible remedio de los males que aquejan a la república;* for material on Gutiérrez's life, see José C. Valadés, "José María Gutiérrez de Estrada (1800-1867)," in *Enciclopedia yucatanense*, VII, 141-204.

52. In 1847 Gutiérrez, now living in Europe, wrote the following pamphlet to bolster his case: *Le Mexique et l'Europe ou exposé de la situation actuelle du Mexique et des dangers qui peuvent en résulter pour l'Europe si elle ne*

prend des mesures efficaces pour y remédier. Also see, Jorge Gurria Lacroix, *Las ideas monárquicas de don Lucas Alamán.*

53. See particularly *El Universal, El Orden,* and *El Omnibus;* Hale, *Mexican Liberalism,* p. 30.

54. For details of this period see Justo Sierra, *Political Evolution of the Mexican People,* pp. 248-265.

Chapter 3: The Reform Leadership

1. Richard A. Johnson, *The Mexican Revolution of Ayutla, 1854-1855,* especially pp. 38-62, 100-112.

2. This summary of the Santa Anna dictatorship is derived from Johnson, *Revolution of Ayutla,* especially pp. 14-37; José María Vigil, *La Reforma,* vol. 5 of *México a través de los siglos,* edited by Vicente Riva Palacio; Wilfrid Hardy Callcott, *Church and State in Mexico, 1822-1857,* especially pp. 202-233; Fernando Díaz y Díaz, *Caudillos y caciques,* pp. 232-278.

3. For forces undermining the dictatorship see Johnson, *Revolution of Ayutla,* pp. 87-99.

4. Cited in Guillermo Prieto, *Circular del ministro de hacienda . . . á los gobernadores de los estados,* p. 5. Also see Johnson, *Revolution of Ayutla,* p. 16, n. 3. For the various centralization laws see Manuel Dublán and José María Lozano, eds., *Legislación mexicana ó colección completa de las disposiciones legislativas expedidas desde la independencia de la República,* VI, 366-368, 395-399, 455, 525-526.

5. For Comonfort's side of the removal see his correspondence in UTLAC, Comonfort Papers, folder 17, especially April, May, June, and July 1853.

6. Both plans in *Archivo mexicano,* I, 3-18; Benito Juárez, *Documentos, discursos y correspondencia,* II, 13-24.

7. For Alvarez's view see Juan Alvarez to Melchor Ocampo and José María Mata, 4 August 1855, AHMA, legajo 50, caja A, expediente 23, doc. 4. Also see Alvarez to Ocampo, 22 June 1854, ibid., doc. 2.

8. Mario de la Cueva, "Prólogo" to *Plan de Ayutla: Conmemoración de su primer centenario,* edited by B. de Silva, pp. ix-x. For a critique of the "official Jacobin" view of the Ayutla movement as a precursor of social reform see Edmundo O'Gorman, "Precedentes y sentido de la revolución de Ayutla," in ibid., pp. 176-177. Also see Andrés Molina Enríquez, *Juárez y la Reforma,* pp. 102-103.

9. For a list and relevant data see Appendix A. Unless otherwise noted all biographical information was taken from the following sources: *Diccionario Porrúa de historia, biografía y geografía de México;* Marcos Arroniz, *Manual de biografía mejicana;* Gabriel Agraz García de Alba, *Ofrenda a México: Compendio de geografía, historia y biografía mexicanas;* Miguel Angel Peral, *Diccionario biográfico mexicano;* Francisco Sosa, *Biografías de mexicanos distinguidos.* Many other individuals could have been chosen to include in the analysis, but biographical information was too fragmentary to be of much

use. The few data that do exist seem to confirm the general patterns discussed in the remainder of this chapter.

10. A fundamental assumption here is that political activity is in large measure influenced by social, economic, and cultural environments. For an elaborate justification see David Apter, "A Comparative Method for the Study of Politics," *American Journal of Sociology* 64 (November 1958): 221-237, in which he argues that the basic motivation for political activism is the desire for social and economic mobility. For Latin America see William A. Welsh, "Methodological Problems in the Study of Political Leadership in Latin America," *Latin American Research Review* 5, no. 3 (Fall 1970): 3-33.

11. Agustín Cué Cánovas, in *La reforma liberal en México*, p. 11, refers to the Ayutla leadership as "the new liberal generation."

12. Brading, "Creole Nationalism," pp. 185-186.

13. Francisco Zarco, *Historia del Congreso extraordinario Constituyente, 1856-1857*, p. 557 (italics in original).

14. Harry Bernstein, *Modern and Contemporary Latin America*, pp. 70-71; Luis Medina Ascencio, S. J., "El clero jalisciense y la Reforma," in *La Reforma en Jalisco y el Bajío*, pp. 105-125.

15. David A. Brading, "The Structure of Agricultural Production in the Mexican Bajío in the Eighteenth Century," presented at the 40th International Congress of Americanists, Rome, 1972; Jan Bazant, "Peones, arrendatarios y aparceros, 1868-1904," *Historia Mexicana* 24, no. 1 (July-September 1974): 94-121; Luis González, *San José de Gracia*, pp. 3-54, and "La situación social de Jalisco en vísperas de la Reforma," in *La Reforma en Jalisco y el Bajío*, pp. 34-41.

16. Andrés Molina Enríquez, *Juárez y la reforma*, p. 115. On race mixture, see Moisés González Navarro, "Mestizaje in Mexico during the National Period," in *Race and Class in Latin America*, edited by Magnus Mörner, pp. 145-169.

17. Ignacio Altamirano, *Discurso pronunciado . . . en la ciudad de Guerrero el 16 de septiembre de 1866*, in BNRB.

18. Manuel Payno, *Memoria sobre la revolución de diciembre de 1857 y enero de 1858*. Two years later Payno, in an attempt to stop the European intervention, claimed that "in no part of America are found fewer Negroes, fewer mulattoes and fewer mestizos than in Mexico." *México y el Sr. Embajador don Joaquín Francisco Pacheco*, pp. 40-43.

19. *El Siglo XIX*, 14, 21 April 1853.

20. Ignacio Ramírez, "Discurso cívico pronunciado . . . el 16 de septiembre de 1861 . . . " in *Discursos pronunciados en las funciones cívicas del año de 1861*, pp. 22-23.

21. Miguel Rul, *Consulta del Diputado . . . dirigida a sus colegas en el 7° Congreso Constitucional*, pp. 6-7.

22. Melchor Ocampo, "Mis quince días de ministro," *Obras*, II, 58.

23. *Diálogo entre Martín y Juan Diego.*

24. Guillermo Prieto, *Circular del ministro de hacienda . . . á los gobernadores de los estados,* p. 8.

25. José María Lafragua, Circular of the Minister of Gobernación.

26. *El Siglo XIX,* 18 November 1856.

27. Juan José de la Garza, Circular of the Governor of Tamaulipas, printed in ibid., 3 March 1856.

28. *El Republicano,* 1 July 1856.

29. Beníto Juárez, "Apuntes para mis hijos," AGN, Conjunto de documentos sobre Juárez, doc. 1; Juárez, *Documentos,* I, 46-49.

30. Juárez, "Apuntes," AGN, Conjunto, doc. 1; Juárez, *Documentos,* I, 92-97; also see René Avilés, *Juárez y la educación en México,* pp. 13-51, and Josefina Vázquez de Knauth, *Nacionalismo y educación en México,* pp. 17-43.

31. Unfortunately no study of the secular institutes exists, but see José Bravo Ugarte, *La educación en México,* pp. 109-130, and Abraham Talavera, *Liberalismo y educación,* I, 9-130.

32. Alfonso Teja Zabre, *Leandro Valle, un liberal romántico,* pp. 25-26.

33. Juárez, "Apuntes," AGN, Conjunto, doc. 1; Juárez, *Documentos,* I, 134-137. For a somewhat different translation, see Roeder, *Juárez,* I, 57.

34. The polemics are found in Ocampo, *Obras,* I, 1-392, and reprinted in Ocampo, *La religión, la iglesia y el clero.*

35. Moisés González Navarro, ed., *Vallarta en la Reforma,* pp. xvii-xxiv, and Vallarta's essay "¿Tiene la potestad secular poder para impedir la enajenación de los bienes eclesiásticos?" pp. 3-12.

36. On Doblado see William J. Ross, III, "The Role of Manuel Doblado in the Mexican Reform Movement, 1855-1860," pp. 1-37; Luis González Obregón, "D. Manuel Doblado," in Enrique M. de los Ríos, ed., *Liberales ilustres mexicanos de la reforma y la intervención;* Ignacio Ramírez López, *Cronología de Manuel Doblado.*

37. The literature on Juárez's life is immense. For Juárez's own evaluation, see his "Apuntes," in Juárez, *Documentos,* I, 24-272. The best biographies are Justo Sierra, *Juárez, su obra y su tiempo,* and Ralph Roeder, *Juárez and His Mexico.* Both are sympathetic and both fail to identify their sources.

38. On Ocampo see José C. Valadés, *Don Melchor Ocampo, reformador de México;* Jesús Romero Flores, *Don Melchor Ocampo, el filósofo de la Reforma;* Agustín Cué Cánovas, "Melchor Ocampo y el liberalismo en Michoacán," *Universidad Michoacán* 34 (February 1960): 9-13, 19-21; Salvador Piñeda, *Vida y pasión de Ocampo: Ocho estampas del reformador;* Eduardo Ruiz, *Biografía del ciudadano Melchor Ocampo.* For the collected works see Melchor Ocampo, *Obras completas.* For a list of Ocampo's library in 1848, see "Catálogo de los libros de Melchor Ocampo . . . ," AHMA, legajo 17, caja 3, expediente 11, documento 9.

39. See Vicente Fuentes Díaz, *Santos Degollado, el santo de la Reforma;* Harry Bernstein, "Mocedades de Matías Romero," *Historia Mexicana* 10 (April-June 1961): 588-612. The Riva Palacio papers are found in UTLAC,

as are the de la Fuente papers.

40. José Miguel Quintana, *Lafragua, político y romántico*, pp. 7-30; González Navarro, *Vallarta*, pp. vii-xxxiii.

41. Works on Arriaga are scarce, the best being Manuel Ramírez Arriaga, *Ponciano Arriaga el desconocido*.

42. On Ramírez, see Ignacio Altamirano, "Biografía de Ignacio Ramírez," in Ignacio Ramírez, *México en pos de la libertad*, pp. 10-70; also see Ignacio Ramírez, *Obras*. On Vigil, see José María Vigil, *José María Vigil: Prólogo, notas, y composición*.

43. See José María Iglesias, *Autobiografía*, and Martin Quirarte's "Datos biográficos" in *Revistas históricas sobre la intervención francesa en México*, pp. xxv-xlii.

44. Raymond C. Wheat, *Francisco Zarco, el portavoz liberal de la Reforma;* Oscar Castañeda Batres, *Francisco Zarco*.

45. The best biography of Prieto is Malcolm D. McLean, *Vida y obra de Guillermo Prieto*. Also see Carlos J. Sierra, *Guillermo Prieto;* Salvador Ortiz Vidales, *Don Guillermo Prieto y su época*. For Prieto's autobiography see his *Memorias de mis tiempos*.

46. Ivie E. Cadenhead, Jr., *Jesús González Ortega and Mexican National Politics*.

47. Guillermo Colin Sánchez, *Ignacio Zaragoza: Evocación de un héroe;* Israel Cavazos Garza, *Mariano Escobedo: El glorioso soldado de la república;* Carleton Beals, *Porfirio Díaz, Dictator of Mexico;* Agustín Rivera y Sanromán, *Pinceladas sobre la vida i gobierno del C. General Porfirio Díaz*, pp. 1-2; Teja Zabre, *Leandro Valle*.

48. Ray F. Broussard, "Mocedades de Comonfort," *Historia Mexicana* 13 (January-March 1964): 379-393); Rosaura Hernández Rodríguez, *Ignacio Comonfort. Trayectoria política. Documentos*.

49. See Frank A. Knapp, *The Life of Sebastián Lerdo de Tejada: A Study of Influence and Obscurity;* Ezequiel Montes, "Pérdida irreparable. Muerte de Don Miguel Lerdo de Tejada . . ." in *La Independencia*, 23 March 1861.

50. Juárez, Mata, and José María Gómez to Ocampo and Arriaga, 28 February 1855, AGN, Conjunto, doc. 29; Juárez, *Documentos*, II, 25-26.

51. Melchor Ocampo to Juan B. Ceballos, 25 September 1852, AHMA, leg. 50, 0-3, doc. 13.

52. Júarez to Ocampo, 30 November 1854, ibid., leg. 50, J-5, doc. 9.

53. Ocampo to M. Robles, 4 March 1854, ibid., leg. 50, 0-3, doc. 15.

54. Juárez to Ocampo, 28 February 1855, ibid., leg. 50, J-5, doc. 14.

55. Juan B. Cebollas, Miguel María Arrioja, Ponciano Arriaga, Melchor Ocampo, "Sobre una pretendida traición a México" (New Orleans, 10 May 1854) in LAF 663.

Chapter 4: The Constitution of 1857

1. Ignacio Comonfort to Governor of the State of Aguascalientes, 12

December 1855, UTLAC, Comonfort Papers, folder 17.

2. *El Siglo XIX,* 27 February 1856.

3. Guillermo Prieto, *Oración cívica pronunciada . . . en la Alameda de México.*

4. José María Lafragua, Decree of the Minister of Gobernación, 22 December 1855, in LAF 398; Lafragua, Manuel Payno, Ezequiel Montes, Manuel Sileceo, Luis de la Rosa, Decree of the Cabinet, 22 December 1855, in ibid. For Lafragua's early views on constitutions see his *Discurso pronunciado . . . contra el proyecto de constitución,* reprinted in *El Siglo XIX,* 9 October 1842.

5. Mariano Riva Palacio to Juan Alvarez, 21 August 1855, UTLAC, M. Riva Palacio Papers, García 169, folder 18, doc. 5729. Also see docs. 5756 and 5768 for similar expressions.

6. Benito Juárez to Manuel Doblado, 17 June 1861, UTLAC, Doblado Typescripts, vol. 2.

7. Much of the following discussion of social composition and roll-call voting behavior appeared in my article "The Mexican Constitutional Congress, 1856-57: A Statistical Analysis," *HAHR* 53, no. 1 (February 1973): 1-26. The best studies of the Constitutional Congress are Emilio Rabasa, *La constitución y la dictadura;* Daniel Cosío Villegas, *La Constitución de 1857 y sus críticos.* For the debates see Francisco Zarco, *Historia del Congreso extraordinario Constituyente (1856-1857).* Also see Colegio de Abogados de México, *El constituyente de 1856 y el pensamiento liberal mexicano;* Manuel Loza Macías, *El pensamiento económico y la Constitución de 1857.* For a comparison with the Constitution of 1917, see H. N. Branch, trans., *The Mexican Constitution of 1917 Compared with the Constitution of 1857.*

8. Jesús Romero Flores, *Comentarios a la historia de México, 1821-1861,* pp. 152, 154-155.

9. Francisco Bulnes, *Juárez y las revoluciones de Ayutla y de la Reforma,* p. 215. Bulnes goes on to suggest that most of those who practiced law did so in the pay of the government because (1) ecclesiastical lawyers handled the big cases and (2) there were too many lawyers for the small job market.

10. Walter V. Scholes, "Church and State at the Mexican Constitutional Convention, 1856-1857," *The Americas* 4 (1948-1949): 151-174. Also see Callcott, *Church and State in Mexico,* pp. 268-269.

11. Socioeconomic data for this study were taken from biographical dictionaries. Among the most useful were: *Diccionario Porrúa de historia, biografía, y geografía de México;* Alberto Leduc and Luis Laray Pardo, *Diccionario de geografía, historia, y biografías mexicanas.* A total of 71 state biographical dictionaries were consulted. The absence of a formal archive made the task of gathering socioeconomic data extremely difficult.

Although the data are extremely sketchy and must be used with great caution, they are more valuable than appears. Rarely did more than 90 delegates vote on a roll call, and in general, it is for these men that data exist. These data must, therefore, be taken as a general order of magnitude rather than as a precise tabulation.

12. The official list of delegates and the states they represented is in Zarco, *Historia,* pp. 21-25. Cross-tabulations using a NUCROS computer program of several socioeconomic variables (age, occupation, region, number of years in political activity) and "participant" categories (number of votes and number of participations in debates) failed to identify significant relationships.

13. For the *convocatoria,* which deliberately excluded the clergy from participation, see Zarco, *Historia,* pp. 13-20.

14. Ibid., pp. 34-35. Also see Emilio Rabasa, *La constitución,* pp. 30-45.

15. Zarco, *Historia,* p. 87; also see pp. 75-76. It should be noted that the Constituent Congress was both a constitution-writing body and a working legislature.

16. Ibid., pp. 31-32.

17. See, for examples, Bulnes, *Juárez,* pp. 162-185; Scholes, "Church and State," p. 152, n. 3; Cosío Villegas, *Constitución,* pp. 82-83; Rabasa, *Constitución,* pp. 30-45.

18. Scholes, "Church and State," p. 152, n. 5.

19. Justo Sierra, *The Political Evolution of the Mexican People,* p. 270.

20. *Actas oficiales del Congreso Constituyente (1856-1857).*

21. For techniques of selecting votes for roll-call analysis see Lee F. Anderson et al., *Legislative Roll-Call Analysis,* pp. 77-86. The criterion used to select votes from the total sample was that to be included a vote had to have at least 10 percent opposition voting. The Riker Index proved inadequate for selecting the final 70 because the number of voting delegates fluctuated radically during the Congress, thus skewing "significance" chronologically. For a computer program to compute the Riker Index, see ibid., p. 186.

22. The best work on factor analysis is R. J. Rummel, *Applied Factor Analysis,* but also see Benjamin Fruchter, *Introduction to Factor Analysis* Anderson et al., *Roll-call Analysis,* ch. 7.

23. The votes were coded in the following manner: yes $= +1$, not voting $= 0$, no $= -1$. The table is drawn from the results obtained using the packaged computer program MESA1 of the University of Texas Computation Center. This technique produced a matrix of Pearson product-moment correlations and used the highest squared multiples in the diagonals of the correlation matrix. This matrix was factored by the principal components procedure. The matrix included only the votes of the 70 delegates who voted more than 50 times. As a check on the validity of this technique, I ran four EDSTAT programs with 1's in the diagonals using all 134 voting delegates, using only the 70 "participant" delegates, excluding missing data, and including missing data. In all runs 15 factors with positive eigenvalues of $\rangle$ 1.5 were extracted, which accounted for 67.9 percent of the total variance in MESA1. In all five runs, the same votes loaded highly on Factor I. The reason the MESA1 results are being used in this study is that they more clearly delineated Factors II through V than did the EDSTAT program. For the purposes of this study,

the orthogonally rotated (VARIMAX) factor matrix was more useful than the unrotated matrix. In the unrotated matrix Factor I remained essentially the same; in the rotated matrix Factors II through V became more clearly delineated. (See Rummel, *Applied,* ch. 16, for orthogonal rotation discussion.) Oblique rotation was not used since I was looking for "independent" dimensions of conflict. It should be noted that in the final MESA1 run, vote no. 70 had to be dropped from the matrix for mathematical reasons. This procedure seemed acceptable since the vote had low loadings in all the EDSTAT results.

24. Zarco, *Historia,* p. 568.

25. Ibid., pp. 549-551.

26. Ibid., p. 630.

27. Ibid., pp. 718. It is important to note that the naming of Factor I would have been impossible without the debates. Only through a careful study of the debates did the underlying dimensions of the votes that loaded highly on Factor I become clear. On the techniques and artistry needed to name factors, and the difficulties involved, see Rummel, *Applied,* pp. 472-489.

28. Zarco, *Historia,* pp. 741-750.

29. Ibid., pp. 1073-1077.

30. Ibid., pp. 320-322, 835-843.

31. For debates on the location of the Federal District see ibid., pp. 1110-1115.

32. Ibid., pp. 405-408.

33. *El Siglo XIX,* 14 July 1861; Knapp, "Parliamentary Government," p. 76.

34. León Guzmán, "El Congreso Constituyente a la nación, 5 February 1857, in Zarco, *Historia,* pp. 1290-1294; Juárez, *Documentos,* II, 232-236; *El Siglo XIX,* 6 February 1857.

35. See Zarco, *Historia,* pp. 782-789, 1208-1209.

36. For a discussion of the unanimous and near-unanimous votes see Bulnes, *Juárez,* pp. 182-185.

37. Jesús Reyes Heroles, *El liberalismo mexicano,* III, 46-58.

38. See Hale, *Liberalism,* pp. 72-107.

39. Zarco, *Historia,* p. 319.

40. Varios Yucatecos, *Programa del Partido Liberal;* Varios Liberales, *Rápida ojeada sobre la revolución y el General Comonfort,* p. 4; José María Alatorre, "Reformas," in *El Aguila Roja,* 14 February 1856.

41. Zarco, *Historia,* p. 1291.

42. Ignacio Ramírez, "Oración pronunciada . . . el 5 de febrero de 1863," in *El Monitor Republicano,* 6 February 1863. Also see similar sentiments in Benito Juárez, "Discurso del Señor Governador al rendir la protesta ante el Honorable Congreso del Estado," Juárez, *Documentos,* II, 250-252.

43. Zarco, *Historia,* pp. 387-404.

44. The only informal list I was able to locate of the moderates and radicals is found in Cosío Villegas, *Constitución,* p. 79. The difficulty with using his

list in a factor analysis is that, with the exception of Marcelino Castañeda, the men listed as moderates had fewer than 50 votes.

45. The factor scores are taken from the EDSTAT program using the 70 participant delegates. They were not transformed and are derived from the rotated factor matrix.

46. A Q-factor analysis consists of factor analyzing a matrix in which "variables" refers to entities, in this case the 70 participant delegates. The loadings thus measure association among delegates on a given factor. See Rummel, *Applied*, pp. 195-196, 241-243; Anderson et al., *Roll-Call Analysis*, pp. 142-143, 165.

47. Guillermo Prieto to Ignacio Comonfort, 14 July 1857, UTLAC, Comonfort Papers, folder 17.

48. Ezequiel Montes to Joaquín Moreno, 4 March 1857, UTLAC, Documentos relativos a la Reforma y a la Intervención Francesa, 1850-1867, García 28.

49. Zarco, *Historia*, p. 1360, Juárez, *Documentos*, II, 237, 240, 250; Juramento de la Constitución de 1857 por Gral. Don Juan Alvarez, 26 April 1857, UTLAC, M. Riva Palacio Papers, García 170, folder 19, doc. 6454.

50. For opposition to the oath see ibid., docs. 6301, 6344, 6387, and 6454; as an example of those who feared the oath would produce anarchy see José de la Piedra to M. Riva Palacio, 9 April 1857, ibid., doc. 6405.

Chapter 5: The Constitutional Dictatorship

1. Plan of Ayutla in *Archivo mexicano*, I, 3-10; Juárez, *Documentos*, II, 13-18.

2. The Acapulco revision in *Archivo mexicano*, I, 10-18; Juárez, *Documentos*, II, 19-24. For an excellent discussion of this paradox see Edmundo O'Gorman, "Precedentes y sentido de la Revolución de Ayutla," in *Plan de Ayutla: Conmemoración de su primer centenario*, pp. 171-204.

3. Manuel Payno, *Memoria sobre la revolución de diciembre de 1857 y enero de 1858.*

4. Manuel Doblado, Decree, n. d. [December? 1857?], in LAF 394; also see Pedro Escudero to Mariano Riva Palacio, 8 September 1857, UTLAC, M. Riva Palacio Papers, García 172, folder 21, doc. 6938.

5. Benito Juárez, Melchor Ocampo, Manuel Ruiz, León Guzmán, Guillermo Prieto to the Mexican People, *Luz de la Libertad* (Guadalajara), 16 March 1859.

6. *El Siglo XIX*, 14 February 1858.

7. Circular de Juan de Dios Arias a los gobernadores, 31 December 1860, in LAF 396 and Juárez, *Documentos*, III, 104-105.

8. From Florencio María del Castillo, "Entrada del ejército liberal a la ciudad de México," ibid., pp. 105-109.

9. *El Siglo XIX*, 18 May 1861, and similar statement by Manuel María

Zamacona, ibid., 26 April 1861.

10. Circular of the Minister of Foreign Relations, 20 January 1861, in LAF 396, doc. 139; Juárez, *Documentos*, IV, 151.

11. *La Independencia Mexicana* (San Luis Potosí), 14 November 1863; Juárez, *Documentos*, VIII, 390. Also see Manifiesto del Congreso de la Unión a sus comitentes, in Dublán and Lozano, *Legislación mexicana*, IX, 660-662.

12. Dublán and Lozano, *Legislación mexicana*, IX, 698-699; Juárez, *Documentos*, IX, 581-583.

13. Dublán and Lozano, *Legislación mexicana*, IX, 718-720.

14. *La Sociedad*, 14 December 1865; Juárez, *Documentos*, X, 378-379.

15. Jesús González Ortega to Sebastián Lerdo de Tejada, 21 December 1865, in Juárez, *Documentos*, X, 386-387. For the Juárez-González Ortega conflict see Ivie E. Cadenhead, "González Ortega and the Presidency of Mexico," *HAHR* 33 (August 1952): 331-346. González Ortega defended his position in "Manifiesto de González Ortega contra la prórroga," 26 December 1865, in Juárez, *Documentos*, X, 387-419.

16. Guillermo Prieto to Lorenzo Vega, 23 December 1865, AJ, caja 10, doc. 1308; Juárez, *Documentos*, X, 419.

17. Juárez, *Documentos*, X, 422-424.

18. *New York Herald*, 16 December 1866; Juárez, *Documentos*, XI, 636.

19. *El Siglo XIX*, 17 December 1867.

20. Dublán and Lozano, *Legislación mexicana*, X, 26-28.

21. Untitled manifesto, 10 January 1861, in LAF 394 and Juárez, *Documentos*, IV, 136-138.

22. Francisco Zarco, Circular of the Minister of Foreign Relations, LAF 396, doc. 139; Juárez, *Documentos*, IV, 151-153. On 24 January 1861 Juárez lifted the state of siege. See Dublán and Lozano, *Legislación mexicana*, IX, 17-18.

23. Ibid., pp. 34-37.

24. Ibid., pp. 228-229; *El Siglo XIX*, 14 June, 1 August 1861.

25. José María Mata to Francisco Zarco in *El Siglo XIX*, 15 November 1861.

26. Dublán and Lozano, *Legislación mexicana*, IX, 317.

27. Ibid., p. 334; *El Siglo XIX*, 14 December 1861; Juárez, *Documentos*, V, 342-347.

28. Felipe Buenrostro, ed., *Historia del primero y segundo congresos de la república mexicana*, II, 82-85; Juárez, *Documentos*, V, 404-407. For an expression of sentiment against the growing presidential power see Ignacio Altamirano's speech to Congress in *El Siglo XIX*, 8 September 1861.

29. *La Voz Nacional* (Guanajuato) quoted in *El Siglo XIX*, 8 April 1862. For an example of Juárez's desire for parliamentary government, see his complaint of excessive executive authority (in Juárez, *Documentos*, II, 188-190) dated 1856; for an early example of liberal hopes for strong government see José María Godoy to Mariano Riva Palacio, 24 November 1857, UTLAC, M. Riva Palacio Papers, García 172, folder 21, doc. 7154.

30. *El Siglo XIX,* 14 April 1862.

31. Benito Juárez to Manuel Alas, 10 June 1862, AJ, caja 3, doc. 183; Jorge L. Tamayo, ed., *Epistolario de Benito Juárez,* p. 167.

32. Law of 27 October 1862 and 27 May 1863 in Dublán and Lozano, *Legislación mexicana,* IX, 548-549, 622.

33. Guillermo Prieto, *Guillermo Prieto a sus amigos.*

34. Juárez, *Documentos,* X, 363-369. For an extended defense of the prorogation see Lerdo's circular of 30 April 1866, ibid., 833-857.

35. Francisco Zarco to Benito Juárez, 14 July 1866, AJ, caja 13, doc. 2030.

36. Ignacio Vallarta to Benito Juárez, 2 January 1867, ibid., doc. 4132.

37. Dublán and Lozano, *Legislación mexicana,* X, 44-48; Juárez, *Documentos,* XII, 325-332.

38. Dublán and Lozano, *Legislación mexicana,* X, 49-65; *El Siglo XIX,* 14 August 1867; Juárez, *Documentos,* XII, 332-341. Expressions of support can be found in Ezequiel Montes, *Discurso pronunciado . . . defendiendo el dictamen de la comisión de puntos constitucionales;* Guillermo Prieto, *Discurso . . . en la cuestión del senado.*

39. *El Siglo XIX,* 22 August 1867.

40. Ibid., 9 December 1867.

41. Cosío Villegas, *La República Restaurada: La vida política,* pp. 230-236. Much of the following discussion is based on this singularly important work.

42. Law of 8 May 1868 discussed in ibid., pp. 336-350.

43. Ibid., pp. 261-268.

44. On 20 May 1875 Lerdo asked for an extension of the suspension and it was granted by a vote of 115 to 26. For details of the laws and the debates in Congress see ibid., pp. 270-311. Also see Knapp, *Sebastián Lerdo de Tejada,* pp. 167-193.

45. For the relevant documents on the Senate, see Juárez, *Documentos,* XIV, 382-442; for discussion see Knapp, *Sebastián Lerdo de Tejada,* pp. 186-192.

Chapter 6: Arms, Politics, and Caudillos

1. Ignacio Altamirano, "Discurso pronunciado en el teatro nacional de México la noche de 15 setiembre de 1861," in *Discursos pronunciados en las funciones cívicas del año de 1861,* in LAF 136.

2. Apter, *Modernization,* p. xii.

3. Huntington, *Political Order,* pp. 142-143; Binder, *Crises and Sequences,* pp. 207-210.

4. See William S. Stokes, "Violence as a Power Factor in Latin American Politics," *Western Political Quarterly* 5 (September 1952): 445-468.

5. This analysis of caudillismo as a system is based on Eric R. Wolf and Edward Hansen, "Caudillo Politics: A Structural Analysis," *Comparative*

Studies in Society and History 9, no. 2 (January 1968): 168-179.

6. Richard N. Morse, "Towards a Theory of Spanish-American Government," *Journal of the History of Ideas* 15 (1954): 79.

7. François Chevalier, " 'Caudillos' et 'caciques' en Amérique: Contribution a l'étude des liens personnels," *Mélanges offerts a Marcel Bataillon par les Hispanistes Français, Bulletin Hispanique,* 64 bis (1962), 30-47.

8. Wolf and Hansen, "Caudillo Politics," pp. 173-177. Also see Hugh M. Hamill, Jr., ed., *Dictatorship in Spanish America,* pp. 3-25.

9. Huntington, *Political Order,* p. 198.

10. Juan Alvarez to Joaquín Moreno, 27 July 1856, UTLAC, Documentos Relativos a la Reforma, García 28.

11. Mariano Riva Palacio to Antonio de Haro y Tamariz, August 1855, UTLAC, M. Riva Palacio Papers, García 169, folder 18, doc. 5716.

12. José María Lafragua, Circular of the Minister of Gobernación, 24 January 1856, in LAF 398.

13. *Observaciones sobre la ley de 26 de Febrero y sobre su reglamento,* p. 27.

14. José María Lafragua, Circular of the Minister of Gobernación, 8 January 1956, in LAF 398.

15. José María Pérez Hernández, *Estadística de la república mexicana,* pp. 215-225. One of the subjects most in need of study is the Mexican military. For a beginning, see Jorge H. Lozoya, *El ejército mexicano (1911-1965),* ch. 1.

16. José María Lafragua, Circular of the Minister of Gobernación, 22 October 1856, in LAF 398.

17. *El Aguila Roja* (Guadalajara), 7 March 1856.

18. Juan Antonio de la Fuente, *Discurso que formó por encargo de la junta patriótica,* p. 16.

19. *El Siglo XIX,* 12 May 1856; also see *La Opinión* (Querétaro) quoted in ibid., 22 January 1856, and Ignacio de la Llave to Antonio de Haro y Tamariz, 27 January 1856, in ibid., 9 February 1856.

20. See Lyle N. McAlister, *The "Fuero Militar" in New Spain, 1764-1800,* for a good discussion of the military *fuero.* During the colonial period there were 31 different major court systems and many minor *fueros.* The Mexican Constitution of 1824 reduced the number of *fueros* to two—military and ecclesiastical.

21. Ley sobre la administración de justicia, 23 November 1855, in *Archivo mexicano,* I, 164-197; Juárez, *Documentos,* II, 98-115; Dublán and Lozano, *Legislación mexicana,* VIII, 565-626. On the *comandancias generales* see Zarco in *El Siglo XIX,* 7 June 1856, and Zarco, *Historia,* pp. 99, 114, 190-195, 205, 229, 725.

22. *El Siglo XIX,* 23 February 1856, 4 April 1856.

23. Ibid., 23 May 1856, 20 January 1861.

24. *Archivo mexicano,* I, 33-34, 49-50, 97, 111.

25. Ibid., 77-79.

26. For 1856 budget see ibid., pp. 262-388 (summary on p. 381). For selected budgets from 1826 to 1855 see Manuel Payno, *Ley de presupuestos generales de la república.* Although these figures are for *projected* budgets only, they are useful indicators of intentions if not actuality. For a discussion of the utility of budgets for measuring political ideology see James W. Wilkie, *The Mexican Revolution: Federal Expenditure and Social Change,* pp. 3-10.

27. For mounting complaints of ex-soldiers' becoming criminals, see *El Monitor Republicano,* 1 May 1856.

28. Juárez refused to make deals with chiefs of rebel armies. Juan E. Pasavan to B. Juárez, 8 November 1860, AJ, caja 1, doc. 115; Juárez, *Documentos,* III, 38-39.

29. Jesus González Ortega a los habitantes de la república, 27 December 1860, in *El Siglo XIX,* 16 January 1861.

30. Ibid., 7 May 1856. Zarco completely ignored the fact that the Gadsden Treaty of 1853 nullified the provisions of Guadalupe-Hidalgo.

31. Ibid., 7 November 1855; Juan Antonio de la Fuente, *Discurso,* p. 16.

32. *Archivo mexicano,* I, 227-228.

33. Zarco, *Historia,* pp. 905-913. The constitution did not make enlistment compulsory as Olvera desired.

34. Secretaría del Estado y del Despacho de Relaciones Exteriores, *Memoria . . . correspondiente a la administración provisional en los años de 1841, 42, y 43,* p. 55; Agustín Escudero to Mariano Riva Palacio, 22 January 1850, UTLAC, M. Riva Palacio Papers, García 165, folder 14, doc. 3760.

35. *Archivo mexicano,* II, 677. For a copy of the law with Lafragua's handwritten comments on the influence of the Spanish *guardia civil,* see *Ley orgánica de la guardia de la república mexicana.*

36. *Archivo mexicano,* V, 616-618; Dublán and Lozano, *Legislación mexicana,* IX, 206-207.

37. For a detailed study of the rurales, see Paul J. Vanderwood, "The Rurales: Mexico's Rural Police Force, 1861-1914" (Ph.D. dissertation, The University of Texas at Austin, 1970), pp. 1-140.

38. Although not actually a "law," the Ley Fuga had legal precedents. See *Archivo mexicano,* II, 537-556, and V, 616-618.

39. For the rurales in the French intervention, see *Memoria de Gobernación, 1873,* doc. 15, p. 58.

40. Vanderwood, "Rurales," pp. 65-71; Pantaleón Tovar, ed., *Historia parlamentaria del cuarto congreso constitucional,* I, 810 and III, 1098; Dublán and Lozano, *Legislación mexicana,* X, 568. For analysis of the debates see Cosío Villegas, *La República Restaurada: La vida política,* pp. 368-397.

41. During the revolt of Tuxtepec the rurales supported Lerdo against Díaz. See ibid., pp. 900-925.

42. For the 20 November 1866 law that stripped all disloyal military men of their rank and subjected them to trial as traitors, see Dublán and Lozano, *Legislación mexicana,* IX, 744.

43. Actas de las sesiones de la junta revolucionaria mexicana, Brownsville, Texas, 22 May, 23 May, 30 May, 1 June 1855, Juárez, *Documentos,* II, 31, 33, 36-37; Guillermo Prieto to Manuel Doblado, 5 September 1855, ibid., pp. 57-58; Ignacio Comonfort to Manuel Doblado, 7 September 1855, ibid., 59-60.

44. *El Siglo XIX,* 27 February 1856, also 8 March, 10 April, and 26 May 1856.

45. Zarco, *Historia,* pp. 191-195, 236-252; Scholes, *Mexican Politics,* pp. 8-9. The committee did not give outright approval to Vidaurri but instead offered to delay action—a move tantamount to approval.

46. See, for example, Vidaurri to Benito Juárez, 31 October 1855, in Santiago Vidaurri, *Correspondencia particular de don Santiago Vidaurri,* p. 5; and in Juárez, *Documentos,* II, 85, in which Vidaurri gets Juárez's title mixed up.

47. Juárez to Vidaurri, 29 January 1858, and Vidaurri to Juárez, 31 January 1858, in Vidaurri, *Correspondencia,* pp. 8-11; and Juárez, *Documentos,* II, 299, 300-302.

48. Vidaurri to Juárez, 27 December 1858, in Vidaurri, *Correspondencia,* pp. 16-17; and Juárez, *Documentos,* II, 404-405.

49. Vidaurri to Juárez, 10 August 1859, in Vidaurri, *Correspondencia,* pp. 26-28; and Juárez, *Documentos,* II, 536-537.

50. The documentation for this conflict is scarce, but see Andrés Treviño to Juárez, 1 January 1860, AJ, caja 2, doc. 36; Juárez, *Documentos,* II, 573; Vidaurri to Ignacio Zaragoza, 1 September 1859, in Ignacio Zaragoza, *Epistolario Zaragoza-Vidaurri,* pp. 108-109, in which Vidaurri hints at rebellion against the liberal government; for official disgust with Vidaurri see José María Mata to Melchor Ocampo, 12 September 1859, AHMA, 2nd series, legajo 8, and Juárez, *Documentos,* III, 695; Scholes, *Mexican Politics,* p. 29.

51. Vidaurri to Editor of the *Southern Intelligencer,* 28 February 1861, in *El Heraldo,* 21 March 1861, and Juárez, *Documentos,* IV, 282; see Vidaurri to Juárez, 24 March 1861, in Juárez, *Documentos,* IV, 300-301, for an example of Vidaurri's complaints. Also Vidaurri to Ignacio Comonfort, 30 May and 15 July 1862, UTLAC, Comonfort Papers, folder 20-B.

52. For the correspondence see Vidaurri, *Correspondencia,* pp. 120-184; Scholes, *Mexican Politics,* p. 89. For Vadaurri's unsuccessful attempt to purchase an hacienda from the Sánchez Navarros, see Harris, *Mexican Family Empire,* pp. 173-174.

53. *El Siglo XIX,* 21 July 1862.

54. Ray F. Broussard, "Vadaurri, Juárez and Comonfort's Return from Exile," HAHR 49, no. 2 (May 1969): 268-280. See *El Siglo XIX*'s strong anti-Vidaurri editorials of 10 November, 14 November, and 10 December 1862.

55. Juárez to Pedro Santacilia, 10 December 1863, in Benito Juárez, *Archivos privados de D. Benito Juárez y D. Pedro Santacilia,* pp. 16-18; Scholes, *Mexican Politics,* pp. 102-103. In 1861 Juárez was rumored to have said: "For my friends, everything; for my enemies, justice . . . if possible." See

Bulnes, *Juárez*, pp. 428-429.

56. Iglesias to Vidaurri, 20 January, 28 January, 30 January, 3 February 1864 in Juárez, *Documentos*, VIII, 643-650. Vidaurri to Iglesias, 1 and 3 February 1864, ibid., pp. 648-651.

57. For pertinent documents see ibid., pp. 651-659; Guillermo Prieto, *Lecciones de historia patria escritas para los alumnos del colegio militar*, p. 503; Scholes, *Mexican Politics*, pp. 103-104.

58. Dublán and Lozano, *Legislación mexicana*, IX, 673-679; Juárez, *Documentos*, VIII, 659-661, 668-670.

59. Cosío Villegas, *La República Restaurada: La vida política*, pp. 118-119; Harris, *Mexican Family Empire*, pp. 305-306.

60. Manifesto of José López Uraga, 28 March 1864, AJ, caja 8, doc. 999; Juárez, *Documentos*, VIII, 698-700. The liberals also feared Lozada's seizure of haciendas in Nayarit. See Jean Meyer, *Problemas campesinos y revueltas agrarias, 1821-1910*, pp. 102-115.

61. Ramón Corona to Benito Juárez, 18 December 1866, AJ, caja 11, doc. 1488; Juárez, *Documentos*, XI, 650-651. No reply from Juárez was located.

62. Juárez to Corona, 15 October 1867, AJ, caja S, doc. 255; Juárez, *Documentos*, XII, 598.

63. Lozada to Corona, 29 May 1867, AJ, caja 17, doc. 2542; Juárez, *Documentos*, XII, 20-22. Juárez, in a letter to Corona, says Lozada's plea came as no surprise since Lozada only wants to save his "correligionarios." Juárez to Corona, 17 June 1867, AJ, caja S, doc. 259; Juárez, *Documentos*, XII, 166-167.

64. Domingo Rubí to Juárez, 26 September 1867, AJ, doc. 3948; Juárez, *Documentos*, XII, 524.

65. Corona to Juárez, 15 October 1867, AJ, doc. S-198; Juárez, *Documentos*, XII, 597-598. Juárez refused to transfer Corona, who may have wanted access to the customs revenues of Tepic's port, San Blas. If so, Juárez may have feared Corona as much as Lozada.

66. Rubí to Juárez, 23 February 1870, AJ, doc. 8880; Juárez, *Documentos*, XIV, 315-316. Also see Juan N. Rábago to Juárez, 14 February 1870, AJ, doc. 8799; Juárez, *Documentos*, XIV, 310-312. Lozada refused to support Vega's activities openly, for two reasons: self-protection should he fail, and his increasing physical sickness and morbid fear of death.

67. Jean Meyer, "El ocaso de Manuel Lozada," *Historia Mexicana* 18 (April-June 1969): 535-544.

68. Ibid., pp. 543, 560-561.

69. Ibid., pp. 553-557.

70. Ibid., pp. 558-559. The struggle with Lozada was also linked to the desires of Jalisco to dominate western Mexico—something the liberals had no intention of permitting. For details, see Harry Bernstein, *Modern and Contemporary Latin America*, pp. 87-91.

71. Varios Liberales, *Rápida ojeada*, p. 4.

Chapter 7: Church and State: Search for Compromise
1. Robert Ricard, *La "Conquête spirituelle" du Mexique*, pp. 273 ff;
Charles Gibson, *The Aztecs under Spanish Rule*, p. 490, note 5; Alfonso
Toro, *La iglesia y el estado en México: Estudio sobre los gobiernos mexicanos
desde la independencia hasta nuestros días*, p. 101 ff.
2. Lázaro de la Garza y Ballesteros to Benito Juárez, 27 November 1855,
LAF 537. For a good discussion of clerical attitudes see Robert J. Knowlton,
"Clerical Response to the Mexican Reform, 1855-1875," *Catholic Historical
Review* 50, no. 4 (January 1965): 509-528.
3. Garza y Ballesteros to Ezequiel Montes, 7 July 1856, in *Contestaciones
entre el illmo. Sr. Arzobispo de México, Dr. D. Lázaro de la Garza y Ballesteros, y el exmo. Sr. Ministro de Justicia, Negocios Eclesiásticos é Instrucción
Pública, Lic. D. Ezequiel Montes, con motivo de la ley espedida en 25 de junio
de 1856, sobre la desamortización de los bienes de las corporaciones civiles y
eclesiásticas de la República*, p. 8. For similar sentiments, see Pedro Espinosa,
Bishop of Guadalajara, *Circular*.
4. Pelagio Antonio de Labastida y Dávalos to Ezequiel Montes, 2 April
1856 in *Representación del Obispo de Puebla y Contestación*, p. 15. Also in
Zarco, *Historia*, p. 136. For an analysis of ecclesiastical inflexibility see Robert
J. Knowlton, "La iglesia mexicana y la Reforma: Respuesta y resultados,"
Historia Mexicana 18 (April-June 1969): 516-534.
5. W. Eugene Shiels, "Church and State in the First Decade of Mexican
Independence," *Catholic Historical Review* 28 (July 1942): 210. For colonial
origin of patronage see Charles Gibson, *Spain in America*. Gibson makes the
observation that Patronato did more than give the crown power over the clergy;
it also allowed the clergy to interfere in the political life of the state.
6. For a law to restrict the practice see *Colección de los aranceles de obvenciones y derechos parroquiales que han estado vigentes en los obispados de la
República Mexicana y que se citan en el supremo decreto de 11 de abril de
1857*. The popular name for the law was Ley Iglesias, which Callcott (*Church
and State in Mexico, 1822-1857*, p. 257) incorrectly translates as "the Church
Law" but which was actually named after its author, José María Iglesias. For
a conflict within the liberal group over the role of the state in church collections see Mariano Riva Palacio to Ignacio Comonfort, 21 April 1857, UTLAC,
M. Riva Palacio Papers, 170/19, doc. 6452; M. Riva Palacio, Circular of the
Governor of the State of Mexico, 21 April 1857, ibid., doc. 6453; Comonfort
to M. Riva Palacio, 7 May 1857, ibid., 171/20, doc. 6532.
7. Shiels, "Church and State," p. 206. Also see Alamán, *Historia*, V,
686-690.
8. *Abusos y desordenes en materias eclesiásticas*, p. v.
9. José María Pérez Hernández, *Estadística de la república mexicana*, pp.

245-257. Government income for 1861 was 20.8 million pesos, 700,000 less than the church's.

10. Michael P. Costeloe, "The Administration, Collection and Distribution of Tithes in the Archbishopric of Mexico, 1800-1860," *The Americas* 23 (July 1966): 3-27; José Guadalupe Navarro R., "Los diezmos en México durante el tiempo de la colonia," *Boletín Eclesiástico de la Arquidiócesis de Guadalajara,* época 5, año 9 (1938): 380. For the fall in tithe revenue see Alexander von Humboldt, *Political Essay on the Kingdom of New Spain,* III, 96. Costeloe, *Church Wealth in Mexico: A Study of the "Juzgado de Capellanías" in the Archbishopric of Mexico, 1800-1856,* p. 17, shows 1821 tithe revenue one-third its eighteenth-century high. Also see Callcott, *Church and State,* pp. 12-19.

11. Jan Bazant, *Alienation of Church Wealth in Mexico,* pp. 14-39.

12. Miguel Lerdo de Tejada, *Memoria de Hacienda,* pp. 75, 82-83; Miguel Lerdo de Tejada, *Noticia de las fincas pertenecientes a corporaciones civiles y eclesiásticas del distrito de México.* For official estimates of monastic wealth see AGN, Justicia Eclesiástica, vol. 48, exp. 24-26. Charles R. Berry, "The Fiction and Fact of the Reform: The Case of the Central District of Oaxaca, 1856-1867," *The Americas* 26, no. 3 (January 1970): 277-290, found the church owned over 72 percent of the houses in Oaxaca.

13. The most sophisticated recent analysis, by Jan Bazant *(Alienation,* pp. 12-13, 270), concludes that the total church wealth was less than 80 million pesos out of a total of about 340 million pesos, or 23.5 percent. For the exaggerated estimate of 620 million, see M. Binet, "Mémoire sur les biens du Clergé," MS in the Ministère des Affaires Etrangères, Paris, France, cited in Francisco López Cámara, *La estructura económica y social de México en la época de la Reforma,* p. 198.

14. Costeloe, *Church Wealth,* pp. 30-58.

15. See Potash, *El Banco de Avío.*

16. José María Vigil, *La Reforma,* V; *México a través de los siglos,* edited by Vicente Riva Palacio, p. 49. At independence the clergy numbered 13-14,000. See Humboldt, *Political Essay,* I, 229-232.

17. Pérez Hernández, *Estadística,* pp. 245-250; Phipps, *Aspects,* p. 47.

18. See, for example, Juárez, "Apuntes para mis hijos," AGN, Conjunto de documentos sobre Juárez, doc. 1; Juárez, *Documentos,* I, 44-49. Also see debate between Melchor Ocampo and Agustín Dueñas, parish priest of Maravatío, in Ocampo, *Obras,* I, 33-390; Bazant *(Alienation,* p. 39) calculates 2,537 regular clergy.

19. Pronunciamiento de Huasca, 13 August 1855. UTLAC, M. Riva Palacio Papers, Archivo 169, folder 18, doc. 5708.

20. Francisco de Paula Arrangoiz y Berzabal, *México desde 1808 hasta 1867,* II, 24-25; Callcott, *Church and State,* p. 45.

21. For its effect on the liberal group, see Ocampo, *Obras,* II, 235.

22. J. Lloyd Mecham, *Church and State in Latin America,* pp. 29-30.

23. For the provincial reforms, see Reyes Heroles, *Liberalismo mexicano*, III, 67-146.

24. For an excellent discussion of the 1833-1834 reforms, see Hale, *Mexican Liberalism*, pp. 108-147. For more details, see Callcott, *Church and State*, pp. 92-98; Costeloe, *Church Wealth*, pp. 10-11; Toro, *Iglesia y estado*, pp. 101-119.

25. For the expropriation law, see Dublán and Lozano, *Legislación mexicana*, V, 246-252. For a participant, Guillermo Prieto, *Memoria de mis tiempos*, II, 138-140.

26. Michael P. Costeloe, "The Mexican Church and the Rebellion of the Polkos," *HAHR* 46, no. 2 (May 1966): 178.

27. *El Siglo XIX*, 16 January 1856, 20 April 1857, 16 September 1857. Also see *El Monitor Republicano*, 25 January 1856.

28. Los redactores de *La Democracia, Contestación a la manifestación del Sr. Arzobispo de México*, p. 11.

29. *El Siglo XIX*, 19 August 1862. For similar doubts about the loyalty of the clergy to Mexico, see *México y la intervención*, p. 109.

30. On early liberalism see Hale, *Mexican Liberalism*, pp. 108-147, and Reyes Heroles, *Liberalismo mexicano*, III, 67-245.

31. Hale, *Mexican Liberalism*, pp. 11-38, 129.

32. *Abusos y desórdenes en materias eclesiásticas*, p. 51.

33. Guillermo Prieto to Ignacio Comonfort, 14 July 1857, in UTLAC, Correspondence of I. Comonfort, folder 17. Reglamento provisional de la libertad de prensa, Mexico, 28 December 1855, in LAF 398. Also see Prieto, Circular of the Minister of Hacienda, 1855, in LAF 72. Lafragua called attacks on the church "irresponsible" (see Circular of the Minister of Gobernación, 28 December 1855, in LAF 398), and José María Iglesias called them against "buenas costumbres" (see *El Siglo XIX*, 20 January 1856).

34. Discurso patriótico pronunciado . . . en la ciudad de Oaxaca, 16 September 1840, in Angel Pola, *Miscelánea*, pp. 1-15; Juárez, *Documentos*, I, 479-484.

35. El Ciudadano Benito Juárez, Gobernador Constitucional del Estado . . . de Oaxaca, a los habitantes del mismo, 29 October 1847, in Pola, *Miscelánea*, pp. 71-74; Juárez, *Documentos*, I, 503-504. Juárez also said justice "is the primordial base of society." Juárez to Oaxaca Congress, 29 February 1848, in Pola, *Miscelánea*, pp. 15-20; Juárez, *Documentos*, I, 522-525.

36. Rafael Martínez de la Torre to Manuel Doblado, 24 October 1855, in Genaro García, ed., *La Revolución de Ayutla según el archivo del General Doblado*, p. 250; Juárez, *Documentos*, II, 84.

37. Ley sobre la administración de justicia, 23 November 1855, *Archivo mexicano*, I, 164-196; Juárez, *Documentos*, II, 98-115; Dublán and Lozano, *Legislación mexicana*, VIII, 565-626.

38. Juárez to Garza y Ballesteros, 30 November 1855, Juárez, *Documentos*, II, 116-117. On 3 December Juárez warned Garza of the harsh consequences of disobedience. Ibid., p. 122. On 5 December he similarly cautioned

the bishop of Michoacán. Ibid., pp. 122-123. For a favorable opinion on the *fuero* law see the congressional report of [Francisco] G[arcía] Anaya, [Eulogio] Barrera, Dictamen sobre la Ley Juárez, 12 April 1856 in ibid., pp. 169-171; Zarco, *Historia*, pp. 96-98. For liberal press support see *El Siglo XIX*, 5 and 15 April 1856.

39. For the constitutional debate on the Juárez Law, see Zarco, *Historia*, pp. 116-128; Juárez, *Documentos*, II, 171-184. For Arriaga see Zarco, *Historia*, p. 121; for Escudero, p. 120; for Aguado, p. 124. The best discussion of the church-state issue at the Constituent Congress is Walter Scholes, "Church and State at the Mexican Constitutional Convention, 1856-1857," *The Americas* 4 (October 1947): 151-174.

40. On the expulsion of the Jesuits see Magnus Mörner, ed., *The Expulsion of the Jesuits from Latin America;* on the consolidation laws see Costeloe, *Church Wealth*, pp. 110-115, and Romeo Flores Caballero, "La consolidación de vales reales en la economía, la sociedad y la política novohispanas," *Historia mexicana* 18 (January-March 1969): 334-378; on the pre-Ayutla reforms see Mecham, *Church and State*, pp. 340-359, and Agustín Cué Cánovas, *La reforma liberal en México*, pp. 20-22. For evidence that Miguel Lerdo de Tejada, author of the Mexican law, was influenced by Mora, see Manuel Payno, *Memoria sobre la revolución de diciembre de 1857 y enero de 1858*, pp. 40-50, in LAF 311. On the Spanish disamortization law see Cué Cánovas, *Reforma liberal*, pp. 23-29, and for its influence in Congress see Zarco, *Historia*, p. 432.

41. Ley de desamortización de bienes de la Iglesia y de corporaciones civiles, 25 June 1856, in *Archivo mexicano*, II, 187-198; Juárez, *Documentos*, II, 197-203; Zarco, *Historia*, pp. 423-427; *Leyes de reforma*, pp. 24-34.

42. The preamble, undoubtedly written by Miguel Lerdo, is found in all the sources listed in note 41.

43. Miguel Lerdo de Tejada, Circular of the Minister of Hacienda, 28 June 1856, in Zarco, *Historia*, pp. 427-430; Juárez, *Documentos*, II, 203-206; *El Siglo XIX*, 28 June 1856.

44. Manuel Payno, *México y el Sr. Embajador don Joaquín Francisco Pacheco*, p. 70.

45. Ezequiel Montes to Joaquín Moreno, 18 March 1857, in UTLAC, Documentos relativos a la Reforma y a la Intervención Francesa, 1850-1867, folder 28. Others called the Lerdo Law a "true revolution." See Manuel Sileceo to Doblado, 25 June 1856, in Genaro García, ed., *Los gobiernos de Alvarez y Comonfort, según el Archivo del General Doblado*, pp. 210-211.

46. José María Lafragua to Santiago Vidaurri, 5 July 1856, in LAF 398. For similar comments see Francisco Benítez to Melchor Ocampo, 8 June 1857 in AHMA, 1st series, legajo 50, B-9-45.

47. Quoted in Cué Cánovas, *Reforma liberal*, pp. 32-33.

48. Hubert H. Bancroft, *History of Mexico*, V, 686; Vigil, *La reforma*, p. 148.

49. Montes to Garza y Ballesteros, 15 July 1856, in *Contestaciones entre*

el . . . Dr. D. Lázaro de la Garza y Ballesteros y el . . . Lic. Ezequiel Montes, p. 40. For clerical decrees threatening excommunication and denying the sacraments to those buying church property see AGN, Justicia Eclesiástica, vols. 181-188, 127.

50. Jan Bazant's conclusions in *Alienation* support Ramírez's contention. Also see his "The Division of Some Mexican Haciendas during the Liberal Revolution, 1856-1862," *Journal of Latin American Studies* 3 (May 1971): 25-37.

51. Ocampo to Juárez, 22 October 1859, in Ocampo, *Obras Completas,* II, 152-153; Juárez, *Documentos,* IV, 221-234.

52. Lafragua's copy of the Ley orgánica del registro del estado civil, 27 January 1857, is found in LAF 398; *El Siglo XIX,* 14 February 1857.

53. For an example see *Guerra al clero.* For anti-toleration pamphlets from the years 1833-1834, see LAF 540.

54. Lázaro de la Garza y Ballesteros, *Exposición que el Illmo. Sr. Arzobispo de México eleva al soberano Congreso Constituyente pidiendo la reforma del artículo 15 del proyecto de constitución,* and his *Pastoral sobre tolerancia religiosa.* Also see *El Monitor Republicano,* 12 November 1855.

55. Pedro Barajas, *Exposiciones que el Illmo. Sr. Obispo eleva al S. Congreso pidiendole se repruebe el artículo 15 del proyecto de constitución que establece la tolerancia de cultos en la República.*

56. *Representación que las Señoras mexicanas elevaron al Congreso Constituyente pidiendo no se establezca en la República la tolerancia de cultos.*

57. José María Lafragua, *Discurso pronunciado . . . contra el artículo 15 del proyecto de la constitución;* Zarco, *Historia,* pp. 625-634. Speech given August 1, 1856.

58. The quoted words are Lafragua's. For other antitoleration statements see Zarco, *Historia,* pp. 453-454, 461-467, 477-479, 548-561, 577-579, 586-593, 597-602, 608-614, 620-625, 635-643, 664-669. For summary see Scholes, "Church and State," pp. 164-169.

59. Zarco, *Historia,* pp. 561-568 and 658-664. For summary of other speeches in favor of freedom of worship, see Scholes, "Church and State," pp. 171-172. There were a few pamphlets in favor of article 15; for example *Representación que varios individuos de la capital del Estado de Jalisco, amantes del progreso y mejores materials del país, dirijen al soberano Congreso Constituyente en favor del artículo 15 del proyecto de constitución.*

60. Zarco, *Historia,* pp. 1220-1224.

Chapter 8: Secularizing the State

1. Montes to Pelagio Antonio de Labastida y Dávalos, 18 April 1856, in *Representación del Obispo de Puebla y Contestación,* pp. 16-25; Zarco, *Historia,* pp. 136-141.

2. Juárez to Lafragua, 7 February 1856, in Pola, *Miscelánea,* pp. 207-208;

Juárez, *Documentos,* II, 167.

3. Lafragua, Circular of the Secretary of Gobernación, 6 May 1856, in LAF 398.

4. *El Siglo XIX,* 2 April 1856.

5. José Primo de Rivera, Secretary of the Ecclesiastical Cabildo of the Archbishopric of Mexico, to the Mexican Public, 29 March 1857, AJ, caja 1, doc. 3; Juárez, *Documentos,* II, 241-242. The decree stated that "those who have sworn loyalty to the Constitution cannot be absolved." A formal retraction was required if the oath had already been taken. It read: "I, _____ , wanting to live and die in the bosom of the Catholic, Apostolic, and Roman Church into which I have had the good fortune to be born, retract everything I voluntarily or involuntarily did or said against the truths and precepts of said Church, and especially I retract the solemn promise I made to uphold the Constitution and the Reform Laws . . . and it is my desire from now on, as I do now, to do everything in my power to repair the scandal I have caused and to strive to my maximum effort with absolute and complete submission to divine and ecclesiastical laws never to part again, either with words or actions, from the doctrines taught by the Church." UTLAC, Documentos relativos, folder 28.

6. Manuel Soto to M. Riva Palacio, 29 March 1857, UTLAC, M. Riva Palacio Papers, 170, folder 19, doc. 6353. Soto was indignant and declared that "fear of the devil is antidemocratic."

7. Joaquín Noriega to M. Riva Palacio, 27 March 1857, ibid., doc. 6348; Noriega to M. Riva Palacio, 11 August 1857, ibid., 171, f. 20, doc. 6804; José de la Piedra to M. Riva Palacio, 9 April 1857, ibid., 170, f. 19, doc. 6405; Francisco Arroyo to M. Riva Palacio, 22 April 1857, ibid., doc. 6454; M. Limón to M. Riva Palacio, 27 April 1857, ibid., doc. 6479.

8. *El Siglo XIX,* 11 April 1857.

9. Ibid., 20 April 1857.

10. Ibid., 25 April 1857.

11. Manifiesto del gobierno a la nación (Mexico City, 4 March 1857), in LAF 1519, pp. 796-803. For descriptions of the oath-taking see AGN, Ramo de Gobernación, legajo 160 (Actos de juramento de la Constitución de 1857), expediente 1.

12. Some of the moderates supported the Tacubaya revolt in the hope of achieving compromise. See Manuel Payno, *Memoria sobre la revolución,* pp. 77-78.

13. The Supreme Government of the Republic to all Mexicans, in *Diario Oficial del Supremo Gobierno,* 30 January 1858, LAF 394 and 120. Also see *El Siglo XIX,* 29 January 1858. Callcott's version (*Church and State,* p. 315) of the plan is actually an anti-Zuloaga tract and not the true plan. Pius IX to Félix Zuloaga, 18 March 1858, in *El Siglo XIX,* 13 May 1858.

14. See Robert J. Knowlton, "Some Practical Effects of Clerical Opposition to the Mexican Reform, 1856-1860," *HAHR* 45, no. 2 (May 1965): 251-

256. Also see Miguel Galindo y Galindo, *La gran década nacional, ó relación histórica de la guerra de reforma, intervención extrangera y gobierno del Archiduque Maximiliano,* I, 435-440. During times of war both liberals and conservatives tapped clerical wealth; the position of the church would, of course, be substantially improved with a conservative victory.

15. Lafragua to Ocampo, 30 September 1858, AHMA, 1st series, legajo 50, L-2-1.

16. Lafragua to Ocampo, 9 June 1859, ibid., L-2-2.

17. See chapter 7, note 33.

18. Prieto to Ocampo, 16 July 1858, AHMA, 1st series, legajo 50, P-25-17; also letters P-25-18, P-25-30.

19. Quoted in Callcott, *Liberalism,* p. 24.

20. *Archivo mexicano,* IV, 54-81; Juárez, *Documentos,* II, 485-500; *Diario de Avisos,* 21 July 1859, in LAF 394. For a good discussion see Scholes, *Mexican Politics,* pp. 43-47.

21. *Archivo mexicano,* IV, 93-101; Juárez, *Documentos,* II, 501-505; Dublán and Lozano, *Legislación mexicana,* VIII, 680-683; *Leyes de reforma,* pp. 101-108.

22. Manuel Ruiz, Circular, 12 July 1859, in *Archivo mexicano,* IV, 82-93; Juárez, *Documentos,* II, 505-510; *Leyes de reforma,* pp. 90-100.

23. Juan Antonio de la Fuente, *Discurso que formó por encargo de la junta patriótica . . . ,* p. 16.

24. Juárez to Pedro Santacilia, 12 July 1859, AJ, S-12; Juárez, *Documentos,* II, 511. Also see Juárez to Santiago Vidaurri, 14 July 1859, in Juárez, *Documentos,* II, 519. Lafragua said the law was the result of the misery created by the clergy "with their eternal resistence and their stupid manifestos." Lafragua to Ocampo, 31 August 1859, AHMA, 1st series, legajo 50, L-23.

25. Law issued 23 July 1859. *Archivo mexicano,* IV, 122-132; Juárez, *Documentos,* II, 526-532; Dublán and Lozano, *Legislación mexicana,* VIII, 688-695; *Leyes de reforma,* pp. 115-125. For this reason, today in Mexico a couple usually has two weddings: a civil and a religious ceremony.

26. Manuel Ruiz, Circular, 23 July 1859. *Archivo mexicano,* IV, 116-121; Juárez, *Documentos,* II, 522-524. For the equality of women see article 15 of the law.

27. Law issued 28 July 1859. *Archivo mexicano,* IV, 137-154; *Leyes de reforma,* pp. 126-140; LAF 663 contains all the Reform Laws of July and August, 1859. Prieto described the law as "divine." Prieto to Ocampo, AHMA, 1st series, legajo 50, P-25-43.

28. Issued 31 July 1859. *Archivo mexicano,* IV, 154-160; Juárez, *Documentos,* II, 532-536; *Leyes de reforma,* pp. 141-146.

29. Ocampo, Circular, 6 August 1859, in Ocampo, *Obras,* II, 229-239; *Leyes de reforma,* pp. 149-158; LAF 663.

30. Law issued 11 August 1859. *Archivo mexicano,* IV, 172-173; Juárez,

Documentos, II, 536-537.

31. Ocampo to Manuel Castillo Portugal, 3 August 1859, in *Leyes de reforma,* pp. 147-148; LAF 663. For the diplomatic problems with the Vatican see Ezequiel Montes to Juárez 18 July 1858, AJ, caja 1, doc. 33 and 34; Juárez, *Documentos,* II, 373-376, 393. Also Montes to Juárez, 9 May 1859, AJ, caja 1, doc. 59; Juárez, *Documentos,* II, 460-461. As of this date, Mexico still does not have diplomatic relations with the Vatican.

32. Registration certificate of Jerónima Francisca Juárez Maza, 10 October 1860. Copy in Juárez, *Documentos,* III, 23-24. Original on display in Sala de Cabildos del Ayuntamiento de Veracruz.

33. González Ortega to the inhabitants of Zacatecas, 31 July 1859, in LAF 426.

34. *Archivo mexicano,* IV, 340-348; *Leyes de reforma,* pp. 190-198; Juárez, *Documentos,* III, 76-82; LAF 663, 426.

35. Juan Antonio de la Fuente, Circular, 4 December 1860, in *Archivo mexicano,* IV, 309-339; *Leyes de reforma,* pp. 163-189.

36. Juárez, *Discurso en la solemne apertura de las sesiones del Congreso de la Unión,* 9 May 1861; *El Siglo XIX,* 9 May 1861. Justo Benítez, governor of Oaxaca, said, "Religion is for men, not governments. . . . this is the great Reform." Governor of Oaxaca to Congress, 16 February 1861, in LAF 490 and 463.

37. *La Independencia,* 1 March, 2 March 1861. Also see Vicente Riva Palacio, *A la memoria del General Leandro Valle, mártir de la libertad,* in UTLAC, Vicente Riva Palacio Papers, 183, folder 1.

38. *El País* (Guadalajara), 13 October 1861. Also see *El Siglo XIX,* 20 June, 22 June, 14 August 1861.

39. Nicolás Pizarro, *Catecismo político constitucional,* pp. 46-47.

40. Ocampo, Circular of the Minister of Hacienda, 3 January 1861, in Ocampo, *Obras,* II, 239-241; Juárez, *Documentos,* IV, 134; *Archivo mexicano,* V, 5-7.

41. Ocampo to Luis Clementi, Archbishop of Damascus, 12 January 1861, in Juárez, *Documentos,* IV, 141; *El Siglo XIX,* 15 January 1861; *Archivo mexicano,* V, 42-43. Also see Francisco Zarco to Secretary of Foreign Relations of the Vatican, 27 February 1861, in AHRE, H/110 "861" 73:0, ff. 44-45. Juárez, *Documentos,* IV, 281.

42. See *Leyes de reforma,* pp. 201-234. Juzgado law in LAF 120.

43. This summary based on Callcott, *Liberalism,* pp. 43-76; Sierra, *Evolución política del pueblo mexicano,* pp. 307-360; Mecham, *Church and State,* pp. 369-375; Egon Caesar Corti, *Maximilian and Charlotte of Mexico;* Cué Cánovas, *Reforma liberal,* pp. 187-194; Toro, *Iglesia y estado,* pp. 302-341; Manuel Rivera Cambas, *Historia de la intervención europea y norteamericana en México y del imperio de Maximiliano de Hapsburgo; La Corte de Roma y el Emperador Maximiliano . . . ;* Bazant, *Alienation,* pp. 256-286.

44. *La Idea Republicana* (Zacatecas), quoted in *El Siglo XIX,* 7 July 1862.

45. *La Chinaca,* 27 March 1863.
46. Carlos de Gagern, *Apelación de los mexicanos a la Europa bien informada de la Europa mal informada,* p. 9.
47. Ignacio Ramírez, "Oración pronunciado . . . el 5 de febrero de 1863," printed in *El Monitor Republicano,* 6 February 1863.
48. For church-state relations during the final years of the Juárez administration see Scholes, *Mexican Politics,* pp. 118-148, 166-176.
49. For the Lerdo administration see Knapp, *Sebastián Lerdo de Tejada,* pp. 214-222. Also see *Exposición del Obispo de León contra el proyecto de elevar a constitucionales las Leyes de Reforma* and *Ley orgánica de las adiciones y reformas constitucionales expedida por el Congreso General en 10 de diciembre de 1874.*
50. For the Díaz years see Karl Schmitt's articles: "The Díaz Conciliation Policy on State and Local Levels, 1876-1911," *HAHR* 40 (November 1960): 513-532; "Catholic Adjustment to the Secular State: The Case of Mexico, 1867-1911," *Catholic Historical Review* 48 (July 1962): 182-204; and "The Mexican Positivists and the Church-State Question, 1876-1911," *Journal of Church and State* 8 (Spring 1966): 200-213. Also see Joseph R. Juárez, "Conflict and Cooperation between Church and State: The Archbishopric of Guadalajara during the Porfiriato, 1876-1911," Ph.D. dissertation, The University of Texas at Austin, 1967.

Chapter 9: Nationalism in a World of Nations
1. Turner, *Mexican Nationalism,* p. 22; John J. Johnson, "The New Latin American Nationalism," *Yale Review* (Winter 1965): 187-204. See also Kalman H. Silvert, "Nationalism in Latin America," *The Annals of the American Academy of Political and Social Science* 334 (1961): 1-9.
2. Binder et al., *Crises and Sequences,* pp. 101-134.
3. Carl Sartorius, *Importancia de México para la emigración alemana;* Luis González, "Notas sobre el nacionalismo mexicano," *América Indígena* 29 (April 1969): 420-429.
4. Manuel Doblado to the citizens of Guanajuato, 17 June 1848, LAF 394.
5. Juan Alvarez a las tropas de su mando, in Anselmo de la Portilla, *Historia de la revolución de México contra la dictadura del general Santa Anna,* p. xliii.
6. *El Republicano,* 6 October 1855.
7. José María Lafragua, Manuel Payno, Ezequiel Montes, Manuel Siliceo, Luis de la Rosa al pueblo mexicano, 22 December 1855, in LAF 398.
8. *El Siglo XIX,* 20 February 1856.
9. Juárez to Matías Romero, 15 November 1856, AMR, fol. 70; Juárez, *Documentos,* II, 220.
10. José María Lafragua, Circular of the Minister of Gobernación, 16 January

1856, in LAF 398.

11. Matías Romero to Benito Juárez, 1 November 1856, AMR, fol. 67; Juárez, *Documentos,* II, 214-217; Tamayo, *Epistolario,* pp. 55-57. Also see Juárez to Romero, 7 August 1856, AMR, doc. 62; Juárez, *Documentos,* II, 208-209. For Degollado trial and important documents see Zarco, *Historia,* pp. 1296-1342. Degollado was exonerated.

12. *El Siglo XIX,* 1 March, 2 March 1857; Juárez, *Documentos,* II, 252-253. Zarco saw foreign conspiracy in every event; he described Apache raids as advanced parties for American filibusterers in *El Siglo XIX,* 7 May 1856.

13. Benito Juárez to Matías Romero, 15 June 1856, AMR, doc. 57; Juárez, *Documentos,* II, 195; *El Siglo XIX,* 9 September 1856, 18 November 1856.

14. Zarco, *Historia,* pp. 790-793.

15. Ibid., pp. 793-799.

16. Manifiesto del gobierno a la nación (4 March 1857) in *Archivo mexicano,* III, 72-133, and in LAF 1519.

17. *El Siglo XIX,* 14 February 1857.

18. Melchor Ocampo, *Discurso pronunciado en la Alameda de la H. C. de Veracruz . . . ,* p. 11 ff.

19. See, for example, *Algunas indicaciones acerca de la intervención Europea en México,* and a reply by Genaro Rus de Cea (pseud. Andrés Ocegura), *Observaciones acerca de la intervención europea en México,* which said Mexicans would do everything possible "to safeguard peace, life, and property and defend national honor and independence" against foreign intervention (p. 5). Also see Rafael de Castro, *La cuestión mexicana o exposición de las causas que hacían indispensable la intervencion europea . . . ,* and *Voto en favor de la intervención de la nación francesa en la República de los Estados Unidos Mexicanos,* both of which conclude Mexicans are incapable of governing themselves.

20. Benito Juárez, "El Presidente interino Constitucional de la República a los Mexicanos" (31 October 1858), in Juárez, *Documentos,* II, 398-402; *El Siglo XIX,* 18 January 1858, contains excerpts from provincial papers.

21. *El Siglo XIX,* 6 April 1858. To demands that Mexico become an American protectorate, *El Siglo* replied that the whole idea was "treasonous" and an "attack on Mexican nationality." Ibid., 8 April 1858.

22. Melchor Ocampo al gobernador del estado de . . . , 28 April 1859, in LAF 417.

23. J. M. Lafragua to Ocampo, 5 October and 22 October 1859, AJ, S-439 and S-439-II; Juárez, *Documentos,* II, 545-548.

24. Melchor Ocampo, Circular de la Secretaría de Relaciones Exteriores, 28 April 1859, in Ocampo, *Obras,* II, 222.

25. El gobierno constitucional a la nación, 30 January 1860; Juárez, *Documentos,* II, 587-590, and *Archivo mexicano,* IV, 243-250.

26. William R. Henry to B. Juárez, 13 June 1858, and Juárez to Henry, 3 August 1858, AJ, 1-25, 1-26; Juárez, *Documentos,* II, 380, 392-393; also

Juárez to Andrés Treviño, 18 January 1860, AJ, 2-136; Tamayo, *Epistolario*, p. 108.

27. Santos Degollado to Melchor Ocampo, 1 February 1860, AHRE, H/ 131/2405, hojas 22-23; Juárez, *Documentos*, II, 599-600.

28. Text of treaty found in many sources, some of which are: Juárez, *Documentos*, III, 751-825; Agustín Cué Cánovas, *El Tratado McLane-Ocampo*, pp. 159-169; José Fuentes Mares, *Juárez y los Estados Unidos*, pp. 227-234.

29. See especially Alejandro Villaseñor y Villaseñor, *Antón Lizardo—el tratado McLane-Ocampo—el brindis del desierto;* Alberto María Carreño, ed., *La diplomacia extraordinaria entre México y Estados Unidos;* Fuentes Mares, *Juárez y los Estados Unidos*, pp. 101-188.

30. Cué Cánovas, *Tratado.*

31. See ibid., pp. 41-50; also see ibid., pp. 17-21, for details of the antecedents of the American claim to Tehuantepec. For relevant documents, see Juárez, *Documentos*, III, 111-345.

32. See Juárez, *Documentos*, III, 353-387, for correspondence and drafts of the treaties. Also see Fuentes Mares, *Juárez y los Estados Unidos*, pp. 50-58, and Cué Cánovas, *Tratado*, pp. 85-92.

33. Sebastián Lerdo de Tejada to John Forsyth, 12 September 1857, Juárez, *Documentos*, III, 387-388. Forsyth's comment is found in letter to Cass, 15 September 1857, in William R. Manning, ed., *Diplomatic Correspondence of the United States, 1831-1860*, IX, 929-932; Juárez, *Documentos*, III, 390.

34. Juárez, *Documentos*, III, 391.

35. Ibid., pp. 403-446.

36. For the Churchwell memoranda see Manning, *Correspondence*, IX, 1024 ff; Juárez, *Documentos*, III, 475-526.

37. Cited in Cué Cánovas, *Tratado*, p. 98.

38. Relevant documentation in Juárez, *Documentos*, III, 527-727. See, in particular, McLane's letter to Cass, 25 June 1859, explaining the intense Mexican opposition to sale of national territory, pp. 647-649.

39. John Forsyth to William L. Marcy, 8 November 1856, in Manning, *Correspondence*, IX, 854-856; Juárez, *Documentos*, III, 338-340. See Mexican protest in Juárez, *Documentos*, III, 461.

40. Quoted in Cué Cánovas, *Tratado*, p. 85, and Fuentes Mares, *Juárez y los Estados Unidos*, p. 166.

41. Quoted in Cué Cánovas, *Tratado*, p. 119.

42. Fuentes Mares, *Juárez y los Estados Unidos*, p. 144.

43. Cué Cánovas, *Tratado*, p. 128.

44. *El Siglo XIX*, 4 March 1861.

45. Juárez, *Discurso*, p. 852.

46. For law see *Archivo mexicano*, V, 596-599, and copy in LAF 417; for public support see *El Siglo XIX*, 18 April 1861.

47. "El Gobierno Constitucional á la Nación," in *El Diario de Avisos*, 21 July 1859; Juárez, *Documentos*, IX, 490-491.

48. Ramírez, *Discurso cívico*, p. 25.

49. *El Progreso* (Veracruz), cited in *El Siglo XIX*, 7 July 1861; *La Libertad* (Durango), cited in ibid., 21 December 1861; *El Monitor Republicano*, 11 November 1861.

50. Ignacio Zaragoza to José María Arteaga, 31 October 1861, and Arteaga Decree, 5 November 1861, cited in *El Siglo XIX*, 21 November 1861.

51. Manuel Payno, "Discurso pronunciado en la plaza del pueblo de San Angel . . . el 16 de setiembre," in *El Monitor Republicano*, 28 September 1862.

52. *El Siglo XIX*, 16 December 1861.

53. Manuel Ruiz to J. M. Arteaga, 1 November 1861, in *El Monitor Republicano*, 14 November 1861.

54. *El Monitor Republicano*, 27 January 1862.

55. *El Siglo XIX*, 26 January 1863.

56. Altamirano, *Discurso cívico*.

57. Ibid.

58. *El Siglo XIX*, 22 April 1862.

59. Ibid., 20 April 1862 (italics in original).

60. Manuel Payno, "Discurso pronunciado en el pueblo de San Angel . . . el 16 de setiembre," in *El Monitor Republicano*, 28 September 1862.

61. Manuel Doblado, "Circular del Ministro de Gobernación," 12 April 1862, in *El Siglo XIX*, 14 April 1862.

62. Fuente, *Discurso*, especially p. 9.

63. *El Boletín de Noticias* (Tampico), quoted in *El Siglo XIX*, 28 March 1862.

64. *La Chinaca*, 12 March 1863. See also *La Campaña* as cited in *El Siglo XIX*, 18 January 1862.

65. José María Iglesias, *Refutación del discurso pronunciado por Mr. Billault, ministro sin cartera en el cuerpo legislativo francés sobre la política del emperador en México*, pp. 3-4. Also *El Siglo XIX*, 7 September 1861, expresses similar sentiments, as does Ignacio Ramírez, "Oración pronunciada . . . el 5 de febrero de 1863," in *El Monitor Republicano*, 6 February 1863.

66. *El Monitor Republicano*, 9 January 1862.

67. Manuel Payno, *México y el Sr. Embajador Don Joaquín Francisco Pacheco*, p. 43.

68. Gagern, *Apelación de los mexicanos*, pp. 3-4.

69. For battle cry see *El Monitor Republicano*, 26 January 1862; for bullfight see *El Siglo XIX*, 7 March 1862; for violence see *El Siglo XIX*, 23 December 1861.

70. *La Chinaca*, 24 March, 7 April, 8 May 1863; *El Siglo XIX*, 12 April 1862; Juan Antonio de la Fuente to Thomas Corwin, 3 October 1862, Juárez, *Documentos*, VII, 68-69.

71. Matías Romero to Minister of Foreign Affairs, 1 February 1862, Romero, *Correspondencia*, II, 32-34; Juárez to Matías Romero, 26 January 1865, Juárez, *Documentos*, IX, 617-168. See the excellent analysis of this problem

by Romero to Minister of Foreign Affairs, 12 November 1864, Juárez, *Documentos*, IX, 450-452.

72. Juárez, *Documentos,* IX, 741.

73. S. Lerdo to M. Romero, 29 March 1865, ibid., pp. 746-747.

74. B. Juárez to P. Santacilia, 6 April 1865, AJ, S-47; Juárez, *Documentos,* IX, 753-755.

75. M. Romero to B. Juárez, 22 August 1865, AMR, caja 3, hoja 724; B. Juárez to P. Santacilia, 25 August 1865, AJ, S-71; B. Juárez to M. Romero, 25 August 1865, Juárez, *Documentos,* X, 179.

76. Dublán and Lozano, *Legislación mexicana,* IX, 734.

77. Juárez used the word *nacionicidio* to describe Maximilian's crime in *Manifiesto justificativo de los castigos nacionales en Querétaro,* p. 35.

78. J. Terán to S. Lerdo de Tejada, 20 April 1865, Juárez, *Documentos,* X, 29; S. Lerdo to J. Terán, 22 July 1865, ibid., p. 30.

79. *El Siglo XIX,* 9 December 1867; see also Zarco's analysis of the speeches in ibid., 11 and 12 December 1867.

80. Knapp, *Lerdo de Tejada,* p. 201. For the policy's effect on the foreign debt see Bazant, *Historia de la deuda exterior de México, 1823-1946,* pp. 84-107.

81. Daniel Cosío Villegas, "La doctrina Juárez," *Historia Mexicana* 11, no. 4 (April-June 1962): 529. An excellent analysis of the role of foreign intervention in producing national unity is Vicente Riva Palacio's "Discurso que pronunció en la alameda . . . por encargo de la Junta Patriótica," in *El Monitor Republicano,* 20 September 1867.

82. For these and other treason laws see Dublán and Lozano, *Legislación mexicana,* IX, 588-589, 652-654.

83. *La convocatoria, la circular con que se acompañó a los gobiernos de los estados, y el manifiesto del ciudadano presidente de la República,* especially articles 22 and 23.

84. See, as examples, *Vindicación del pueblo mexicano en la invasión francesa;* José María del Castillo Velasco, *Aniversario del cinco de mayo de 1862,* pp. 4-5; Emilio Castro, *¿Quienes son los traidores?,* pp. 5-6; *Los traidores juzgados á la luz de la razón.*

85. Ernesto de la Torre Villar, "Visión de México y los mexicanos en algunos intervencionistas," *Humanitas* 4 (1963): 521.

Chapter 10: The Legacies of the Reform

1. Hale, *Liberalism,* pp. 258-261.

2. José María Lafragua, *Memoria de Relaciones Exteriores,* p. 67.

3. Zarco, *Historia,* pp. 386-404.

4. For local reforms see Donald J. Fraser, "La política de desamortización en las comunidades indígenas, 1856-1872," *Historia Mexicana* 21, no. 4 (April-June 1972): 623; Mora's attitude about Indians in Mora, *México,* I, 65-67;

Hale, *Liberalism*, p. 218. Liberals wrote editorials and pamphlets urging destruction of Indian communities. See Wheat, *Zarco*, p. 74, and Y. O., *La Reforma social de México deducida del aspecto político que él presenta y fundada en la experiencia de cuarenta y cinco años*, pp. 11-14. Even conservatives agreed that the Indian communities needed to be dissolved for economic reasons. See Alamán, *Historia*, V, 433.

5. See Miguel Lerdo de Tejada, *Memoria de Hacienda, 1857*, Doc. No. 149 and Appendix, Table III-1.

6. Bazant, *Alienation*, p. 114; *Memoria 1857*, p. 10; Berry's description of Oaxaca buyers ("Fiction and Fact," pp. 285-286) conforms to Bazant's findings in Mexico City and the states of Veracruz, San Luis Potosí, Michoacán, and Jalisco.

7. Bazant, *Alienation*, pp. 287-290.

8. See Phipps, *Some Aspects*, pp. 112-113; Eyler N. Simpson, *The Ejido: Mexico's Way Out*, pp. 29-31; Molina Enríquez, *La Reforma*, p. 75. By looking at laws and not archives Reyes Heroles (*Liberalismo*, III, 637-644) argues that ejidos were exempt from the law.

9. Labastida, *Colección*, pp. 28-29. Lerdo did eliminate taxes on sales under 200 pesos. For an analysis of Lerdo's attitude, see Fraser, "Desamortización," pp. 635-647. See the Riva Palacio archive (UTLAC), esp. docs. 5960, 6320, 6329, 6335, 6387, for early 1857. The situation was further complicated by the complex land-owning patterns of the villages, in which existed (1) *fondo legal*—actual village and its houses, (2) *ejido*—common lands for pasture and recreation, (3) *terrenos de repartimiento*—common land granted to individuals, (4) *propios*—land whose produce supported village expenses, often rented, and (5) *montes y aguas*—used for cutting wood, gathering fruit, and drawing water.

10. Dublán and Lozano, *Legislación mexicana*, VIII, 330-342.

11. Powell, *Liberalismo y el campesinado*.

12. Ibid., pp. 140-144; Calderón, *La República Restaurada: Vida económica*, pp. 333-340.

13. UTLAC—M. Riva Palacio, Doc. 8331.

14. Projected budgets in E. Busto, *Estadística de la república mexicana*, p. xcii. Actual expenditures were undoubtedly much larger.

15. Luiz González et al., *La República Restaurada: Vida social*, p. 133.

16, Moisés González Navarro, "Tenencia de la tierra y población agrícola, 1877-1960," *Historia Mexicana* 19, no. 1 (July-September 1969): 62-86; Jan Bazant, "Peones, arrendatarios y aparceros, 1868-1904," *Historia Mexicana* 24, no. 1 (July-September 1974): 94-121.

17. *Documentos relativos á la exposición general de industria verificada en el año de 1856*, p. 22.

18. Dawn Keremitsis, *La industria textil*, pp. 41-76; Bitar Letayf, *La vida económica de México de 1824-1867 y sus proyecciones*, pp. 154-225; Calderón, *República Restaurada: Vida económica*, pp. 85-86.

19. Calderón, *República Restaurada: Vida económica*, pp. 608-670. Enrique Florescano and María del Rosario Lanzagorta, "Política económica," in Luis González et al., eds., *La economía mexicana en la época de Juárez*, pp. 59-102.

20. Calderón, *República Restaurada: Vida económica*, pp. 712-732.

21. *Archivo mexicano*, IV, 61.

22. Bravo Ugarte, *Educación*, p. 110.

23. For a discussion of the debate on education at the Constitutional Congress, see Abraham Talaver, *Liberalismo y educación*, II, 34-39.

24. Dublán and Lozano, *Legislación mexicana*, IX, 208; Avilés, *Juárez*, pp. 125-132.

25. For organic law see *Escuelas laicas, textos y documentos;* for report see *Memoria que el secretario . . .*

26. Vázquez de Knauth, *Nacionalismo*, pp. 51-53.

27. Ibid., pp. 72-80.

28. For an assessment of the contradictions in political liberalism see Laurens B. Perry, "El modelo liberal y la política práctica en la República Restaurada, 1867-1876," *Historia Mexicana* 23, no. 4 (April-June 1974): 646-699.

Bibliography

Note: Because many of the pamphlets cited in the bibliography are found exclusively in the Lafragua Collection (Biblioteca Nacional, Mexico City), they will be indicated parenthetically, after the publication data, by the notation LAF followed by the volume number.

Abusos y desórdenes en materias eclesiásticas. Mexico City: 1855. (LAF 345.)

Actas oficiales y minutario de decretos del Congreso Extraordinario Constituyente de 1856-1857. Mexico City: El Colegio de México, 1957.

Adorno, Juan Nepomuceno. *Análisis de los males de México y sus remedios practicables.* Mexico City: 1858.

_____. *Catecismo de la providencialidad del hombre. Deducida de los sentimientos de religiosidad, moralidad, sociabilidad y perfectabilidad, propios de la especie humana, e indicantes del destino de ésta sobre la tierra.* Mexico City: 1862.

Agraz García de Alba, Gabriel. *Ofrenda á México: Compendio de geografía, historia y biografía mexicanas.* Guadalajara: 1958.

Aguilar, Gustavo F. *Los presupuestos mexicanos desde los tiempos de la colonia hasta nuestros días.* Mexico City: Impreso Departamento Gráficas, 1940.

Aguilar de Bustamante, Javier. *Ensayo político, literario, teológico dogmático.* Mexico City: 1862.

Aguirre, G. *Algunas reflexiones sobre la ley orgánica de las adiciones y reformas a la constitución.* Mexico City: 1875.

Alamán, Lucas. *Documentos diversos.* 4 vols. Mexico City: Editorial Jus, 1945-1947.

_____. *Disertaciones sobre la historia de la república mejicana, desde la época de la conquista que los españoles hicieron . . . hasta la independencia.* 3 vols. Mexico City: 1844-1845.

_____. *Historia de Méjico desde los primeros movimientos que prepararon su independencia en el año de 1808 hasta la época presente.* 5 vols. Mexico City: 1849-1852.

————. *Memoria sobre el estado de la agricultura é industria de la república en el año de 1844.* Mexico City: 1845.

————. *Semblanzas e ideario.* Edited by Arturo Arnáiz y Freg. 2nd ed. Mexico City: Universidad Nacional Autónoma de México, 1963.

Algunas indicaciones acerca de la intervención europea en México. Paris: 1859.

Almond, Gabriel, and James Coleman, eds. *The Politics of the Developing Areas.* Princeton: Princeton University Press, 1960.

Altamirano, Ignacio Manuel. *Algunas palabras acerca de Mr. Wagner ministro de Prusia en México.* Mexico City: 1862.

————. *Discurso cívico pronunciado en la Alameda de México el 16 de setiembre de 1862...* Mexico City: 1862.

————. *Discurso pronunciado ... en la ciudad de Guerrero el 16 de septiembre de 1866.* Guerrero?: 1866?

————. "Discurso pronunciado en el teatro nacional de México la noche de 15 de septiembre de 1861." In *Discursos pronunciados en las funciones cívicas del año de 1861.* Mexico City: 1861. (LAF 136.)

————. *Historia y política de México (1821-1882).* Mexico City: Empresas Editoriales, 1947.

American Universities Field Staff. *Expectant Peoples: Nationalism and Development.* New York: Random House, 1963.

Anderson, Lee F., et al. *Legislative Roll-Call Analysis.* Evanston, Ill.: Northwestern University Press, 1966.

Apter, David. "A Comparative Method for the Study of Politics." *American Journal of Sociology* 64 (November 1958): 221-237.

————. *The Politics of Modernization.* Chicago: University of Chicago Press, 1965.

El archivo mexicano. Colección de leyes, decretos y circulares. 6 vols. Mexico City: 1856-1862.

Arnade, Charles W. "The Porfirio Díaz Papers of the William Clements Library." *Hispanic American Historical Review* 33, no. 2 (May 1953): 324-325.

Arrangoiz y Berzábal, Francisco de Paula. *México desde 1808 hasta 1867.* 4 vols. Madrid: 1871-1872.

Arrillaga, Basilio J., ed. *Recopilación de leyes, decretos, bandos.* 9 vols. Mexico City: 1861-1866.

Arroniz, Marcos. *Manual de biografía mejicana.* Paris: 1857.

Avilés, René. *Juárez y la educación en México.* Mexico City: Sociedad Mexicana de Geografía y Estadística, 1972.

Bancroft, Hubert Howe. *History of Mexico.* 6 vols. San Francisco: 1883-1888.

————. *Vida de Porfirio Díaz.* San Francisco: 1887.

Barajas, Pedro. *Exposiciones que el Illmo. Sr. Obispo eleva al S. Congreso pidiendole se repruebe el artículo 15 del proyecto de constitución que establece la tolerancia de cultos en la República.* San Luis Potosí: 1856. (LAF 1405.)

Barba González, Silvano. *Manuel Lozada.* Mexico City: 1956.

Bassols, Narciso, ed. *Leyes de reforma que afectan al clero publicadas por órden cronológica.* Puebla: Imp. de Convictorio, 1902.

Bazant, Jan. *Alienation of Church Wealth in Mexico: Social and Economic Aspects of the Liberal Revolution, 1856-1875.* Edited and translated by Michael P. Costeloe. Cambridge, England: Cambridge University Press, 1971.

———. "La desamortización de los bienes corporativos de 1856." *Historia Mexicana* 16, no. 2 (October-December 1966): 193-212.

———. "The Division of Some Mexican Haciendas during the Liberal Revolution, 1856-1862." *Journal of Latin American Studies* 3 (May 1971): 25-37.

———. *Historia de la deuda exterior de México, 1823-1946.* Mexico City: El Colegio de México, 1968.

———. "Peones, arrendatarios y aparceros, 1868-1904." *Historia Mexicana* 24, no. 1 (July-September 1974): 94-121.

———. "Tres revoluciones mexicanas." *Historia Mexicana* 10 (October-December 1960): 220-242.

Beals, Carleton. *Porfirio Díaz, Dictator of Mexico.* Philadelphia: J. B. Lippincott Co., 1932.

Beals, Ralph L. "Social Stratification in Latin America." *American Journal of Sociology* 58 (1953): 327-339.

Bellah, R. N. "Religious Aspects of Modernization in Turkey and Japan." *American Journal of Sociology* 64 (July 1958): 1-9.

Bendix, Reinhard. *Nation-Building and Citizenship: Studies of Our Changing Social Order.* New York: Wiley and Sons, 1964.

———. "Tradition and Modernity Reconsidered." *Comparative Studies in Society and History* 9, no. 3 (April 1967): 292-346.

Bernstein, Harry. "Mocedades de Matías Romero." *Historia Mexicana* 10 (April-June 1961): 588-612.

———. *Modern and Contemporary Latin America.* Philadelphia: J. B. Lippincott Co., 1952.

———. "Regionalism in the National History of Mexico." In *Latin American History: Essays on Its Study and Teaching, 1898-1965,* edited by Howard F. Cline. 2 vols. Austin: University of Texas Press, 1967, vol. 1, 389-394.

———. "El secreto de Matías Romero." *Historia Mexicana* 11, no. 1 (July-September 1961): 119-123.

Bernstein, Marvin D. *The Mexican Mining Industry, 1890-1950.* Albany: State University of New York, 1965.

Berrueto Ramón, Federico. *Ignacio Zaragoza.* Mexico City: Instituto de Estudios Históricos de la Revolución Mexicana, Secretaría de Gobernación, 1962.

Berry, Charles R. "The Fiction and Fact of the Reform: The Case of the Central District of Oaxaca, 1856-1867." *The Americas* 26, no. 3 (January 1970): 277-290.

Berusse, Edward J. "The Origins of the MacLane-Ocampo Treaty of 1859." *The Americas* 14, no. 3 (January 1958): 223-245.

Binder, Leonard, et al. *Crises and Sequences in Political Development.* Princeton, N.J.: Princeton University Press, 1976.

Binkley, Robert C. *Realism and Nationalism, 1852-1877.* New York: Harper and Row, 1935.

Black, Cyril E. *The Dynamics of Modernization: A Study in Comparative History.* New York: Harper and Row, 1966.

Blanco Martínez, Rosilda. *El pensamiento agrario en la Constitución de 1857.* Mexico City: Librería Ediciones Botas, 1957.

Borah, Woodrow. "Race and Class in Mexico." *Pacific Historical Review* 23 (1954): 331-342.

Bosch García, Carlos. *Historia de las relaciones entre México y los Estados Unidos, 1819-1848.* Mexico City: Escuela Nacional de Ciencias Políticas y Sociales, 1961.

Bottomore, T. B. *Elites and Society.* New York: Basic Books, 1964.

Boyer, Richard E., and Keith A. Davies. *Urbanization in 19th-Century Latin America: Statistics and Sources.* Los Angeles: Latin American Center, University of California, 1973.

Brading, David A. "Creole Nationalism and Mexican Liberalism." *Journal of Interamerican Studies and World Affairs* 15, no. 2 (May 1973): 139-190.

————. "Government and Elite in Late Colonial Mexico." *Hispanic American Historical Review* 53, no. 3 (August 1973): 389-414.

————. *Miners and Merchants in Bourbon Mexico, 1763-1810.* Cambridge, England: Cambridge University Press, 1971.

————. "The Structure of Agricultural Production in the Mexican Bajío in the Eighteenth Century." Papers of the 40th International Congress of Americanists, Rome, 1972.

Branch, H. N., trans. *The Mexican Constitution of 1917 Compared with the Constitution of 1857.* Philadelphia: The American Academy of Political and Social Science, 1917.

Bravo Ugarte, José. *Historia de México.* 3 vols. Mexico City: Editorial Jus, 1941-1959.

————. *La educación en México.* Mexico City: Editorial Jus, 1966.

Broussard, Ray F. "Ignacio Comonfort: His Contribution to the Mexican Reform." Ph.D. dissertation, The University of Texas at Austin, 1959.

————. "Mocedades de Comonfort." *Historia Mexicana* 13, no. 3 (January-

March 1964): 379-393.

_____. "Vidaurri, Juárez and Comonfort's Return from Exile." *Hispanic American Historial Review* 49, no. 2 (May 1969): 268-280.

Buenrostro, Felipe. *Historia del primero y segundo congresos constitucionales de la república mexicana.* 9 vols. Mexico City: 1874-1882.

Bulnes, Francisco. *Las grandes mentiras de nuestra historia; la nación y el ejército en las guerras extranjeras.* Mexico City: Librería de la Vda. de C. Bouret, 1904.

_____. *Juárez y las revoluciones de Ayutla y de Reforma.* Mexico City: Antigua Imprenta de Murguía, 1905.

_____. *El verdadero Juárez y la verdad sobre la intervención y el imperio.* Mexico City: Librería de la Vda. de C. Bouret, 1904.

Burgoa, Ignacio. *El juicio de amparo.* 6th ed. Mexico City: Editorial Porrúa, 1968.

Bustamante, Carlos María. *Cuadro histórico de la revolución mexicana.* 3 vols. Mexico City: 1823-1832.

Busto, E. *Estadística de la república mexicana.* Mexico City: 1880.

Cadenhead, Ivie E., Jr. "González Ortega and the Presidency of Mexico." *Hispanic American Historical Review* 32, no. 3 (August 1952): 331-346.

_____. *Jesús González Ortega and Mexican National Politics.* Texas Christian University monographs in History and Culture, no. 9. Fort Worth: Texas Christian University Press, 1972.

Calderón, Francisco R. *La República Restaurada: La vida económica.* Vol. 2 of *Historia moderna de México,* edited by Daniel Cosío Villegas. 9 vols. Mexico City: Editorial Hermes, 1955-1971.

Caldwell, Edward Maurice. "The War of 'La Reforma' in Mexico, 1858-1861." Ph.D. dissertation, The University of Texas at Austin, 1935.

Callcott, Wilfrid Hardy. *Church and State in Mexico, 1822-1857.* Durham, N.C.: Duke University Press, 1926.

_____. *Liberalism in Mexico, 1857-1929.* Stanford, Calif.: Stanford University Press, 1931.

Carreño, Alberto María, ed. *Archivo del General Porfirio Díaz: Memorias y documentos.* 15 vols. Mexico City: Editorial "Elede," 1947-1951.

_____. *La diplomacia extraordinaria entre México y los Estados Unidos, 1789-1947.* 2 vols. Mexico City: Editorial Jus, 1951.

Carrión, Jorge. "Efectos psicológicos de la Guerra de '47 en el hombre de México." *Cuadernos Americanos,* Año 7, 37, no. 1 (January-February 1948): 116-132.

Castañeda, Carlos E., ed. *La guerra de reforma según el archivo del General D. Manuel Doblado, 1857-1860.* San Antonio, Texas: Casa Editorial Lozano, 1930.

_____, and Jack A. Dabbs. *Guide to the Latin American Manuscripts in The University of Texas Library.* Cambridge, Mass.: Harvard University Press, 1939.

————, ————. *Independent Mexico in Documents: Independence, Empire, and Republic*. Mexico City: Editorial Jus, 1955.

Castañeda Batres, Oscar. *Francisco Zarco*. Mexico City: Club de Periodistas de México, 1961.

————. *Francisco Zarco ante la intervención francesa y el imperio, 1863-1864*. Mexico City: Publicaciones de la Secretaría de Relaciones Exteriores, Dirección General de Prensa y Publicidad, 1958.

Castillo Velasco, José María del. *Aniversario del cinco de mayo de 1862*. Mexico City: 1868. (LAF 362.)

————. *Juárez, la intervención y el imperio; refutación á la obra "El verdadero Juárez" de Bulnes*. Mexico City: Herrera Hermanos, 1904.

Castro, Emilio. *¿Quienes son los traidores?* Mexico City: 1868. (LAF 758.)

Castro, Rafael de. *La cuestión mexicana o exposición de las causas que hacían indispensable la intervención europea . . .* Mexico City: 1864. (LAF 877.)

Cavazos Garza, Israel. *Mariano Escobedo: El glorioso soldado de la república*. Monterrey: Gobierno del Estado, 1949.

Chapman, C. E. "The Age of Caudillos: A Chapter in Hispanic American History." *Hispanic American Historical Review* 12 (1932): 281-300.

Chávez Orozco, Luis. *Historia económica y social de México: Ensayo de interpretación*. Mexico City: Ediciones Botas, 1938.

Chevalier, François. " 'Caudillos' et 'caciques' en Amérique: Contribution a l'étude des liens personnels." *Mélanges offerts a Marcel Bataillon par les Hispanistes Français, Bulletin Hispanique* 64 bis (1962): 30-47.

————. "Conservateurs et libéraux au Mexique. Essai de sociologie et géographie de l'indépendance a l'intervention française." *Cahiers d' Histoire Mondiale* 8 (1964): 456-474.

————. *La Formation des grands domaines au Mexique: Terre et société aux XVIe-XVIIe siècles*. Paris: Université de Paris, 1952. Translated by Leslie Byrd Simpson as *Land and Society in Colonial Mexico, The Great Hacienda*. Berkeley: University of California Press, 1963.

————. "Suivances seigneuriales et présages de la revolution agraire dans le nord du Mexique, fin du XVIIIéme et XIXéme siècles." *Revue Historique* 222 (1959): 1-18.

La Chinaca.

Colección de leyes, decretos y circulares expedidas por el Supremo Gobierno de la República, 1863-1867. 3 vols. Mexico City: 1867.

Colección de los aranceles de obvenciones y derechos parroquiales que han estado vigentes en los obispados de la República Mexicana y que se citan en el supremo decreto de 11 de abril de 1857. Mexico City: 1857. (LAF 539.)

Colegio de Abogados de México. *El constituyente de 1856 y el pensamiento liberal mexicano*. Mexico City: Librería de M. Porrúa, 1960.

Coleman, James. "Modernization: Political Aspects." *International Encyclo-*

pedia of the Social Sciences, edited by David C. Sills, X, 395-402. 17
vols. New York: Macmillan, 1968.

Colin Sánchez, Guillermo. *Ignacio Zaragoza: Evocación de un héroe.* Mexico
City: Editorial Porrúa, 1963.

El Comité Local de Durango. *Al Benemérito C. Benito Juárez.* Durango:
1906.

*Contestaciones entre el illmo. Sr. Arzobispo de México, Dr. D. Lázaro de la
Garza y Ballesteros, y el exmo. Sr. Ministro de Justicia, Negocios Eclesiásticos é Instrucción Pública, Lic. D. Ezequiel Montes, con motivo de
la ley espedida en 25 de junio de 1856, sobre la desamortización de los
bienes de las corporaciones civiles y eclesiásticas de la República.* Mexico
City: 1856. (LAF 536.)

*La convocatoria, la circular con que se acompañó a los gobiernos de los estados,
y el manifiesto del ciudadano presidente de la República.* Mexico City:
1867.

La Corte de Roma y el Emperador Maximiliano . . . Mexico City: 1870. (LAF
664.)

Corti, Egon Caesar. *Maximilian and Charlotte of Mexico.* Translated by
Catherine Alison Phillips. 2 vols. New York: Knopf, 1929.

Cosío Villegas, Daniel. *La Constitución de 1857 y sus críticos.* Mexico City:
Editorial Hermes, 1957.

_____. "La Doctrina Juárez." *Historia Mexicana* 11, no. 4 (April-June
1962): 527-545.

_____. *La historiografía política del México moderno.* Mexico City: 1953.

_____. "El Porfiriato: Era de consolidación." *Historia Mexicana* 13, no. 1
(July-September 1963): 76-87.

_____. "Sebastián Lerdo de Tejada, mártir de la República Restaurada."
Historia Mexicana 17, no. 2 (October—December 1967): 169-199.

_____, ed. *Historia moderna de Mexico.* 9 vols. Mexico City: Editorial
Hermes, 1955-1971.

Costeloe, Michael P. "The Administration, Collection and Distribution of
Tithes in the Archbishopric of Mexico, 1800-1860." *The Americas* 23
(July 1966): 3-27.

_____. "Church-State Financial Negotiations in Mexico during the American
War, 1846-1847." *Revista de Historia de América* 60 (July-December
1965): 91-123.

_____. *Church Wealth in Mexico: A Study of the "Juzgado de Capellanías"
in the Archbishopric of Mexico, 1800-1856.* Cambridge, England:
Cambridge University Press, 1967.

_____. "The Mexican Church and the Rebellion of the Polkos." *Hispanic
American Historical Review* 46, no. 2 (May 1966): 170-178.

Crevenna, Theo, ed. *Materials para el estudio de la clase media en la América
Latina.* 6 vols. Washington, D.C.: Pan American Union, Departamento
de Asuntos Culturales, 1950-1951.

Cué Cánovas, Agustín. "Melchor Ocampo y el liberalismo en Michoacán." *Universidad Michoacana* 34 (February 1960): 9-13, 19-21.

————. *El Tratado McLane-Ocampo: Juárez, los Estados Unidos y Europa.* 2nd ed. Mexico City: Editorial América Nueva, 1959.

————. *El Tratado Mon-Almonte: Miramón, el Partido Conservador, y la Intervención Europea.* Mexico City: Ediciones Los Insurgentes, 1960.

————. *La reforma liberal en México.* Mexico City: Ediciones Centenario, 1960.

Cuevas, Luis Gonzaga. *Porvenir de México.* 3 vols. Mexico City: 1851-1857.

Cuevas, Mariano. *Historia de la iglesia en México.* 5 vols. Mexico City: Imp. del Asilo "Patricio Sanz," 1921-1928.

Cumberland, Charles. *Mexico: The Struggle for Modernity.* New York: Oxford University Press, 1968.

Dabbs, Jack Autrey. *The French Army in Mexico, 1861-1867: A Study in Military Government.* The Hague: Mouton, 1963.

Decreto constitucional para la libertad de la América Mexicana. Mexico City: 1814.

Delgado, Jaime. *España y México en el siglo XIX.* 3 vols. Madrid: Instituto Gonzalo Fernández de Oviedo, 1950-1954.

Deutsch, Karl W. "Some Problems in the Study of Nation-Building." In *Nation-Building*, edited by Karl W. Deutsch and William J. Foltz. New York: Atherton Press, 1963.

Diálogo entre Martín y Juan Diego. Mexico City: 1855. (LAF 1405.)

Diario de Avisos.

Diario de los Debates. Quinto Congreso Constitucional de la Unión. 4 vols. Mexico City: 1871.

Diario de los Debates. Sexto Congreso Constitucional de la Unión. 4 vols. Mexico City: 1871-1873.

Diario Oficial del Supremo Gobierno.

Díaz, Porfirio. *Memorias de Porfirio Díaz, 1830-1915.* 2nd ed. 2 vols. Mexico City: El Libro Francés, 1922-1923.

Díaz y Díaz, Fernando. *Caudillos y caciques: Antonio López de Santa Ana y Juan Alvarez.* Mexico City: El Colegio de México, 1972.

Diccionario Porrúa de historia, biografía y geografía de México. 2 vols. Mexico City: Editorial Porrúa, 1964-1966.

Discursos pronunciados en las funciones cívicas del año de 1861. Mexico City: 1861.

di Tella, Torcuato S. "The Dangerous Classes in Early Nineteenth-Century Mexico." *Journal of Latin American Studies* 5, no. 1 (May 1973): 79-105.

Documentos para la historia contemporánea de México. 2 vols. in one. Mexico City: Tipografía Mexicana, 1967-1968.

Documentos relativos a la exposición general de industria verificada en el año de 1856. Mexico City: 1856.

Dublán, Manuel, and José María Lozano, eds. *Legislación mexicana ó colección completa de las disposiciones legislativas expedidas desde la independencia de la República.* 34 vols. Mexico City: 1876-1904.

Durkheim, Emile. *The Division of Labor in Society.* Translated by George Simpson. Glencoe, Ill.: The Free Press, 1949.

Edinger, L. J., and D. S. Searing. "Social Background in Elite Analysis: A Methodological Inquiry." *American Political Science Review* 61 (1967): 428-445.

Eisenstadt, S. N. *Modernization: Protest and Change.* Englewood Cliffs, N.J.: Prentice-Hall, 1966.

————. "Sociological Aspects of Political Development in Underdeveloped Countries." *Economic Development and Cultural Change* 5 (1957): 283-307.

Escuelas laicas, textos y documentos. Mexico City: Empresas Editoriales, 1948.

Espinosa y Dávalos, Pedro. *Circular del gobierno eclesiástico de Guadalajara.* Guadalajara: 18 July 1856. (LAF 1405.)

Examen racional analítico de los males públicos. Mexico City: 1848. (LAF 929.)

Exposición del Obispo de León contra el proyecto de elevar a constitucionales las Leyes de Reforma. León, Guanajuato: 1873. (LAF 1920.)

Farriss, Nancy M. *Crown and Clergy in Colonial Mexico, 1759-1821: The Crisis of Ecclesiastical Privilege.* London: Athlone Press, 1968.

Fisiología de la cosa pública. Mexico City: 1850. (LAF 929.)

Flores Caballero, Romeo. "La consolidación de vales reales en la economía, la sociedad y la política novohispanas." *Historia Mexicana* 18 (January-March 1969): 334-378.

————. *Counterrevolution: The Role of the Spaniards in the Independence of Mexico, 1804-1838.* Translated by Jaime E. Rodríguez O. Lincoln, Nebraska: University of Nebraska Press, 1974.

Florescano, Enrique, and María del Rosario Lanzagorta. "Política económica." In *La economía mexicana en la época de Juárez,* edited by Luis González et al. Mexico City: Secretaría de Industria y Comercio, 1972.

Florstedt, Robert F. "Mora y la génesis del liberalismo burgués." *Historia Mexicana* 2 (1961): 207-223.

Fraser, Donald J. "La política de desamortización en las comunidades indígenas, 1856-1872." *Historia Mexicana* 21, no. 4 (April-June 1972): 615-652.

Friedrich, Carl J. "Nation Building?" In *Nation-Building,* edited by Karl W. Deutsch and William J. Foltz. New York: Atherton Press, 1963.

Fruchter, Benjamin. *Introduction to Factor Analysis.* New York: Van Nostrand, 1954.

Fuente, Juan Antonio de la. *Discurso que formó por encargo de la junta patriótica...* Veracruz: 1860. (LAF 137.)

Fuentes Díaz, Vicente. *La intervención norteamericana en México: 1847.* Mexico City: Imprenta Nuevomundo, 1947.

————. *Santos Degollado, el santo de la reforma.* Mexico City: 1959.

Fuentes Mares, José. *Juárez y el imperio.* Mexico City: Editorial Jus, 1963.

————. *Juárez y la intervención.* Mexico City: Editorial Jus, 1962.

————. *Juárez y la República.* Mexico City: Editorial Jus, 1965.

————. *Juárez y los Estados Unidos.* Mexico City: Libro Mex, 1960. 4th ed. Mexico City: Editorial Jus, 1964.

Gagern, Carlos de. *Apelación de los mexicanos a la Europa bien informada de la Europa mal informada.* Mexico City: 1862. (LAF 353.)

Galindo y Galindo, Miguel. *La gran década nacional, ó relación histórica de la guerra de reforma, intervención extranjera y gobierno del Archiduque Maximiliano.* 3 vols. Mexico City: Secretaría de Fomento, 1904-1906.

García, Genaro, ed. *Correspondencia secreta de los principales intervencionistas mexicanos, 1860-1862.* 3 vols. Mexico City: Vda. de C. Bouret, 1905-1907.

————. *Los gobiernos de Alvarez y Comonfort, según el archivo del General Doblado: Documentos inéditos.* Mexico City: Vda. de C. Bouret, 1910.

————. *La revolución de Ayutla según el archivo del General Doblado: Documentos inéditos.* Mexico City: Vda. de C. Bouret, 1909.

García Cantú, Gastón. "Las dos políticas exteriores de México." *Cuadernos Americanos* 56 (September-October 1959): 41-55.

García Cubas, Antonio. *La república mexicana en 1876.* Mexico City: 1876.

García Granados, Ricardo. *Historia de México desde la restauración de la república en 1867 hasta la caída de Profirio Díaz.* 4 vols. Mexico City: A. Botas e hijo, 1928.

García Granados, Ricardo. *La constitución de 1857 y las leyes de reforma en México: Estudio histórico-sociológico.* Mexico City: Tipografía Económica, 1906.

García Tapia, Jesús. *Tratados Ocampo-McLane.* Mexico City: Editorial Uayangareo, 1951.

Garza y Ballesteros, Lázaro de la. *Esposición que el Illmo. Sr. Arzobispo de México eleva al soberano Congreso Constituyente pidiendo la reforma del artículo 15 del proyecto de constitución.* Mexico City: 1856. (LAF 540.)

————. *Libro de inscripción del Ven. Clero Mexicano el año de 1851,* in Archivo General de la Nación, Papeles de Bienes Nacionales, Leg. 127, Exp. 2.

————. *Pastoral sobre tolerancia religiosa.* Mexico City: 1855. (LAF 540.)

General Juan Alvarez. Mexico City: [1855?]

Gibson, Charles. *The Aztecs under Spanish Rule: A History of the Indians of the Valley of Mexico, 1519-1810.* Stanford, California: Stanford University Press, 1964.

————. *Spain in America.* New York: Harper and Row, 1966.

————. "The Transformation of the Indian Community in New Spain, 1500-1810." *Journal of World History* 2 (1955): 581-607.

González, Luis. "Notas sobre el nacionalismo mexicano." *América Indígena* 29 (April 1969): 420-429.

————. "El optimismo nacionalista como factor de la independencia de México." In *Estudios de Historiografía Americana,* edited by Isabel Gutiérrez Arroyo. Mexico City: El Colegio de México, 1948, pp. 153-215.

————. *San José de Gracia: Mexican Village in Transition.* Translated by John Upton. Austin, Texas: University of Texas Press, 1972.

————, et al. *La economía mexicana en la época de Juárez.* Mexico City: Secretaría de Industria y Comercio, 1972.

————, et al. *La República Restaurada: La vida social.* Vol. 3 of *Historia moderna de México,* edited by Daniel Cosío Villegas. 9 vols. Mexico City: Editorial Hermes, 1955-1971.

González García, José. "El derecho de propiedad y la propiedad de manos muertas en el pensamiento del constituyente mexicano de 1856 y 1857." Mexico City: Thesis, Universidad Nacional Autónoma de México, 1965.

González Navarro, Moisés. "Instituciones indígenas en México independiente." In *Métodos y resultados de la política indigenista en México,* by Alfonso Caso et al. Mexico City: Instituto Nacional Indigenista, 1954.

————. "Mestizaje in Mexico during the National Period." In *Race and Class in Latin America,* edited by Magnus Mörner. New York: Columbia University Press, 1970, pp. 145-169.

————. *El pensamiento político de Lucas Alamán.* Mexico City: El Colegio de México, 1952.

————. *Raza y tierra. La guerra de castas y el henequén.* Mexico City: El Colegio de México, 1971.

————. "La situación social de Jalisco en visperas de la Reforma." In *La Reforma en Jalisco y el Bajío.* Guadalajara: Librería Font, 1959.

————. "Tenencia de la tierra y población agrícola, 1877-1960." *Historia Mexicana* 19, no. 1 (July-September 1969): 62-86.

————, ed. *Vallarta en la Reforma.* Mexico City: Universidad Nacional Autónoma de México, 1956.

Grajales Ramos, Gloria, comp. *México y la Gran Bretaña durante la intervención, 1861-1862.* Mexico City: Secretaría de Relaciones Exteriores, Dirección General de Prensa y Publicidad, 1962.

————. *Nacionalismo incipiente en los historiadores coloniales: Estudio historiográfico.* Mexico City: Universidad Nacional Autónoma de México, 1961.

Griffin, Charles C. "An Essay on Regionalism and Nationalism in Latin American Historiography." *Journal of World History* 8, no. 2 (1964): 371-379.

————. *The National Period in the History of the New World.* Mexico City:

Instituto Panamericano de Geografía, 1961.

Guerra al clero. Mexico City: 1855. (LAF 424.)

Gusfield, Joseph R. "Tradition and Modernity: Misplaced Polarities in the Study of Social Order." In *Political Modernization: A Reader in Comparative Political Change,* edited by Claude E. Welch, Jr. Belmont, Calif.: Wadsworth Pub. Co., 1967, pp. 47-62.

Gutiérrez, Blas José. *Leyes de reforma.* 2 vols. Mexico City: 1870.

Gutiérrez de Estrada, José María. *Carta dirigida al escmo Sr. presidente de la república sobre la necesidad de buscar en una convención el posible remedio de los males que aquejan á la república.* Mexico City: 1840.

——— . *Le Mexique et l'Europe ou exposé de la situation actuelle du Mexique et des dangers qui peuvent en résulter por l'Europe si elle ne prend des mesures efficaces pour y remédier.* Paris: 1847.

Guzmán y Raz Guzmán, Jesús. *Bibliografía de la Reforma, la Intervención y el Imperio.* Mexico City: Imprenta de la Secretaría de Relaciones Exteriores, 1930-1931.

Hale, Charles A. "Alamán, Antuñano y la continuidad del liberalismo." *Historia Mexicana* 11, no. 4 (October-December 1961): 224-245.

——— . "José María Luis Mora and the Structure of Mexican Liberalism." *Hispanic American Historical Review* 45, no. 2 (May 1965): 196-227.

——— *Mexican Liberalism in the Age of Mora, 1821-1853.* New Haven: Yale University Press, 1968.

——— . "The War With the United States and the Crisis in Mexican Thought." *The Americas* 14 (1957): 153-173.

Hamill, Hugh M., Jr. *The Hidalgo Revolt: Prelude to Mexican Independence.* Gainesville: University of Florida Press, 1966.

——— . "The Virgin of Guadalupe and the Origins of Mexican Nationalism." Paper read before the Ohio Academy of History, April 1961.

——— . *Dictatorship in Spanish America.* New York: Knopf, 1965.

Harris, Charles H., III. *A Mexican Family Empire: The Latifundio of the Sánchez Navarros, 1765-1867.* Austin: University of Texas Press, 1975.

El Heraldo.

Hernández Rodríguez, Rosaura. "Comonfort y la intervención francesa." *Historia Mexicana* 13, no. 1 (July-September 1963): 59-75.

——— *Ignacio Comonfort: Trayectoria política. Documentos.* Mexico City: Universidad Nacional Autónoma de México, Instituto de Investigaciones Históricas, 1967.

Hidalgo, José Manuel. *Proyectos de monarquía en México.* Mexico City: F. Vázquez, 1962.

Historia de la Revolución de México contra la dictadura del General Santa-Anna, 1953-1855. Mexico: 1856.

Hobsbawm, Eric J. *Social Bandits and Primitive Rebels: Studies in Archaic Forms of Social Movement in the 19th and 20th Centuries.* Glencoe, Ill.: The Free Press, 1969.

Huerta Hernández, Martina. *Juárez fundador de una sociedad civil.* Mexico City: 1968.

Humbolt, Alexander. *Ensayo político sobre el reino de la Nueva España.* Edited by Juan A. Ortega y Medina. Mexico City: Editorial Porrúa, 1966.

———. *Political Essay on the Kingdom of New Spain.* Translated by J. Black. 4 vols. London: 1811.

Huntington, Samuel P. *Political Order in Changing Societies.* New Haven: Yale University Press, 1968.

Ibarra, Guillermo. *El periodismo en la Reforma.* Mexico City: Valores Humanos, 1957.

La Idea Republicana (Zacatecas).

Iglesias, José María. *Autobiografía.* Mexico City: 1893.

———. *Discurso pronunciado por . . . en la Alameda de México el 5 de mayo de 1863.* Mexico City: 1863.

———. *Refutación del discurso pronunciado por Mr. Billaut, ministro sin cartera en el cuerpo legislativo francés sobre la política del emperador en México.* Mexico City: 1862. (LAF 335.)

———. *Revistas históricas sobre la intervención francesa en México.* 3 vols. Mexico City: 1867-1869. Reprinted in 1 vol., Mexico City: Editorial Porrúa, 1966.

Iguínez, Juan B. *Bibliografía biográfica mexicana.* Mexico City: Imprenta de la Secretaría de Relaciones Exteriores, 1930.

La Independencia.

La Independencia Mexicana (San Luis Potosí).

Iturriaga, José E. *La estructura social y cultural de México.* Mexico City: Fondo de Cultura Económica, 1951.

Jaguaribe, Helio. *Political Development: A General Theory and a Latin American Case Study.* New York: Harper and Row, 1973.

Johnson, John J. "The New Latin American Nationalism." *Yale Review* (Winter 1965): 187-204.

Johnson, Richard Abraham. *The Mexican Revolution of Ayutla, 1854-1855: An Analysis of the Evolution and Destruction of Santa Anna's Last Dictatorship.* Rock Island, Ill.: Augustana College Library Publications, 1939.

Juárez, Benito. *Apuntes para mis hijos.* Mexico City: Editorial Cronos, 1955.

———. *Archivos privados de D. Benito Juárez y D. Pedro Santacilia.* Mexico City: Secretaría de Educación Pública, 1928.

———. *Decretos espedidos por el Exmo. governador del estado Don Benito Juárez.* [Oaxaca?]: 1856.

———. *Discurso en la solemne apertura de las sesiones de Congreso de la Unión.* Mexico City: 1861. (LAF 1519.)

———. *Documentos, discursos y correspondencia.* Edited by Jorge L. Tamayo. 14 vols. Mexico City: Secretaría del Patrimonio Nacional, 1964-

1969.

————. *Manifiesto justificativo de los castigos nacionales en Querétaro.* Guadalajara: 1868.

————. *Miscelánea: Comunicados, respuestas, iniciativas, dictámenes, informes, brindis, etc.* Edited by Angel Pola. Mexico City: A. Pola, 1906.

Juárez, Joseph R. "Conflict and Cooperation between Church and State: The Archbishopric of Guadalajara during the Porfiriato, 1876-1911." Ph.D. dissertation, The University of Texas at Austin, 1967.

Kedourie, Elie. *Nationalism.* London: Hutchinson, 1960.

Keremitsis, Dawn. *La industria textil mexicana en el siglo XIX.* Mexico City: Secretaría de Educación Pública, 1973.

Knapp, Frank Averill. *The Life of Sebastián Lerdo de Tejada: A Study of Influence and Obscurity.* Austin: University of Texas Press, 1951. Reprinted, New York: Greenwood Press, 1968.

————. "Parliamentary Government and the Mexican Constitution of 1857." *Hispanic American Historical Review* 33 (1953): 65-87.

Knowlton, Robert J. *Church Property and the Mexican Reform, 1856-1910.* De Kalb, Ill.: Northern Illinois University Press, 1967.

————. "Clerical Response to the Mexican Reform, 1855-1875." *The Catholic Historical Review* 50, no. 4 (January 1965): 509-528.

————. "The Disamortization and Nationalization of Ecclesiastical Property in Mexico, 1856-1910." Ph.D. thesis, State University of Iowa, 1963.

————. "La iglesia mexicana y la Reforma: Respuesta y resultados." *Historia Mexicana* 18 (April-June 1969): 516-534.

————. "Some Practical Effects of Clerical Opposition to the Mexican Reform, 1856-1860." *Hispanic American Historical Review* 45, no. 2 (May 1965): 246-256.

Kohn, Hans. "Nationalism." In *International Encyclopedia of the Social Sciences,* edited by David C. Sills. 17 vols. New York: Macmillan, 1968.

————. *The Idea of Nationalism: A Study in Its Origins and Background.* New York: Macmillan, 1944.

Labastida, Luis G. *Colección de leyes, decretos, reglamentos, circulares, órdenes y acuerdos relativos a la desamortización de los bienes de corporaciones civiles y religiosas y a la nacionalización de los que administraron las últimas.* Mexico City: 1893.

Labastida y Dávalos, Pelagio Antonio de. *Representación del Obispo de Puebla y contestación* [Mexico City?: 1856?].

Lacroix, Jorge Gurría. *Las ideas monárquicas de don Lucas Alamán.* Mexico City: Instituto de Historia, 1951.

Ladd, Doris M. *The Mexican Nobility at Independence, 1780-1826.* Austin, Texas: Institute of Latin American Studies, 1976.

Lafragua, José María. *Discurso pronunciado . . . contra el artículo 15 del proyecto de la constitución.* Mexico City: 1842. (LAF 398.)

————. *Memoria de Relaciones Exteriores.* Mexico City: 1847.

Laqueur, Walter. "Revolution." In *International Encyclopedia of the Social Sciences*, edited by David C. Sills. 17 vols. New York: Macmillan, 1968.

biografías mexicanas. Mexico City: Vda. de C. Bouret, 1910.

Lerdo de Tejada, Miguel M. *Cuadro sinóptico de la república mexicana en 1856.* Mexico City: 1856.

_____. *Memoria de Hacienda.* Mexico City: 1857.

_____. *Noticia de las fincas pertenecientes a corporaciones civiles y eclesiásticas del distrito de México.* Mexico City: 1856. (LAF 117.)

Letayf, Bitar. *La vida económica de México de 1824-1867 y sus proyecciones.* Thesis, Universidad Nacional Autónoma de México, 1964.

Levy, Marion. *The Structure of Society.* Princeton, N.J.: Princeton University Press, 1952.

Ley orgánica de la guardia de la república mexicana. Mexico City: 1857. (LAF 397.)

Ley orgánica del registro del estado civil. Mexico City: 27 January 1857.

Ley orgánica de las adiciones y reformas constitucionales expedida por el Congreso General en 10 de diciembre de 1874. Mexico City: 1874.

Leyes de Reforma, gobiernos de Ignacio Comonfort y Benito Juárez. Mexico City: Empresas Editoriales, 1947. (LAF 120.)

La Libertad (Durango).

López Cámara, Francisco. *La estructura económica y social de México en la época de la Reforma.* Mexico City: Siglo Veintiuno Editores, 1967.

Loza Macías, Manuel. *El pensamiento económico y la Constitución de 1857.* Mexico City: Editorial Jus, 1959.

Lozoya, Jorge Alberto. *El ejército mexicano, 1911-1965.* Mexico City: Centro de Estudios Internacionales, 1970.

Luz de la libertad (Guadalajara).

McAlister, Lyle N. *The "Fuero Militar" in New Spain, 1764-1800.* Gainesville: University of Florida Press, 1957.

McBride, George McCutchen. *The Land Systems of Mexico.* New York: American Geographical Society, 1923.

McLean, Malcolm Dallas. *Vida y obra de Guillermo Prieto.* Mexico City: El Colegio de México, 1960.

MacNeil, Ann W. "The Supreme Harmonizing Power, 1837-1841." M.A. thesis, The University of Texas at Austin, 1969.

Maine, Henry. *Ancient Law: Its Connection with the Early History of Society, and Its Relation to Modern Ideas.* London: 1861.

Manning, William R., ed. *Diplomatic Correspondence of the United States: Inter-American Affairs, 1831-1860.* 12 vols. Washington, D.C.: Carnegie Endowment for International Peace, 1932-1939.

Marshall, C. E. "The Birth of the Mestizo in New Spain." *Hispanic American Historical Review* 19 (1939): 161-184.

Mecham, J. Lloyd. *Church and State in Latin America; A History of Politico-Ecclesiastical Relations.* 2nd ed., rev. Chapel Hill: University of North

Carolina Press, 1966.

Medina, Hilario, et al. *El liberalismo y la reforma en México.* Mexico City: Universidad Nacional Autónoma de México, 1957.

Medina Ascencio, Luis, S.J. "El clero jalisciense y la Reforma." In *La Reforma en Jalisco y el Bajío.* Guadalajara: Librería Font, 1959.

Mejía Zúñiga, Raúl. *Benito Juárez y su generación.* Mexico City: Sepsetentas, 1972.

Melo Abarrátegui, Andrés. "Los orígenes del constitucionalismo mexicano." Thesis, Universidad Nacional Autónoma de México, 1965.

Mena, Mario. *Melchor Ocampo.* Mexico City: Editorial Jus, 1959.

Méndez, Ignacio. *Síntomas de una grán revolución social. Medios de precaverla.* Mexico City: 1878.

Memoria de gobernación, 1873. Mexico City: 1874.

Meusel, A. "Revolution and Counter-revolution." In *International Encyclopedia of the Social Sciences,* edited by David C. Sills. 17 vols. New York: Macmillan, 1968.

Mexico, Congreso Constituyente, 1856-1857. *Actas oficiales y minutario de decretos del Congreso extraordinario Constituyente de 1856-1857.* Mexico City: El Colegio de México, 1957.

Mexico, Secretaría de Hacienda y Crédito Público. *Miguel Lerdo de Tejada (1821-1861).* Mexico City: Dirección General de Prensa, Memorias, Bibliotecas y Publicaciones, 1961.

Mexico, Secretaría del Estado y del Despacho de Relaciones Exteriores, etc. *Memoria . . . correspondiente a la administracion provisional, en los años de 1841, 42, 43.* Mexico City: 1844.

México en 1847 [by "Un Mexicano"]. Mexico City: 1847. (LAF 322.)

México y la intervención. Mexico City: 1861. (LAF 447.)

Meyer, Jean. "De colonisation et sous-développement: Vues sur le Mexique au XIXe siècle." *Revue d'histoire moderne et contemporaine* 14 (October-December 1967): 406-423.

————. "El ocaso de Manuel Lozada." *Historia Mexicana* 18 (April-June 1969): 535-568.

————. *Problemas campesinos y revueltas agrarias, 1821-1910.* Mexico City: Secretaría de Educación Pública, 1973.

Ministerio de Fomento. *Memoria, 1857.* Mexico City: 1857.

Miranda, José. "El liberalismo mexicano y el liberalismo europeo." *Historia Mexicana* 8, no. 4 (April-June 1959): 512-523.

Molina Enríquez, Andrés. *Los grandes problemas nacionales.* Mexico City: Imprenta de A. Carranza e hijos, 1909.

————. *Juárez y la Reforma.* Mexico City: Libro Mex, 1956. Originally published as *La Reforma y Juárez.* Mexico City: Tip. de la Viuda de F. Díaz de León, 1906.

El Monitor Republicano.

Monroy, Guadalupe. *Archivo histórico de Matías Romero; Catálogo descriptivo,*

1837-1872. Mexico City: Banco de México, 1965.

Montes, Ezequiel. *Discurso pronunciado . . . defendiendo el dictamen de la comisión de puntos constitucionales.* Mexico City: 1870. (LAF 1037.)

Mora, José María Luis. *Méjico y sus revoluciones.* 4 vols. Paris: 1856.

Moreno, Rafael. "Creación de la nacionalidad mexicana." *Historia Mexicana* 12, no. 4 (April-June 1963): 530-551.

Mörner, Magnus, ed. *The Expulsion of the Jesuits from Latin America.* New York: Knopf, 1965.

————. *Race and Class in Latin America.* New York: Columbia University Press, 1970.

Morse, Richard A. "Towards a Theory of Spanish American Government." *Journal of the History of Ideas* 15, no. 1 (January 1954): 71-93.

Muñoz y Pérez, Daniel. *El general don Juan Alvarez: Ensayo biográfico seguido de una selección de documentos.* Mexico City: Editorial Academia Literaria, 1959.

Navarrete, Félix [pseud. Jesús García Gutiérrez]. *La lucha entre el poder civil y el clero a la luz de la historia.* El Paso, Texas: [Revista Press], 1935.

Navarro, Juan N. *Legislación mexicana.* Mexico City: 1855.

Navarro R., José Guadalupe. "Los diezmos en México durante el tiempo de la colonia." *Boletín Eclesiástico de la Arquidiócesis de Guadalajara,* época 5, año 9 (1938), 29-40, 80-89, 119-126, 171-178, 202-214, 245-252, 306-310, 244-251, 378-390, 420-430, 476-481; época 5, año 10 (1939), 77-83.

New York Herald.

Niosi, Jerome J. "The McLane Mission to Mexico, 1859-1860." Ph.D. dissertation, New York University, 1954.

Observaciones sobre la ley de 26 de Febrero y sobre su reglamento. Mexico City: 1865. (LAF 539.)

Ocaranza, Fernando. *Juárez y sus amigos.* Mexico City: Editorial Polis, 1939.

Ocampo, Melchor. *Discurso pronunciado en la Alameda de la H. C. de Veracruz.* Veracruz: 1858.

————. *Melchor Ocampo al governador del estado de . . . ,* 28 April 1859. (LAF 302.)

————. *Obras completas.* 3 vols. Mexico City: F. Vázquez, 1900-1901.

————. *La religión, la Iglesia y el clero.* Mexico City: Empresas Editoriales, 1948.

O'Gorman, Edmundo. "Precedentes y sentido de la Revolución de Ayutla." In *Plan de Ayutla: Celebración de su primer centenario,* edited by B. de Silva, pp. 171-204. Mexico City: Universidad Nacional Autónoma de Mexico, 1954.

El Omnibus.

El Orden.

Orozco Farías, Rogelio, ed. *Fuentes históricas: México, 1821-1867.* Mexico City: 1964.

[Ortega, Manuel del Carmen.] *La religión, la independencia y la raza.* Mexico City: 1866.

Ortiz Vidales, Salvador. *Don Guillermo Prieto y su época.* Mexico City: Ediciones Botas, 1939.

[Otero, Mariano.] *Consideraciones sobre la situación política y social de la república mexicana en el año 1847.* Mexico City: 1848.

El País (Guadalajara).

Palmer, Robert R. *A History of the Modern World.* 2nd ed., rev. New York: Knopf, 1963.

Parra, Manuel Germán. "Las grandes tendencias de la evolución histórica de la política indigenista." In *Bibliografía indigenista de México y Centroamérica, 1850-1950.* Mexico City: Instituto Nacional Indigenista, 1954.

Parra, Porfirio. *Estudio histórico-sociológico sobre la reforma en México.* Guadalajara: Impr. "La Gaceta de Guadalajara," 1906.

Parsons, Talcott. *The Social System.* Glencoe, Ill.: The Free Press, 1951.

Payno, Manuel. *La reforma social en España y México, apuntes históricos y principales leyes sobre desamortización de bienes eclesiásticos.* Mexico City: Dirección General de Publicaciones, 1958.

————. *Ley de presupuestos generales de la república.* Mexico City: 1855.

————. *Memoria de Hacienda.* Mexico City: 1857.

————. *Memoria sobre la revolución de diciembre de 1857 y enero de 1858.* Mexico City: 1860. (LAF 311.)

————. *México y el Sr. Embajador don Joaquín Francisco Pacheco.* Mexico City: 1862. (LAF 353.)

————, ed. *Colección de las leyes, decretos, circulares y providencias relativas á la desamortización eclesiástica, a la nacionalización de los bienes de corporaciones, y á la reforma de la legislación civil que tenía relación con el culto y con la iglesia.* Mexico City: 1861.

Peral, Miguel Angel, ed. *Diccionario biográfico mexicano.* Mexico City: Editorial P.A.C., 1944.

Pereyra, Carlos. *Juárez discutido como dictador y estadista a propósito de los errores, paradojas y fantasías del Sr. Don Francisco Bulnes.* Mexico City: Tipografía Económica, 1904.

Pérez Hernández, José María. *Estadística de la república mexicana.* Guadalajara: 1862.

Periódico Oficial (Chihuahua y Paso del Norte), 1864-1865.

Perry, Laurens B. "El modelo liberal y la política práctica en la república restaurada, 1867-1876." *Historia Mexicana* 23, no. 4 (April-June 1974): 646-699.

Phipps, Helen. "Some Aspects of the Agrarian Question in Mexico." *University of Texas Bulletin* no. 2515 (April 1925).

Pimentel, Francisco. *Cuadro descriptivo y comparativo de las lenguas indígenas de México.* 2 vols. Mexico City: 1865.

————. *Memoria sobre las causas que han originado la situación actual de la*

raza indígena de México y medios de remediarla. Mexico City: 1864.
(LAF 1409.)

Piñeda, Salvador. *Vida y pasión de Ocampo: Ocho estampas del reformador.*
Mexico City: Libro Mex, 1959.

Pizarro, Nicolás. *Catecismo político constitucional.* Mexico City: 1861. (LAF
311.)

Pletcher, David M. *The Diplomacy of Annexation: Texas, Oregon, and the
Mexican War.* Columbia: University of Missouri Press, 1973.

_____. *Rails, Mines and Progress: Seven American Promoters in Mexico,
1867-1911.* Ithaca, N.Y.: Cornell University Press, 1958.

Pompa y Pompa, Antonio, ed. *Colección de documentos inéditos ó muy
raros relativos a la reforma en México.* 2 vols. Mexico City: Instituto
Nacional de Antropología e Historia, 1957.

Portilla, Anselmo de la. *Historia de la revolución de México contra la dictadura del general Santa-Anna, 1853-1855.* Mexico City: Imprenta de V.
García Torres, 1856.

_____. *Méjico en 1856 y 1857.* New York: Impr. de S. Hallet, 1858.

Potash, Robert A. *El Banco de Avío de México. El fomento de la industria,
1821-1846.* Mexico City: Fondo de Cultura Económica, 1959.

Potter, David. "The Historian's Idea of Nationalism and Vice Versa." *American Historical Review* 67 (1962): 924-950.

Powell, T. G. *El liberalismo y el campesinado en el centro de México, 1850-
1876.* Mexico City: Sepsetentas, 1974.

Priestley, Herbert I. *José de Gálvez, Visitor-General of New Spain, 1765-
1771.* Berkeley: University of California Press, 1916.

Prieto, Guillermo. *Arquilla abierta: Cartas y crónicas de Guillermo Prieto é
Ignacio M. Altamirano.* Selection and notes by Ana Guido de Icaza.
Mexico City: Talleres Gráficos de la Nación, 1952.

_____. *Circular del ministro de hacienda . . . á los gobernadores de los
estados.* Mexico City: 1855. (LAF 72.)

_____. *Discurso de Guillermo Prieto en la cuestión del senado.* Mexico
City: 1870. (LAF 739.)

_____. *Discurso pronunciado en San Andrés Tuxtla por el ciudadano Guiller-
mo Prieto, en la solemnidad el 16 de septiembre de 1858.* Veracruz:
1858.

_____. *Discursos pronunciados en las funciones cívicas del año de 1861 en
la capital de la república . . .* Mexico City: 1861.

_____. *Guillermo Prieto a sus amigos.* San Antonio: 1866. (LAF 744.)

_____. *Lecciones de historia patria escritas para los alumnos del colegio
militar.* Mexico City: 1893.

_____. *Ley sobre bienes nacionalizados.* Mexico City: 1861.

_____. *Memorias de mis tiempos.* 2 vols. Mexico City: Vda. de C. Bouret,
1906.

_____. *Oración cívica pronunciada por el ciudadano Guillermo Prieto en la*

Alameda de México, el día 16 de septiembre de 1855, aniversario del glorioso grito de "Independencia" dado por el cura de Dolores en 1810. Mexico City: 1855. (LAF 756.)

————. *Reglamentación de las leyes de reforma.* Mexico City: 1875.

El Progreso (Veracruz).

Pye, Lucian W. *Aspects of Political Development: An Analytical Study.* Boston: Little, Brown, 1966.

Quintana, José Miguel. *Lafragua, político y romántico.* Mexico City: Editorial Academia Literaria, 1958.

Rabasa, Emilio. *La constitución y la dictadura: Estudio sobre la organización política de México.* Mexico City: Tip. de "Revista de Revotas," 1912.

Ramírez, Ignacio. *Cartas de Ignacio Ramírez (el Nigromante) a Guillermo Prieto (Fidel).* Mexico City: Vargas Rea, 1944.

————. "Discurso cívico pronunciado . . . el 16 de Septiembre de 1861." In *discursos pronunciados en las funciones cívicas del año de 1861.* Mexico City: 1873. (LAF 136.)

————. *México en pos de la libertad.* Mexico City: Empresas Editoriales, 1949.

————. *Obras de Ignacio Ramírez.* 2 vols. Mexico City: 1889.

Ramírez Arriaga, Manuel. *Ponciano Arriaga el desconocido.* Mexico City: Sociedad Mexicana de Geografía y Estadística, 1965.

Ramírez Cabañas, Joaquín. *Las relaciones entre México y el Vaticano.* 2nd ed. Mexico City: Imprenta de la Secretaría de Relaciones Exteriores, 1928.

Ramírez López, Ignacio. *Cronología de Manuel Doblado.* Mexico City: Editorial Libros de México, 1963.

Randall, Robert. *Real del Monte: A British Mining Venture in Mexico.* Austin: University of Texas Press, 1972.

Los redactores de *La Democracia. Contestación a la manifestación del Sr. Arzobispo de México.* Oaxaca: 1859. (LAF 463.)

Reed, Nelson. *The Caste War of Yucatan.* Stanford, Calif.: Stanford University Press, 1964.

La Reforma en Jalisco y el Bajío. Guadalajara: Librería Font, 1959.

Representación del Obispo de Puebla y Contestación. [Mexico City?: 1856?]. (LAF 536.)

Representación que las Señoras mexicanas elevaron al Congreso Constituyente pidiendo no se establezca en la República la tolerancia de cultos. Mexico City: 1856. (LAF 345.)

Representación que varios individuos de la capital del Estado de Jalisco, amantes del progreso y mejores materials del país, dirijen al soberano Congreso Constituyente en favor del artículo 15 del proyecto de constitución. Guadalajara: 1856.(LAF 1405.)

El Republicano.

Reyes Heroles, Jesús. *El liberalismo mexicano.* 3 vols. Mexico City: Universidad Nacional Autónoma de México, Facultad de Derecho, 1957-1961.

_____ . "Economía y política en el liberalismo mexicano," *Cuadernos Americanos* 86, no. 2 (March-April 1956): 180-202.

Ríos, Enrique M. de los. *Liberales ilustres mexicanos de la reforma y la intervención.* Mexico City: 1890.

Ricard, Robert. *La "Conquête spirituelle" du Mexique.* Paris: Institut d' Ethnologie, 1933.

Riva Palacio, Vicente. *A la memoria del General Leandro Valle, mártir de la libertad.* Mexico City: 1861.

_____ . *Discursos cívicos pronunciados en las festividades del 15 y 16 de septiembre de 1867.* Mexico City: 1867.

_____ . *Historia de la administración de don Sebastián Lerdo de Tejada.* Mexico City: 1875.

_____ . *La soberanía de los estados y la suprema corte de justicia.* Mexico City: 1874.

_____ , ed. *México a través de los siglos.* 5 vols. Barcelona: 1889.

Rivera Cambas, Manuel. *Historia de la intervención europea y norteamericana en México y del imperio de Maximiliano de Hapsburgo.* 3 vols. Mexico City: 1888-1895.

_____ . *Historia de la reforma religiosa, política y social en México.* Mexico City: 1875.

Rivera y Sanromán, Agustín. *Anales mexicanos. La reforma i el segundo imperio.* 3 vols. Lagos de Moreno, Jalisco: Tip. de V. Veloz, 1890-1891.

_____ . *Pinceladas sobre la vida i gobierno del C. General Porfirio Díaz.* Lagos de Moreno, Jalisco: López Arce, 1908.

Robertson, Spense. *Iturbide of Mexico.* Durham, N.C.: Duke University Press, 1952.

Roeder, Ralph. *Juárez and His Mexico: A Biographical History.* 2 vols. New York: Viking Press, 1947.

Romero, Matías, ed. *Correspondencia de la legación mexicana en Washington durante la intervención extranjera, 1860-1868.* 10 vols. Mexico City: 1870-1892.

Romero Flores, Jesús. *Comentarios a la historia de Mexico, 1821-1861.* Mexico City: Libro Mex, 1958.

_____ . *Don Melchor Ocampo, el filósofo de la Reforma.* 2nd ed. Morelia, Michoacán: Ediciones de la Universidad Michoacana de San Nicolás de Hidalgo, 1953.

Ross, William J., III. "The Role of Manuel Doblado in the Mexican Reform Movement, 1855-1860." Ph.D. dissertation, The University of Texas, 1967.

Ruiz, Eduardo. *Biografía del ciudadano Melchor Ocampo.* Mexico City: 1857.

Ruiz Catañeda, María del Carmen. *Periodismo político de la reforma en la ciudad de México, 1854-1861.* Mexico City: Instituto de Investigaciones Sociales, Universidad Nacional Autónoma de México, 1954.

Rul, Miguel. *Consulta del Diputado . . . dirigida a sus colegas en el 7º Congreso Constitucional.* Mexico City: 1873. (LAF 654.)

Rummel, R. J. *Applied Factor Analysis.* Evanston, Ill.: Northwestern University Press, 1970.

Rus de Cea, Genaro [pseud. Andrés Ocegura]. *Observaciones acerca de la intervención europea en México.* Paris: 1859.

Salado Alvarez, Victoriano. *Episodios nacionales: Santa Anna. La reforma. La intervención. El imperio.* Mexico City: Colección Málaga, 1945.

Sartorius, Carl Christian Wilhelm. *Importancia de México para la emigración alemana.* Mexico City: 1852.

————. *Mexico about 1850.* Stuttgart: Brockhaus, 1961.

Schmitt, Karl. "Catholic Adjustment to the Secular State: The Case of Mexico, 1877-1911." *Catholic Historical Review* 48 (July 1962): 182-204.

————. "The Díaz Conciliation Policy on State and Local Levels, 1876-1911." *Hispanic American Historial Review* 40 (November 1960): 513-532.

————. "The Mexican Positivists and the Church-State Question, 1876-1911." *Journal of Church and State* 8 (Spring 1966): 200-213.

Scholes, Walter V. "Church and State at the Mexican Constitutional Convention, 1856-1857." *The Americas* 4 (October 1947): 151-174.

————. "El liberalismo reformista." *Historia Mexicana* 2, no. 3 (January-March 1953): 178-191.

————. *Mexican Politics during the Juarez Regime, 1855-1872.* Columbia: University of Missouri Press, 1957.

————. "A Revolution Falters: Mexico, 1856-1857." *Hispanic American Historical Review* 32 (1952): 1-21.

Scott, Robert E. "Nation Building in Latin America." In *Nation-Building,* edited by Karl W. Deutsch and William J. Foltz. New York: Atherton Press, 1963.

Secretaría del Estado y del Despacho de Relaciones esteriores. *Memoria . . . correspondiente a la administración provisional en los años de 1841, 42 y 43.* Mexico City: 1844.

Sepúlveda, César. "Historia y problemas de los límites de México." *Historia Mexicana* 8. no. 1 (July-September 1958): 1-34; 8, no. 2 (October-December 1958): 145-174.

Shafer, Boyd C. *Nationalism: Myth and Reality.* New York: Macmillan, 1955.

Shiels, W. Eugene. "Church and State in the First Decade of Mexican Independence." *Catholic Historical Review* 28 (July 1942): 206-228.

Sierra, Carlos J. *Guillermo Prieto.* Mexico City: Club de Periodistas de México, 1962.

Sierra, Justo. *Evolución política del pueblo mexicano.* Mexico City: Fondo de Cultura Económica, 1950. Translated as *The Political Evolution of the Mexican People* by Charles Ramsdell. Austin, Texas: University of Texas Press, 1969.

_____. *Juárez, su obra y su tiempo.* Edited by Arturo Arnáiz y Freg. Mexico City: Universidad Nacional Autónoma de México, 1948.

El Siglo XIX.

Silva, B. de, ed. *Plan de Ayutla: Celebración de su primer centenario.* Mexico City: Universidad Nacional Autónoma de México, 1954.

Silvert, Kalman H. "Nationalism in Latin America." *The Annals of the American Academy of Political and Social Science* 334 (1961): 1-9.

Simpson, Eyler N. *The Ejido: Mexico's Way Out.* Chapel Hill: University of North Carolina Press, 1937.

Sims, Harold D. "Espejo de caciques: Los Terrazas de Chihuahua." *Historia Mexicana* 18 (January-March 1969): 379-399.

_____. *La expulsión de los españoles de México, 1821-1828.* Mexico City: Fondo de Cultura Económica, 1974.

Sinkin, Richard N. "The Mexican Constitutional Congress, 1856-57: A Statistical Analysis." *Hispanic American Historical Review* 53, no. 1 (February 1972):1-26.

Smart, Charles Allen. *Viva Juárez! A Biography.* Philadelphia: Lippincott, 1962.

Smelser, Neil J. *Theory of Collective Behavior.* Glencoe, Ill.: The Free Press, 1962.

Snyder, Louis Leo. *The Meaning of Nationalism.* New Brunswick, N.J.: Rutgers University Press, 1954.

La Sociedad.

Sosa, Francisco. *Biografías de mexicanos distinguidos.* Mexico City: 1884.

Stabb, Martin S. "Indigenism and Racism in Mexican Thought: 1857-1911." *Journal of Inter-American Studies* 1 (1959): 405-423.

Stein, Stanley and Barbara. *The Colonial Heritage of Latin America: Essays on Economic Dependence in Perspective.* New York: Oxford University Press, 1970.

Stokes, William S. "Violence as a Power Factor in Latin American Politics." *Western Political Quarterly* 5 (September 1952): 445-468.

Symposium nacional de historia sobre la Constitución de Apatzingán. Mexico City: Sección de Historia, Sociedad Mexicana de Geografía y Estadística, 1965.

Talavera, Abraham. *Liberalismo y educación.* 2 vols. Mexico City: Sepsetentas, 1973.

Tamayo, Jorge L., ed. *Antología de Benito Juárez.* Mexico City: Universidad Nacional Autónoma de México, 1972.

_____, ed. *Epistolario de Benito Juárez.* Mexico City: 1957.

_____, ed. *Juárez en Chihuahua.* Mexico City: 1970.

Tavera Alfaro, Xavier, ed. *Tres votos y un debate del Congreso Constituyente, 1856-1857.* Jalapa, Veracruz: Universidad Veracruzana, 1958.

Teja Zabre, Alfonso. *Leandro Valle, un liberal romántico.* Mexico City: Imprenta Universitaria, 1956.

_____. *Vida de Morelos, nueva versión.* Mexico City: Universidad Nacional Autónoma de México, 1959.

Tena Ramírez, Felipe. *El constituyente de 1856 y el pensamiento liberal mexicano.* Mexico City: Editorial Porrúa, 1960.

_____, ed. *Leyes fundamentales de México, 1808-1957.* Mexico City: Editorial Porrúa, 1957.

Tilly, Charles. "The Analysis of a Counter-Revolution." *History and Theory* 3, no. 1 (1963): 30-58.

Timmons, Wilbert Helde. *Morelos: Priest, Soldier, Statesman of Mexico.* El Paso, Texas: Texas Western College Press, 1963.

Tönnies, Ferdinand. *Fundamental Concepts of Sociology.* Translated by Charles Loomis. New York: American Book Co., 1940.

Toro, Alfonso. *La iglesia y el estado en México: Estudio sobre los conflictos entre el clero católico y los gobiernos mexicanos desde la independencia hasta nuestros días.* Mexico City: Talleres Gráficos de la Nación, 1927.

Torre Villar, Ernesto de la. "La visión de México y los mexicanos en algunos intervencionistas." *Humanitas* 4 (1963): 521-541.

_____, ed. *El triunfo de la república liberal, 1857-1860.* Mexico City: Fondo de Cultura Económica, 1960.

Torres, Victor Manuel. "El pensamiento político de Ignacio Ramírez." *Historia Mexicana* 12, no. 2 (October-December 1962): 190-228.

Tovar, Pantaleón, ed. *Historia parlamentaria del cuarto congreso constitucional* 4 vols. Mexico City, 1872.

Los traidores juzgados a la luz de la razón por la revista universal. Mexico City: 1869.

Los traidores pintados por si mismos, libro secreto de Maximiliano. Mexico City, 1867. (LAF 699.)

Turner, Frederick C. "The Compatibility of Church and State in Mexico." *Journal of Inter-American Studies* 9, no. 4 (October 1967): 591-602.

_____. *The Dynamic of Mexican Nationalism.* Chapel Hill: University of North Carolina Press, 1968.

El Universal.

Ursua Cocke, Frances. "Ideología de la reforma: Ensayo de sistematización." Thesis, Universidad Nacional Autónoma de México, 1962.

Valadés, José C. *Alamán, estadista e historiador.* Mexico City: Antigua Librería Robredo J. Porrúa e Hijos, 1938.

_____. *Don Melchor Ocampo, reformador de México.* Mexico City: Editorial Patria, 1954.

_____. "José María Gutiérrez de Estrada, 1800-1867." In *Enciclopedia Yucatanense*, VII, 141-204. 8 vols. Mexico City: 1944-1947.

Vallarta, Ignacio Luis. *Vallarta en la reforma.* Prologue and selection by

Moisés González Navarro. Mexico City: Universidad Nacional Autónoma de México, 1956.

Vanderwood, Paul J. "Genesis of the Rurales: Mexico's Early Struggle for Public Security." *Hispanic American Historical Review* 50, no. 3 (August 1970): 323-344.

————. "The Rurales: Mexico's Rural Police Force, 1861-1914." Ph.D. dissertation, The University of Texas at Austin, 1970.

Varios Liberales. *Rápida ojeada sobre la revolución y el General Comonfort.* Veracruz: 1860. (LAF 311.)

Varios Yucatecos. *Programa del Partido Liberal.* Mérida: 1861. (LAF 490.)

Vázquez de Knauth, Josefina. *Nacionalismo y educación en México.* Mexico City: El Colegio de México, 1970.

Vidaurri, Santiago. *Correspondencia particular de don Santiago Vidaurri, gobernador de Nuevo Leon.* Edited by Santiago Roel. Monterrey, Nuevo León: Universidad de Nuevo León, 1946.

Vigil, José María. *José María Vigil: Prólogo, notas y composición.* Edited by Carlos J. Sierra. Mexico City: Club de Periodistas de México, 1963.

Villaseñor y Villaseñor, Alejandro. *Antón Lizardo—el tratado McLane-Ocampo—el brindis del desierto.* Mexico City: Editorial Jus, 1962.

Vindicación del pueblo mexicano en la invasión francesa de 1862. Mexico City: 1867. (LAF 362.)

Voto en favor de la intervención francesa en la República de los Estados Unidos Mexicanos. Puebla: 1863. (LAF 681.)

La Voz Nacional (Guanajuato).

Weber, Max. *The Protestant Ethic and the Spirit of Capitalism.* Translated by Talcott Parsons. New York: Scribner, 1930.

————. *The Theory of Social and Economic Organization.* Translated by A. M. Henderson and Talcott Parsons. Glencoe, Ill.: The Free Press, 1947.

Weiner, Myron, ed. *Modernization: The Dynamics of Growth.* New York: Basic Books, 1966.

Welsh, William A. "Methodological Problems in the Study of Political Leadership in Latin America." *Latin American Research Review* 5, no. 3 (Fall 1970): 3-33.

Wheat, Raymond Curtis. *Francisco Zarco, el portavoz liberal de la Reforma.* Translated by Antonio Castro Leal. Mexico City: Editorial Porrúa, 1957.

Whitaker, Arthur Preston. *Nationalism in Latin America, Past and Present.* Gainsville: University of Florida Press, 1962.

————, and David C. Jordan. *Nationalism in Contemporary Latin America.* New York: The Free Press, 1966.

Wilkie, James W. *The Mexican Revolution: Federal Expenditure and Social Change Since 1910.* 2nd ed., rev. Berkeley: University of California Press, 1970.

Wolf, Eric Robert. "Closed Corporate Peasant Communities in Mesoamerica and Central Java." *Southwestern Journal of Anthropology* 13 (1957): 1-18.

_____ . "The Mexican Bajío in the 18th Century: An Analysis of Cultural Integration." In *Synoptic Studies of Mexican Culture,* edited by Munro S. Edmonson. New Orleans: Tulane University, Middle American Research Institute Publication 17, 1957.

_____ . *Sons of the Shaking Earth.* Chicago: University of Chicago Press, 1959.

_____ , and Edward C. Hansen. "Caudillo Politics: A Structural Analysis." *Comparative Studies in Society and History* 9, no. 2 (January 1968): 168-179.

Wormuth, Francis Dunham. *The Origins of Modern Constitutionalism.* New York: Harper, 1949.

Y.O. *La reforma social de México deducida del aspecto político que él presenta y fundada en la experiencia de cuarenta y cinco años.* Mexico City: 1855.

Zaragoza, Ignacio. *Cartas y documentos.* Mexico City: Fondo de Cultura Económica, 1962.

_____ . *Epistolario Zaragoza-Vidaurri, 1855-1859.* Mexico City: Primer Congreso Nacional de Historia para el Estudio de la Guerra de Intervención, 1962.

Zarco, Francisco. *Comentarios de Francisco Zarco sobre la intervención francesa (1861-1863).* Mexico City: Publicaciones de la Secretaría de Relaciones Exteriores, 1929.

_____ . *Historia del Congreso extraordinario Constituyente, 1856-1857.* Mexico City: El Colegio de México, 1956.

Zavala, Silvio. "Orígenes coloniales del peonaje en México." *Trimestre Económico* 10 (1944): 711-748.

Zayas Enríquez, Rafael de. *Benito Juárez: Su vida—su obra.* Mexico City: Tipografía de la Viuda de Francisco Díaz de León, 1906. Reprinted, Mexico City: Sepsetentas, 1971.

Index